How Writing Works

From the invention of the alphabet to the explosion of the internet, Dominic Wyse takes us on a unique journey into the process of writing. Starting with seven extraordinary examples that serve as a backdrop to the themes explored, the book pays particular attention to key developments in the understanding of writing and language, including Aristotle's grammar, socio-cultural multimodality, and pragmatist philosophy of communication. Analogies with music are used as a comparator throughout the book, yielding radically new insights into composition processes. The book presents the first comprehensive analysis of the *Paris Review Interviews* with the world's greatest writers such as Louise Erdrich, Gabriel García Márquez, Ted Hughes, and Marilynne Robinson. It critically reviews the most influential guides to styles and standards of language, and presents new empirical research on young people's creativity and writing. Drawing on over twenty years of work, Wyse presents research-informed innovative practices to demonstrate powerfully how writing can be learned and taught.

DOMINIC WYSE is Professor of Early Childhood and Primary Education at University College London Institute of Education. He is author of *The Good Writing Guide for Education Students* and *Teaching English, Language and Literacy*. He has been an invited expert for BBC *Newsnight* and the BBC Radio Four *Today* programme, and for the *Guardian* and *Times* newspapers.

How Writing Works

From the Invention of the Alphabet to the Rise of Social Media

Dominic Wyse
University College London

CAMBRIDGE
UNIVERSITY PRESS

University Printing House, Cambridge CB2 8BS, United Kingdom

One Liberty Plaza, 20th Floor, New York, NY 10006, USA

477 Williamstown Road, Port Melbourne, VIC 3207, Australia

314–321, 3rd Floor, Plot 3, Splendor Forum, Jasola District Centre, New Delhi – 110025, India

79 Anson Road, #06–04/06, Singapore 079906

Cambridge University Press is part of the University of Cambridge.

It furthers the University's mission by disseminating knowledge in the pursuit of education, learning, and research at the highest international levels of excellence.

www.cambridge.org
Information on this title: www.cambridge.org/9781107184688
DOI: 10.1017/9781316882276

First published 2017

Printed in the United Kingdom by TJ International Ltd. Padstow Cornwall

A catalogue record for this publication is available from the British Library.

ISBN 978-1-107-18468-8 Hardback
ISBN 978-1-316-63606-0 Paperback

This book is dedicated to Pascal Wyse, an outstanding composer of music, text and comedy.

Contents

Figures and Tables

Figures

Tables

Acknowledgements

My very grateful thanks to the following people for their invaluable support and advice:

At Cambridge University Press: Andrew Winnard for commissioning the book, and his perceptive decisions on key overall ideas; Stephanie Taylor for her efficient handling of the complex manuscript; and Sarah Lambert and all the production and marketing staff.

Charlie English for his lifelong friendship and for helping me think about the overall focus of the book (as did Patrick Walsh).

Morag Styles and David Whitley, at the University of Cambridge, for their friendship, wisdom and knowledge about poetry and literature.

My University College London colleagues: Lesley Gourlay for some useful reading recommendations; Jan Derry for her expertise in philosophy and for reading and commenting on the theory chapter; Andrew Burn for our work together on the Ministry of Stories project, for his reflections on the history chapter and for many chats about music; Alison Gazzard for her work on computers and their cultural relevance; Paul Standish for reminding me of the importance of Wittgenstein's language games; Andrew Brown, Becky Francis, Lynn Ang, Joe Mintz, Chris Brown and Emily Knight for support during my study leave; Karen Edge for her knowledge about Toronto; and Richard Andrews (now at the University of East Anglia) for his expertise in writing and music.

Jessica Pandya, Cathy Mills and Steve Graham for their collaboration, expertise and their beautifully crafted and humbling endorsements.

David Olson for being so generous with his time and expertise during my visit to Toronto; for his perceptive reading of drafts; and for introducing me to Kathy Broad, Shelley Stagg Peterson, Heather Walters and Carolyn Venema. Dan White for stopping his research on books to take me out for a fine Chinese meal in Toronto.

The inspirational Ben Payne and Lucy MacNab at the *Ministry of Stories*, and the various organisations such as SHINE that funded the creativity and writing research.

The Commonwealth Education Trust, The Centre for Commonwealth Education and the University of Cambridge for funding the Tanzania Research.

Barrie and Vera Wyse for the gifts of music and writing that they passed on to me.

Esther Wyse for her social media expertise; Olly Wyse for 1,2,3,4,5, Once I Caught a Fish Alive!; and Jackie Wyse always my first reader, for listening and understanding (and who typed the A Level computer programme account, figure 0.4, using a manual typewriter!).

Introduction

Written language is a supreme achievement that distinguishes humans from animals. For many millions of people across the world, being literate gives access to vital parts of social and cultural life, and being illiterate results in more limited opportunities. For employment as an academic, journalist, and of course writer, writing is central to the work. For professional people, writing is a main vehicle for getting work done. For other jobs, writing is vital to efficient practices including health and safety. And for many people, writing as a source of pleasure, recreation, and reflection is what they value most. One thing all writers have in common is the challenge to write well. The challenge for a tiny minority is to reach 'immortality' in their writing, but for most people the challenge is making writing effectively reflect the meanings and messages they want to create and communicate. For children, the challenge is learning to write in the first place, and for teachers the challenge is helping their learners to do this. But in spite of the thousands of years of history of writing, and in spite of its global use today, writing has attracted less attention from researchers, particularly compared to oral language and reading.

The beginning of my exploration of writing was informed by both seminal and more recent books written by people with different kinds of relevant expertise, for example by classicists (e.g. Eric Havelock, *The Muse Learns to Write*), philosophers (Aristotle, *On Interpretation*), anthropologists (Jack Goody, *The Interface between the Written and the Oral*), cognitive scientists (Steven Pinker, *The Language Instinct*), psychologists/educationalists (David Olson, *The World on Paper*), linguists (David Crystal, *The Stories of English*), literary/media theorists (Marshall McLuhan, *The Gutenberg Galaxy*), journalists (Lynn Truss, *Eats, Shoots & Leaves*), and accounts by writers (Stephen King, *On Writing*). In answer to a question about the origins of his poems the poet Ted Hughes said:

Well, I have a sort of notion. Just the tail end of an idea, usually just the thread of an idea. If I can feel behind that a sort of waiting momentum, a sense of some charge there to tap, then I just plunge in. What usually happens then – inevitably I would say – is that I go off in some wholly different direction. The thread end of an idea burns away and I'm pulled in – on the momentum of whatever was there waiting. Then that feeling opens up other energies, all the possibilities in my head, I suppose. That's the pleasure – never quite knowing what's there, being surprised. Once I get onto something I usually finish it. In a way it goes on finishing itself while I attend to its needs. It might be days, months. Later, often enough, I see exactly what it needs to be and I finish it in moments, usually by getting rid of things.[1]

Hughes was not only a great poet, he was also interested in how people learn to write, so much so that he published a book on the matter, *Poetry in the Making*, subtitled *A Handbook for Writing and Teaching*. The aims behind Hughes' book prompt a wider question about the ways in which writing and language might be taught and learned. If people are to learn, there needs to be some agreement about things to be taught and the best ways of doing so.

One of the first examples of a book designed to teach English language use was published in no less than 100 editions. The author became a household name in the UK and in the USA, and a citation to his name was even used by Charles Dickens in *Dombey and Son*[2]. And the title of this book?:

WALKER'S
PRONOUNCING DICTIONARY
OF THE
ENGLISH LANGUAGE.
ABRIDGED
FOR THE USE OF SCHOOLS
CONTAINING
A COMPENDIUM OF THE
PRINCIPLES OF ENGLISH PRONUNCIATION
WITH THE
PROPER NAMES
THAT OCCUR IN
THE SACRED SCRIPTURES
TO WHICH IS LIKEWISE ADDED,
A SELECTION OF GEOGRAPHICAL PROPER NAMES AND DERIVATIVES.[3]

The author, John Walker (1732–1807), had a first job as a professional actor, including a run in London's Covent Garden. But his second career was as an educator: initially setting up his own school. After a disagreement with the co-founder of the school, Walker took up the teaching of elocution, at which he excelled. So much so that he was soon educating royalty. His major contribution was a theory of inflections. His attention to the pitch of the voice built on the

[1] Heinz, 'Ted Hughes', 17. [2] Crystal, *Stories of English*, 406.
[3] Planned in 1774 then finally published in 1791.

work of Joshua Steele who had investigated vocal pitch in relation to music.[4] As is clear from the title of Walker's book, he was concerned that young people should learn to use language 'correctly' as he saw it. However, his wasn't a book about the composition of writing but more about other important elements of language. Books directly about writing were to come later.

How Writing Works is about the process of writing: the place of meaning as the driving force of writing; and the 'ear of the writer' that enables writing. The work on the book was driven by the following questions:

In what ways does meaning drive writing?
How should we understand writing theoretically?
How do key moments in the history of writing enable us to reflect on writing now?
What are the relationships between the composition of meaning, and the technical elements of writing such as structure, sentences, words, letters, and sounds?
What are the relationships between oral and written language?
How are conventions and standards of language established and applied, and in what ways do and should they impinge on writing?
What is the nature of creativity in writing?
And consequently: how does writing work and therefore how is writing best taught?

Although the book does make occasional comparisons with other languages, when appropriate, its main focus is on writing in English. My intention is to present a new and more complete account of the process of writing. By way of introduction to some of the themes of the book, and I hope as a means to engage you, I begin with seven short stories of writing.

1

It was a cold morning and the sky was brilliant blue. The crowd waited expectantly. A countdown commenced. At 'zero' the roar of rocket engines vibrated through people's chests. The shuttle moved slowly at first, as if the shackles would stop it escaping, but then with gargantuan force its forward momentum quickened. The white of its tiled hull, and the white smoke from the rockets, contrasted strongly with the blue sky. In a few short minutes, the shuttle was out of sight and had left the earth's atmosphere. At NASA's Mission Control the pictures of the *Columbia* Space Shuttle's orbit were clear, and radio contact with the crew was fully functional.

While one of the NASA mission control team had been watching the launch, he thought he spotted something. On playback of the launch video, 82 seconds in, the scientist saw what looked like a small object bouncing off the wing of the shuttle. He alerted his manager. Emergency meetings were convened. PowerPoint presentations of technical information were discussed.

[4] Beal, 'Walker, John' in Oxford Dictionary of National Biography.

Having considered the PowerPoint slides, high-level NASA officials decided that the *Columbia* was not in danger, and further investigations were not necessary, not even the option of powerful military spy cameras that could have photographed any damage to the Shuttle for further analysis.

Twelve days later, on 1 February 2003, the Columbia disintegrated on re-entry to the earth's atmosphere, killing all seven crew members.

The *Columbia* disaster was a tragic event that highlighted the risks astronauts take in the exploration of space. An uncomfortable aspect of the *Columbia* disaster was that writing, in the particular structural and communicative form of the PowerPoint presentation package, was seen as a contributing factor in the disaster because it resulted in key messages being missed. 'Death by PowerPoint' could never have been more serious or literal.

The problem with PowerPoint involved the ways in which meaning was structured. Bullet points at higher levels, and in the executive summaries, suggested that *Columbia* was safe[5]. Technical points that suggested that fatal damage to the shuttle was a possibility were lower in the textual hierarchy of bullet points. At the same time the PowerPoint slides were being produced, NASA engineers were exchanging emails (more simply structured texts) about what they saw as a credible danger.

A formal report into the tragedy by the Columbia Accident Investigation Board concluded that:

> As information gets passed up an organization hierarchy, from people who do analysis to mid-level managers to high-level leadership, key explanations and supporting information are filtered out. In this context, it is easy to understand how a senior manager might read this PowerPoint slide and not realise that it addresses a life-threatening situation.
>
> At many points during its investigation, the board was surprised to receive similar presentation slides from NASA officials in place of technical reports. The Board views the endemic use of PowerPoint briefing slides instead of technical papers as an illustration of the problematic methods of technical communication at NASA.[6]

2

Pierre was happy. He had finished work for the day and was free to spend a precious hour or two on his hobby. A few months ago, he had found *Arithmetica*, a new translation of ferociously difficult mathematical problems. He had already easily solved seven of the problems in the *Arithmetica*. Most of the problems required extended mathematical proofs written out in lengthy series of equations. But Pierre was impatient to get through, so as a shortcut he would begin the solution to a problem, then when he was certain he could solve

[5] Tufte, *Cognitive Style of Powerpoint*. [6] Tufte, *Cognitive Style of Powerpoint*, 11

it, leave a note, sometimes in the margin of the page he had got to. While solving problem number eight in the *Arithmetica* Pierre realised that there were some intriguing possibilities. One in particular excited him. Having thought about possible solutions his mind was certain. He wrote in the margin:

Cuius rei demonstrationem mirabilem sane detexi hanc marginis exiguitas non caperet. [I have a truly marvellous demonstration of this proposition which this margin is too narrow to contain.][7]

And what was the proposition? There is no whole-number solution to $x^n + y^n = z^n$. In other words, although we can find whole-number solutions to Pythagoras' theorem $x^2 + y^2 = z^2$, it is not possible to solve the equation if ^{n} is a whole number greater than two.

This was how one of the most famous mathematical problems of all time, and an associated prize, was established some 300 years ago as a result of the note from the French mathematician Pierre de Fermat.[8] The proposition became known as Fermat's last theorem.

It is extraordinary enough that a simple handwritten note in the margin of a notebook should attract and challenge the world's greatest mathematicians for 300 years. And the physical survival of Fermat's written notes over such a long period of time is in itself impressive. This was only made possible because Fermat's eldest son, Clément-Samuel, realised the importance of his father's hobby, so he carefully collected and published the notes and thoughts that his father had scribbled onto his copy of *Arithmetica*.

The note Fermat left in the margin is only the starting point for this story. When Andrew Wiles was a child, he came across an account of the riddle of Fermat's last theorem. Unlike most children, Wiles was intrigued straight away. He even made an attempt to solve the problem on the assumption that as Fermat was an amateur mathematician, and as Wiles knew as much mathematics as Fermat knew, he could perhaps solve it. He soon realised, like so many mathematicians throughout history, that the problem was very difficult indeed.

It wasn't until Wiles went to the University of Cambridge that he started to think seriously about what might be involved in the solving of Fermat's last theorem. At first Wiles knew that he had to familiarise himself with major areas of complex mathematics. One area of maths that would one day be useful to him was the *elliptical equations* recommended by his tutor at Cambridge.

An unusual feature of Wiles's approach to the problem was to break with the tradition of collaboration that mathematicians in the modern era have adopted,

[7] An image of the original text can be seen here: http://commons.wikimedia.org/wiki/File:Diophantus-II-8-Fermat.jpg#/media/File:Diophantus-II-8-Fermat.jpg.

[8] The information for this story is taken from Singh, *Fermat's Last Theorem*.

by working alone and with complete secrecy. One of the reasons for this was the fear that if he shared some of his work, having made progress on solving the problem, another mathematician might supply the final piece in the jigsaw and claim the lucrative prize. Wiles even pretended to be working on elliptical equations, and published a series of minor papers so that he would not be suspected of his work on the theorem. But the other reason for his solitude was in order to maintain the high levels of concentration without distraction, over seven years, that Wiles knew would be necessary. In a description of the mental space required for creativity, Wiles said:

> Leading up to that kind of new idea there has to be a long period of tremendous focus on the problem without any distraction. You have to really think about nothing but that problem – just concentrate on it. Then you stop. Afterwards there seems to be a kind of period of relaxation during which the subconscious appears to take over and it's during that time that some new insight comes.[9]

Wiles also described the moment when he finally solved the problem.

> One morning in late May, Nada [his wife] was out with the children and I was sitting at my desk thinking about the remaining family of elliptical equations. I was casually looking at a paper of Barry Mazur's and there was one sentence there that just caught my attention. It mentioned a nineteenth-century construction, and I suddenly realised that I should be able to use that to make the Kolyvagin-Flach method work on the final family of elliptical equations. I went on into the afternoon and I forgot to go down for lunch, and by about three or four o'clock I was really convinced that this would solve the last remaining problem. It got to about tea-time and I went downstairs and Nada was very surprised that I'd arrived so late. Then I told her – I'd solved Fermat's Last Theorem.[10]

Wiles chose to announce his discovery at a conference at the Sir Isaac Newton Institute at the University of Cambridge. In a series of three lectures, it was not obvious in the first two lectures what Wiles was going to announce, but lecture by lecture the rumours grew, and by the time of the third lecture the atmosphere was electric. With the words 'I think I'll stop here', Wiles had solved the riddle.

Or had he? In order for the prize to be awarded Wiles's paper had to go through the standard procedure of peer-review, where experts in the same field review the paper and decide whether its argument is correct. One problem was that no other single person in the world had the same expertise. So the journal editor appointed six reviewers who would each look at one of the six sections of what was a document of more than 100 pages.

One of the referees emailed a series of questions to Wiles which he answered easily. But then there was a question for which his answer did not satisfy the reviewer. Wiles was in turmoil. After seven years of work and a public

[9] Singh, *Fermat's Last Theorem*, 228. [10] Singh, *Fermat's Last Theorem*, 265.

announcement that generated press coverage around the world, it appeared that he had not after all solved the riddle.

Wiles was resigned to simply learning from the mathematics he had successfully done. But after six months of additional work, he had a revelation:

> I realised that, although the Kolyvagin-Flach method wasn't working completely, it was all I needed to make my original Iwasawa theory work. I realised that I had enough from the Kolyvagin-Flach method to make my original approach to the problem from three years earlier work. So out of the ashes of Kolyvagin-Flach seemed to rise the true answer to the problem … It was so indescribably beautiful; it was so simple and so elegant. I couldn't understand how I'd missed it and I just stared at in disbelief for twenty minutes. then during the day I walked around the department, and I'd keep coming back to my desk looking to see if it was still there. It was. I couldn't contain myself. I was so excited. It was the most important moment of my working life. Nothing I ever do again will mean as much.[11]

Wiles' mathematical proof, 108 pages divided into five 'chapters', are notable for the story I have told but also, in themselves, as a variant of written language: the language of very high level maths, which as you can see is not just numbers but has a clear narrative in words (something that is clear from the first page of the published proof, Figure 0.1).

3

In 1979, age 15, I became interested in computer technology. The full extent of computer resources in my secondary school was one 'tele printer' machine. This was the size of a small desk and consisted of an electronic typewriter keyboard and a paper spool (about the width of A4 paper). You typed a line of computer code which then was sent down the telephone line to a mainframe computer (often described as a computer that filled a whole room), then some seconds later the response came back printed on the spool of computer paper that was part of the tele printer. My curiosity was not dimmed by this very basic technology – in fact at the time it seemed rather exciting!

In 1977 one of the first PCs that would reach people's homes was presented at the US West Coast Computer Faire, it was called the *Commodore Pet*[12]. Three years later I was using this computer to write the computer programme for a project as part of the first nationally available *A Level* in computer studies in the UK. One third of the assessment of this A level was a practical project that required the writing of a computer programme.

[11] Singh, *Fermat's Last Theorem*, 298.

[12] Centre for Computing History, 'Commodore International Shows Its Commodore Pet 2001'.

Let f be an eigenform associated to the congruence subgroup $\Gamma_1(N)$ of $\mathrm{SL}_2(\mathbf{Z})$ of weight $k \geq 2$ and character χ. Thus if T_n is the Hecke operator associated to an integer n there is an algebraic integer $c(n, f)$ such that $T_n f = c(n, f)f$ for each n. We let K_f be the number field generated over $\mathbf{Q}$ by the $\{c(n, f)\}$ together with the values of χ and let $\mathcal{O}_f$ be its ring of integers. For any prime λ of $\mathcal{O}_f$ let $\mathcal{O}_{f,\lambda}$ be the completion of $\mathcal{O}_f$ at λ. The following theorem is due to Eichler and Shimura (for $k = 2$) and Deligne (for $k > 2$). The analogous result when $k = 1$ is a celebrated theorem of Serre and Deligne but is more naturally stated in terms of complex representations. The image in that case is finite and a converse is known in many cases.

THEOREM 0.1. *For each prime $p \in \mathbf{Z}$ and each prime $\lambda \mid p$ of $\mathcal{O}_f$ there is a continuous representation*

$$\rho_{f,\lambda}\colon \mathrm{Gal}(\bar{\mathbf{Q}}/\mathbf{Q}) \longrightarrow \mathrm{GL}_2(\mathcal{O}_{f,\lambda})$$

which is unramified outside the primes dividing Np and such that for all primes $q \nmid Np$,

$$\operatorname{trace} \rho_{f,\lambda}(\operatorname{Frob} q) = c(q, f), \qquad \det \rho_{f,\lambda}(\operatorname{Frob} q) = \chi(q)q^{k-1}.$$

We will be concerned with trying to prove results in the opposite direction, that is to say, with establishing criteria under which a λ-adic representation arises in this way from a modular form. We have not found any advantage in assuming that the representation is part of a compatible system of λ-adic representations except that the proof may be easier for some λ than for others.

Assume

$$\rho_0 : \mathrm{Gal}(\bar{\mathbf{Q}}/\mathbf{Q}) \longrightarrow \mathrm{GL}_2(\bar{\mathbf{F}}_p)$$

is a continuous representation with values in the algebraic closure of a finite field of characteristic p and that $\det \rho_0$ is odd. We say that ρ_0 is modular if ρ_0 and $\rho_{f,\lambda} \bmod \lambda$ are isomorphic over $\bar{\mathbf{F}}_p$ for some f and λ and some embedding of $\mathcal{O}_f/\lambda$ in $\bar{\mathbf{F}}_p$. Serre has conjectured that every irreducible ρ_0 of odd determinant is modular. Very little is known about this conjecture except when the image of ρ_0 in $\mathrm{PGL}_2(\bar{\mathbf{F}}_p)$ is dihedral, A_4 or S_4. In the dihedral case it is true and due (essentially) to Hecke, and in the A_4 and S_4 cases it is again true and due primarily to Langlands, with one important case due to Tunnell (see Theorem 5.1 for a statement). More precisely these theorems actually associate a form of weight one to the corresponding complex representation but the versions we need are straightforward deductions from the complex case. Even in the reducible case not much is known about the problem in the form we have described it, and in that case it should be observed that one must also choose the lattice carefully as only the semisimplification of $\overline{\rho_{f,\lambda}} = \rho_{f,\lambda} \bmod \lambda$ is independent of the choice of lattice in $K^2_{f,\lambda}$.

Figure 0.1 One page of Wiles' mathematical proof of the solution of Fermat's last theorem. Wiles, A. 'Modular elliptic curves and Fermat's Last Theorem'. *Annals of Mathematics*, 142, (1995), 443–551. By permission of Andrew Wiles.

The writing of a computer programme, like any writing, first and foremost requires the creation of a purpose for the programme, perhaps a problem to solve. My interest in music, including singing for the local church choir, had led to my involvement in church tower-bell ringing. Bell ringing beyond the most basic stages requires each bell ringer to learn the different bell ringing 'methods'. A method is a particular combination of 'changes' to the sequence of bells rung. So, if there are six church tower bells being rung, the starting sequence is always what are known as 'rounds': bell one, bell two, bell three, four, five, six, with bell one being the smallest highest pitched bell called the 'treble', and the largest and lowest pitched bell called the 'tenor' (and by one of those curious coincidences the 'Tower Captain's' surname was Alan Treble). A bell ringing *method* changes this sequence by allowing the 'movement' of bells from a starting position in the sequence, up or down one place in the sequence. For example, you can see in Figure 0.2 that the person ringing bell number two follows the path shown by the *blue line* (the darker vertical line in figure 0.2).

The path of the blue line for their bell has to be memorised by the bell ringers.[13] My idea for the computer studies project was to create a simulation and teaching package for bell ringers (now inevitably there is a website devoted to this). The programme required the user to input the correct position of their bell using the numbers of the keyboard within a set number of seconds. When a correct answer was supplied, the screen added the relevant segment of the blue line (the bell's path), and a connected amplifier was used to play the synthesised sound of the bells ringing the change. If an incorrect answer was supplied the computer would reveal the correct answer.

At the time of the Commodore PET, storage of programmes was on audio cassettes (small hard drives to fit inside computers had not been developed: at that time a hard drive was the size of a large suitcase). The Commodore's total RAM (Random Access Memory) was 4KB which is 4,000 times less memory than my current mobile phone which has 16 GB.

The programming language I used was BASIC, a language that is still used in variants such as *smart BASIC* today. The writing of the computer programme was built as several 'modules'. Figure 0.3 shows one page of the BASIC language that I wrote for one of the modules. The number 8850 indicates that it is a draft version of the programme at that moment, something corroborated by my note ('255 not completely correct: odd [number] bells?').

Looking at the programme and the report again after more than 30 years, I could barely understand its meaning, certainly not the detail of the logic. I'm assuming that most readers of this book will understand even less of the specific

[13] A 'Bob' is a quick alteration of the path of the method, called by an instruction from the tower captain, if a longer period of ringing than one iteration of the complete method is required. It enables the method to be rung again but with an entirely different set of number sequences. In this kind of bell ringing, the same sequence is not allowed to be repeated.

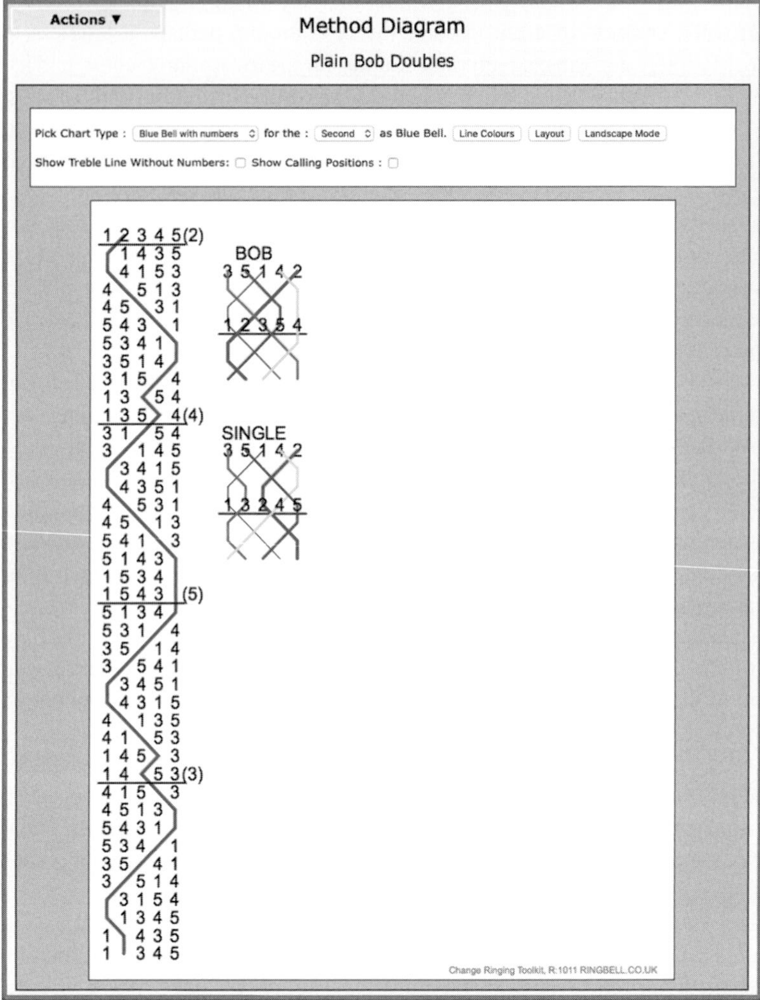

Figure 0.2 A bell-ringing 'method'. Change Ringing Toolkit. 'Method Diagram Plain Bob Minor.' 2016. (Source: Steve Scanlon).

meanings. The submission of the project for the A Level assessment also required an account of the design of the project. Figure 0.4 is an extract from my account of the final version of the programme presented for the submission. Once again my understanding of the detail of the computing logic in Figure 0.4 has largely faded; in fact, it came as something of a surprise to think that I

8850

AN Insight into Campanology

```
10 CLR
20 INPUT"HOW MANY BELLS";B:DIMCO(B-1)
30 INPUT"YOUR BELL";YB
35 REM***COURSING ORDER READ INTO ARRAY***
40 DATA2,4,6,8,10,12,11,9,7,5,3,1
45 C3=1
47 READDA:IFDA)BTHEN47
48 IFDA=YBTHEN47
50 CO(C3)=DA:C3=C3+1:IFC3()BTHEN47
55 REM***STARTING PLACE AND BELL ASSIGNED TO VARIABLES-BRANCH SET,ODD/EVEN***
60 IFINT(YB/2)=YB/2THEN80
70 PB=YB+1:P=YB+1:GOTO100
80 E=1:PB=YB-3:P=YB-1:GOTO100
90 IFPB( OTHENPB=0
95 E=0
100 GOSUB390
115 REM***START BELL PICKED UP IN ARRAY***
117 IFCO(C)=PBTHEN120
118 C=C+1:GOTO117
120 C=C+1:GOTO256
125 REM***STANDARD PLACE MOVEMENT ASSIGNED***
130 IFE()1THEN140
135 P=P-1:GOTO160
140 P=P+1
150 IFP()B+1THEN240
155 E=1:GOTO130
160 IFP=1THEN170
165 GOTO240
167 REM***VARIABLES ON "LEAD" SET***
170 E=0:PB=0:GOTO250
215 REM***RE-START COURSING ORDER***
220 IFC)=BTHENC=1
235 REM***PRECEEDING BELL ASSIGNED***
240 PB=CO(C)
245 EN=EN+1:C=C+1
250 GOSUB390
255 IFEN=(B*2)-3THENEND
256 REM***RE-START COURSING ORDER***
257 IFC)=BTHENC=1
260 GOTO130
380 REM***INPUT FOR USER***
390 INPUT"PLACE";T1
400 IFT1()PTHENGOTO390
410 INPUT"PRECEDING BELL";T2
420 IFT2()PBTHENGOTO410:GOSUB510
421 RETURN
500 REM***
510 IFP=1OR6THEN540
520 IFE()1THEN580
530 POKE(32798+P),78
540 POKE(32798+P),66
550 IFC2=2THEN570
560 IFP()6THEN540
570 C2=0:GOTO590
580 POKE(32798+P),77
590 RETURN
```

Figure 0.3 Extract of BASIC language from A Level project.

had accumulated this technical knowledge. The links between written language and memory are one of the many significant issues that surround moves from oral cultural to written culture. And the rapid developments in technology have already resulted in the need for new means of curation and research.

Breakdown of Program

Lines 7-76 — The module starts with a series of questions designed to set various parameters (detailed in user section). Each question is followed by validation for: illegal alphabetic data, (eg. line 8); illegal carriage return (eg.line7) and other specific validation checks,such as:-

Line 9 — 'D' must be an integer between 1 and 5 inclusive;

Line 16 — 'B' must be an integer between 4 and 12 " ;

Line 60 — 'YB'mmust be an integer between 1 and 'B' " ;

Line 75 — 'T' must be an integer between 1 and 900 " .

Lines 79-113 — This section selects a Random number between 1 and 'B'-1. It then exchanges the element of 'CS' corresponding with the Random number and the element above. It then prints the resultant change at line 106.

Lines 114-156 — This section is a single Bubble Sort. The Bubble Sort is appropriate because every element must move a place at a time.

Line 115 — 'BV' is assigned as the last element in the variable array.

Lines 120-125 — If the element is less than the lower element then an exchange is made. If not then the lower element is picked up, ie. 'BV' is diminished by 1.

Line 130 — Checks to see if 'BV'=1. If it dowsaa pass has been completed.

Lines 140-150 — Exchanges two elements represented by 'TS' and 'CS'('BV'-1). A Flag is also set at one to indicate an exchange has taken place.

Line 155 — If the Flag is 0 then the sort is complete and the program ends.

Line 156 — Resets the Flag to 0.

The next line is the screen output of the 'Call Change.

Line 160 — Sets a Loop to print each element of the array 'CS'.

Lines 170-190 — Data corresponding with the Bell Sounds.

Lines 195-220 — Pokes the sound corresponding with a number in the array 'CS' to the amplifier.

Lines 225-END — Test section - checks if your answer is correct and outputs appropriate messages.

Figure 0.4 Extract from A Level account of computer programme.

4

The King and the Duke, two petty criminals or, as they pronounced themselves, 'world renowned tragedians', had taken an interest in Huck and Jim and joined them on their Mississippi river journey. On one of the many stops along the journey, in Arkansas, the King and the Duke took to the stage for the 'sublime Shakespearian spectacle' in a 'one horse town' in the Deep South of the US.

With no lack of ambition they included in their performance *Romeo and Juliet, Richard III*, and *Hamlet* . . . extracts.

Regrettably for the King and the Duke the presence of a circus meant that only an audience of 12 people turned up. Much to the tragedians' annoyance this small audience laughed all the way through, until they left well before the end of the show, apart from one boy who had fallen asleep. Not to be deterred by these 'Arkansaw lunk-heads' the King and the Duke decided that low comedy was the answer.

AT THE COURT HOUSE
FOR 3 NIGHTS ONLY!
The World-Renowned Tragedians
DAVID GARRICK THE YOUNGER!
AND
EDMUND KEAN THE ELDER
Of the London and Continental Theatres
In their thrilling Tragedy of
THE KINGS CAMELOPARD
OR
THE ROYAL NONESUCH! ! !
Admission 50 cents
LADIES AND CHILDREN NOT ADMITTED.[14]

At first the audience thought the show was hilarious:

When the place couldn't hold no more, the duke he quit tending door and went around the back way and come onto the stage and stood up before the curtain, and made a little speech, and praised up this tragedy, and said it was the most thrillingest one that ever was; and so he went on a-bragging about the tragedy and about Edmund Kean the Elder, which was to play the main principal part in it; and at last when he'd got everybody's expectations up high enough, he rolled up the curtain, and the next minute the king come aprancing out on all fours, naked; and he was painted all over, ring-streaked-and-striped, all sorts of colours, as splendid as a rainbow. And – but never mind the rest of his outfit, it was just wild, but it was awful funny. The people most killed themselves laughing; and when the king got done capering, and capered off behind the scenes, they roared and clapped and stormed and haw-hawed till he come back and done it over again; and after that, they made him do it another time. Well, it would a made a cow laugh to see the shines that old idiot cut.

Then the duke he lets the curtain down, and bows to the people, and says the great tragedy will be performed only two nights more, on accounts of pressing London engagements, where the seats is all sold aready for it in Drury Lane . . .[15]

The audience were outraged: 'What, is it over? Is that *all*?' Just as the stage was to be stormed, a judge who was in the audience suggested that perhaps if

[14] Twain, *Huckleberry Finn*, 162. [15] Twain, *Huckleberry Finn*, 63.

they wanted to avoid being the laughing stock of the town they should tell everyone else how good the show was, 'Then we'll all be in the same boat.'

This scene is just one of the myriad of comic scenes from Twain's masterpiece. According to Ernest Hemingway, 'All modern American literature comes from one book by Mark Twain called *Huckleberry Finn*.'[16] Twain, or Samuel L. Clemens, the writer and his work are of interest for a number of reasons. *Huckleberry Finn* is a great work partly for its reputation as a prime representation of *literary realism*.[17] This realism comes in no small part through Twain's ear as a writer, demonstrated in his authentic representation of the grammar of the vernacular dialect of the Deep South. Twain's voice as a writer was also reflected in the use of his nom de plume: his real name was Samuel Langhorne Clemens. He was an accomplished journalist, and also a travel writer. His travel book *Life on the Mississippi* which drew in part from his experience as a Mississippi steamboat pilot had a strong influence on *Huckleberry Finn* (the name Mark Twain was a Mississippi boating term meaning the mark for two fathoms deep). The nature of *Huckleberry Finn* is also interesting from an educational perspective, or as a *bildungsroman* (from the German for education, *bildung*, and a novel, *roman*), as we see the young characters develop, though Huckleberry Finn's 'educational experiences that result in his final emergence as a mature young man'.[18]

There are many fascinating things about Twain, including his essays and polemical writing, and his trademark all-white suit. But Twain was not just interested in doing the writing, he also was interested in the processes of writing, and more specifically publication, to the extent that his entrepreneurial spirit resulted in him establishing his own publishing company and publishing his own book, as my copy of the Penguin classics edition notes:

> The text of this edition follows that of The Library of America's edition of Mark Twain's *Mississippi Writings* (1982), which in turn was based on that of the first American edition published on February 18, 1885, by Twain's own publishing company.[19]

The final twist in this story comes from when I saw *The Paige Compositor*[20] in the Mark Twain museum in Hartford, Connecticut. Here was another remarkable side to Twain's character, the confidence to take risks, ruinous risks, and his determination in the face of adversity. Twain invested the equivalent of about $6,000,000 of his book profits and his wife's inheritance into a printing machine that turned out to be unable to 'compose pages', forever requiring

[16] Back cover of Penguin Classics edition of *Huckleberry Finn*.

[17] Seelye, J. 'Introduction'. In *Adventures of Huckleberry Finn*.

[18] Ibid., xv.

[19] Twain, *Huckleberry Finn*, xxxv.

[20] An image of the Paige Compositor can be seen here: https://commons.wikimedia.org/wiki/File:Paige_Compositor.jpg.

complex adjustments based on trial and error.[21] Bankruptcy was the result. But what was Twain's response?: to undertake a very successful worldwide lecture tour that returned him to solvency.

5

SALIERI[22]
Come. Let's begin.
He takes his pen.

SALIERI
Confutatis Maledictis.
. . .

MOZART
The Fire.

SALIERI
What time?

MOZART
Common time.
Salieri writes this, and continues now to write as swiftly and urgently as he can, at Mozart's dictation. He is obviously highly expert at doing this and hardly hesitates. His speed, however, can never be too fast for Mozart's impatient mind.

MOZART
Start with the voices. Basses first. Second beat of the first measure – A. (singing the note) Con-fu-ta-tis. (speaking) Second measure, second beat. (singing) Ma-le-dic-tis. (speaking) G-sharp, of course.

SALIERI
Yes.

This is some of the dialogue from a scene in the film *Amadeus*. The composer, Mozart, is in his bed because he is dying. He is desperate to finish his final work: a work that has been described as a Requiem for his own death. Salieri, a lesser composer portrayed as intensely envious of Mozart but also acutely aware of his genius, struggles to scribe the music as Mozart impatiently dictates.

The writer Peter Shaffer had written the script for a successful play which then became a film. The writing of an outstanding screenplay that was

[21] Wikipedia. 'Mark Twain.' Wikipedia, 2016.
[22] Shaffer, P. *Amadeus*, The Internet Movie Script Database, 2016.

nominated for 53 awards and won 25, including 8 Academy Awards and 4 Golden Globes, is itself a memorable story. But it is but a tiny fragment of the astonishing array of stories and meanings expressed as a consequence of Mozart's *Requiem*, one of the greatest artistic works of all time from one of the greatest creative geniuses of all time. And with regard to the many myths and truths that surround the requiem Simon Keefe observes that attention to its *reception* has been underplayed in academic analyses:

> Above all, reception draws attention to a fundamental feature of the Requiem's ontological status, namely that our collective understandings of it derive from our imaginative (and often undifferentiated) engagement with fictional, quasi fictional, and factual circumstances of composition to a degree unrivalled perhaps by any other work in the Western canon.[23]

In 1791 in conditions of secrecy Mozart was commissioned to write a requiem for the wife of Count Walsegg-Stuppach.[24] But as Mozart worked on the *Requiem* he became gravely ill. On the day he died, from his bed he asked for the score to be brought to him. 'Didn't I predict that I would write this Requiem for myself?'[25] And as reported in *Tales from the Stave*[26], having said these words, with tears in his eyes he once more looked through the score attentively; it was a last glance, a painful farewell to his beloved art, a glimpse of immortality. In steady handwriting, but with the ink becoming gradually more faint, the final music Mozart ever wrote was to accompany the words, 'And let them, Lord, pass from death to life' ('Fac eas, Domine, de morte transire ad vitam'). The very last words he wrote were also on the Requiem score. The meaning of Mozart's last words is that the musicians should repeat (Da Capo) the section called 'Quam olim' ('Quam olim Abrahae promisisti et semini ejus': *which was promised to Abraham and his descendants*).

Mozart's last words are part of yet another extraordinary story that happened nearly two hundred years later. At the World's Fair in Brussels in 1958 one of only two original versions of Mozart's *Requiem* score was on display. Someone tore from the page of the score Mozart's handwritten instruction for 'Quam Olim Da Capo', no doubt knowing that this was the very last thing Mozart wrote (Figure 0.5 is a scan from this original score).

Mozart died leaving the *Requiem* unfinished, so the story of its writing continued: who could finish the work? The talented, experienced composer and friend of Mozart's Joseph von Eybler was the first to agree to continue the work, but he gave up. The job then fell to Mozart's inexperienced student,

[23] Keefe, *Mozart's Requiem*, 7. [24] Eisen, 'Mozart'.

[25] There is no evidence that the wonderful scene in the film, quoted from the playscript above, where the composer Salieri notes down Mozart's music is authentic, but it is thought that Salieri did visit while Mozart was dying.

[26] BBC, 'Tales from the Stave'.

Figure 0.5 The last page of music and words Mozart wrote. (Source: National Library of Austria.)[27]

Franz Xavier Süssmayer. Süssmayer completed the score with love and respect but as he was not a particularly good composer some of his writing was clearly not up to the standard of Mozart's. Although the Süssmayer version is the one most often performed, as a result of the dissatisfaction with it there have been six modern completions, each taking a different approach to sources.[28]

The contributions of other composers to Mozart's *Requiem* raises questions of authorship, authenticity and ownership: to what extent is the music by Mozart? On one of the only two original manuscripts, held at the Austrian National Library, Constanza's second husband marked the sections that belonged to Mozart and those that belonged to Joseph Eybler. As a result of studying these markings, and their knowledge more generally about the *Requiem*, Thomas Leibnitz and Nigel Simeone conclude that the heart and substance of the music is by Mozart. Simeone's own parting words on the BBC Radio 4 programme were, 'It is one of the most moving documents I have ever

[27] The last words, and the last page of music that Mozart wrote can be seen in original colour here: Wikipedia. 'Requiem (Mozart).' Wikipedia, 2016. https://commons.wikimedia.org/wiki/File:Mozart_K626_Arbeitspartitur_last_page.jpg.

[28] BBC, 'Tales from the Stave'.

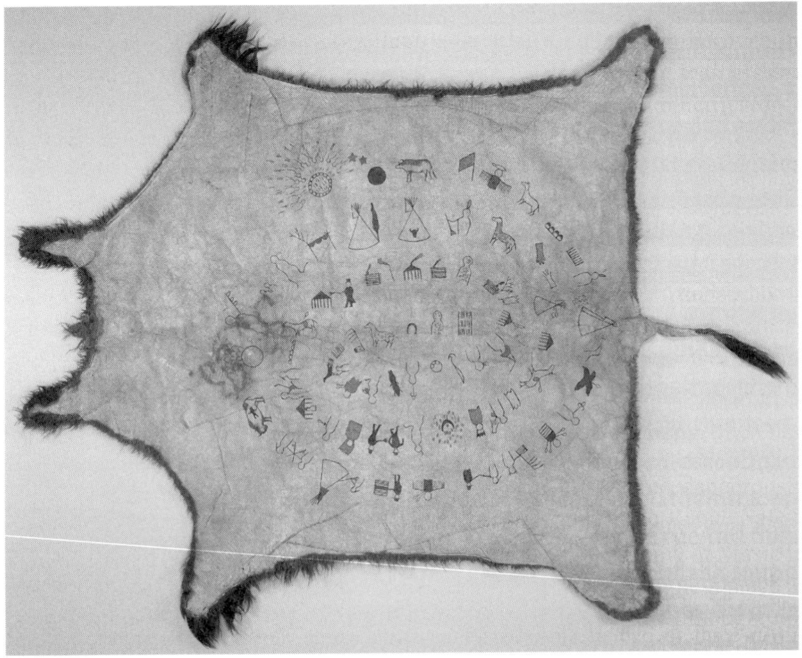

Figure 0.6 The Lone Dog Winter Count. (Source: National Museum of the American Indian, Washington, DC.).

seen . . . heart-breaking . . . to see the last page he ever wrote . . . I just feel like weeping when I look at that page. It is unbearably moving.'

Just as the film script for *Amadeus* would not have been written if Mozart had not composed the *Requiem*, so the composition of the music by Mozart could not have been written without another form of writing, the requiem text. As a major element of the Catholic religion, the requiem text represents a form of standard language and convention. Throughout history, as each new pope has been anointed, he has recommended edits to the requiem text. Musically, the requiem text has resulted in some of the greatest choral music ever written including requiems by Verdi, Fauré, Brahms, and Britten.

6

The writer 'Lone Dog' of the American Yanktonais Nakota community (who were part of the larger tribe known as the Sioux) was the last known keeper of *Winter Count*, a record of time through the counting of winters (starting with the winter of 1800–1801; see Figure 0.6).[29]

[29] Schupman, E, and L. O'Flahavan, *Lone Dog's Winter Count.*

The meaning of each picture on the winter count is a summary, or *mnemonic*, of a whole year of the community's history, from first snowfall one year to first snowfall the next year. The elders would meet to decide one momentous event from the year that would be a reminder of the whole year. The chosen event was then encapsulated in a picture painted on to an animal hide. If you look carefully, you may be able to work out which of the pictures recorded the Leonid Meteor Storm of 1833 that would have been seen by many people round the globe. For the Yanktonais Nakota community, significant shared meaning was expressed through pictures, and each picture summed up a whole year of events. A beautiful object, and a beautiful example of the way that pictures supported what was almost entirely an oral culture dependent on the transmission of the community's history by its elders to each successive generation.

7

The Mozart *Requiem* mass and the example of the *Columbia* disaster that began this introduction, show us writing used to enact and record significant moments in human history. There is writing at our death, and there is writing to record our birth. Because writing is such a powerful part of being human it is also part of the lives of very young children. For the new-born baby, text is just another thing to be observed in the baby's environment, but surprisingly soon it becomes something with which to explore and experiment. And after only a few short years, most young children begin the life-long journey to represent meaning in marks and writing.

Esther was about six years old. She had been asked by her teacher to write a story to prepare for England's national tests in writing. She decided to call the story 'The Tooth Fairy', and it was written along these lines:

> One day the tooth of a little girl called Chloe came loose then fell out of her mouth. Chloe noticed that the tooth was an unusual colour so she decided to show her mum.
>
> 'Oh look, it's orange', said her mum. 'That reminds me of a story. When I was a little girl like you the same thing happened to me. So I said to grandma, shall I throw my tooth away?'
>
> 'Oh no,' said grandma, 'you should throw it into a fire.'
>
> 'Why', I said.
>
> 'Try it and see.'
>
> So I threw my orange tooth into the fireplace, and the fire went out.
>
> The next day Chloe was playing in her garden when she smelled smoke. She looked towards the smoke and saw that the house next door had flames billowing out of the downstairs window. She ran to the low garden fence, pulled her orange tooth out of her pocket, and threw it through the fiery window. And you can guess what happened, the fire went out. A group of worried onlookers shouted, WELL DONE CHLOE!

Esther, as is typical of a girl her age, had enjoyed creating a story that required her to play with ways of making meaning. But it was in the process of the writing that another remarkable story was revealed. The first thing Esther wrote on her blank piece of paper was the title, and she spelled 'Tooth Fairy' as *The Toth Fire*. Her friend took one look at it and said, 'That's not how you spell "fairy"'! Quick as a flash Esther's combative reply was, 'It doesn't say "fairy", it says "fire"'. And, quickly rejecting her first idea for the writing, she proceeded to construct a completely new story that combined the ideas of a tooth and fire. In Esther's mind, it was far better that she did this than concede that her friend was right about the spelling error!

*

The seven stories of writing were selected because they demonstrate the power, richness and diversity that characterise writing and its processes. The seriousness of the impacts of writing was evident in the space shuttle disaster, but also the ways in which text structure is profoundly linked with the expression of very precise meanings. There appeared to be a lack of clear understanding by some at NASA about the ways in which the communication of specific messages requires command and knowledge of not just the words but also the written form and the links between both. The failure to highlight the most important information prominently in a presentation, while also retaining important technical information, is a problem with balancing structural constraints of written form with the need to ensure meaning is clear. This problem is not with PowerPoint per se, it is one of the challenges of all writing.

In the second of my stories the mathematician's struggle with a 300-year-old riddle that began life as a handwritten note in an obscure margin reveals a different form of written communication, mathematical proof, and the seven-year solitude of the lone writer ultimately transformed through engagement with the community of scholars. Because of this written note, the child Andrew Wiles had a dream. As an adult, his writing of a mathematical proof communicated a very special kind of meaning. This meaning was temporarily doubted by his peers, but finally his success was communicated in the writing of the world's media. And the reason I know these stories? Because Simon Singh thought that the story of the solving of Fermat's theorem could be told: and Singh's wonderful book[30] shows the way in which powerful storytelling is not just the preserve of fiction writers.

In recognition that all writers have personal histories of writing, but also to point to a different form of writing, the third story, of my experience of learning to code the computer language BASIC when at school, is a recognition that we

[30] Singh, *Fermat's Last Theorem*.

are only at the beginning of a profound moment in the history of writing, and we continue to experience these digital developments.

The experiences and reflections of expert writers is an important element of the analysis underpinning the book, and the example of Mark Twain, as both exceptional author but also someone so seriously engaged with the processes of writing and publication that he tried to market a printing press, is a glimpse of what we might learn from such writers.

The fifth story, Mozart's *Requiem*, is profoundly interesting for so many reasons. As a creative masterpiece that combines words and music to make meaning, it is in my view unsurpassed. The story of the processes of Mozart's composition are so interesting in their own right that they have provided the stimulus for a play and a film, and repeated engagement by scholars of music. The torn and stolen fragment of manuscript lends yet another depressing story. Forms such as writing do not exist in some decontextualised world. They live and breathe through their meanings and their connections. Connections between composition of music and composition of text are necessarily part of work that combines the languages of music and words, but the connections are also important as a means to reflect upon writing more generally. The history of human creativity shows how powerful stories are realised through multiple reinterpretations that exist in many combinations of forms.

The wonder of the native American Indian's solution to memory, in the sixth story, provides a link with the graphical forms that characterised some of the earliest forms of writing. The history of writing that I address in the second chapter of the book reveals how key developments took humans from pictures to the alphabet and into the digital age.

And finally, in the seventh story the driving force of meaning lies in so many places. The unusual stimulus of the friend's observation provoked real creativity in the establishment of the overall meaning of a completely new story. Meanings were playfully expressed through orange teeth, stories within stories, and a classic childhood rite of passage: losing 'baby' teeth. And the true story about the process of writing showed how spelling is far from a mundane technical feature of writing but instead is inextricably bound up with effective expression of meaning. The example was also chosen as a reflection of our fascination with children's development but also as an early signal of my intention to think about how literacy education might be better, including how governments set literacy policy, and the extent to which such policies reflect rigorous and robust evidence about what works in the teaching of writing.

The Chapters of How Writing Works

In many areas of research, there is growing recognition that advances in knowledge over the next 100 years will come from sophisticated understandings that draw across different academic disciplines and areas of human endeavour. This book's analysis of how writing works draws on philosophy, psychology-neuroscience, social science, education, and the arts. As part of the multidisciplinary focus, and as part of the focus on arts, comparisons with music are drawn periodically throughout the book. Music is an interesting comparator because, like language, it exists in oral and written forms.

'ἄνδρα μοι ἔννεπε, μοῦσα, πολύτροπον'

('Sing to me of the man, Muse, the man of twists and turns').

Debates continue on the place of orality and writing in Homer's *Odyssey*, but long before Homer's epic there were marks and pictures made by human beings that communicated meaning. Starting with the philosophers of Ancient Greece, Chapter 1 presents key theoretical ideas about language and writing, and outlines the multidisciplinary theoretical backdrop to the book's arguments. Humans not only express meanings directly through writing but also have the unique capacity of metacognition, to actively and deliberately reflect *on* writing, and the ways in which meaning is expressed. Even as the ancient Greeks' invention of the alphabet grew in use, they started thinking about what changes writing would bring. Plato suggested that the change was nothing short of revolution: an oral state of mind was to be replaced by a literate state of mind, and the key role in this was played by the Greek alphabet[31]. Socrates explicitly discussed writing with his student Theaetetus, including the minutiae of syllables and letters, in the context of their conversation about knowledge. In modern times, findings from neuroscience suggest that the development of writing (and literacy) in young children permanently changes the brain, a further outcome of the influence of writing on thinking. And more recent thinking in philosophy, from the perspective of pragmatism, also offers important possibilities for understanding writing.

Chapter 2 is a history of writing. Some of the earliest known paintings, depicting animals to be worshipped and hunted, were seen on the walls of caves. The pictures and marks that were the beginnings of writing led ultimately to human beings' greatest invention of all: the alphabet. Without the alphabet most other inventions would be impossible: no general theory of relativity; no jet engine; no solving of Fermat's last theorem. The history of writing, from pictures through to the alphabet, is a story of incremental steps: first, hieroglyphs and pictograms to represent financial transactions; then, the move from *rebuses* to abstract determinatives; and finally, the supreme addition by the Greeks, of five characters to represent vowels added to the Proto-Canaanite alphabet of consonants. All these historical developments were

[31] Havelock, *The Muse Learns to Write*.

driven by humans' constant need to express meaning more clearly, less ambiguously, and in increasingly diverse ways.

The history of writing is also a story of technological changes. A change as important in magnitude as the internet, the invention of the printing press, occurred in the fifteenth century. This was revolutionary for many reasons. It transformed a world of anonymous writers and scribes into a new kind of consumer world with, for the first time, a reading public. The profound changes stimulated by printing included the standardisation of language, the beginnings of the concept of literary fame, the idea of intellectual property, and the change from knowledge controlled by elites towards democratisation of the written word. These trends would continue hundreds of years later, as part of the digital revolution.

If we accept that understanding writing requires a sense of the ways that language changes over time, appropriate ways of thinking about writing, and research from different disciplines, what are the practical lessons for improving writing? As I reveal in Chapter 3, interest in this area, and advice, is not in short supply. There are thousands of texts giving advice about writing (including one I've written myself). What is less common is an analysis of the patterns of guidance that the range of these texts offer. The modern guides to language and writing addressed in this chapter are descendants of John Walker's *Pronouncing Dictionary*, which share the intent to describe and prescribe standards of language and writing.

The accounts of writing by eminent writers are a relatively untapped source of knowledge. From the complexities of creativity and composition, to the pragmatics of the room where writing takes place, there is the potential to learn a great deal. The writing processes of some of the greatest writers, that I analyse in Chapter 4, reveal their attention, first and foremost, to meaning at the level of the whole text. The generation of ideas for writing, the 'problems' that authors invent, the themes of their writing, the creative processes, and ultimately the precision of meaning that is expressed in their careful choice of words, phrases, and sentences, are processes that all writers can learn about and consider applying to their own writing.

Fiction or non-fiction writing is built on creativity, which consists of the pillars of originality and value, the subjects that are explored at the beginning of Chapter 5. Creativity is not unique to writers. Composers of music, artists, choreographers, architects, also create, and in some different ways so do mathematicians and scientists. Like writers, all meaning-makers use their craft to communicate particular meanings, with intended effects, to a desired audience.

Writing's primitive origins teach us much about the central place of meaning. But there is another source of primitive writing: children's writing. The genetic echoes of humans' development of writing are still present in every young child's journey to learn how to write. It is clear that children's natural play with written marks is centred on meaning and its expression. Just as humans moved from oral language to pictures to alphabets, so too do children as part of their development. Research on how children best learn to write, and how they (and older people) can be taught to write, provides another powerful source of knowledge about writing and how to improve it. This is the knowledge from the discipline of education which is the central focus of Chapter 6.

The final chapter of the book features one last analysis of data: my own reflections as a writer of this book, and some of the biography of my work as a writer. The end of this chapter, and the book, draws conclusions about how writing works, and as a consequence how the teaching and learning of writing in a wide range of contexts might be improved.

1 Thinking about Writing and Language

The philosophers of ancient Greece made some of the first academic contributions to understanding written language, as they did for so many aspects of human culture and existence. The invention of the alphabet was a linguistic revolution that quickly began to be felt in Greek society. As a result Plato suggested that an oral state of mind was to be replaced by a literate state of mind.[1] One aspect of the revolution was that the dominance that teachers exerted (through teaching that was part of an oral culture) was fundamentally challenged by the move towards writing. If people became able to access knowledge through written texts, there might be less need for oral transmission of knowledge by teachers.

In more recent times, two main academic loci for thinking about writing have emerged: psychological-neuroscientific, and socio-cultural. The ways in which the brain and mind are engaged, including as part of writing processes, is central to psychological and neuroscientific work.[2] At the same time, the rapid rise of socio-cultural theory has contributed to the growing empirical evidence that the human mind and brain develop as a direct result of social and cultural factors. Although there are clear differences between psychological-neuroscientific and socio-culturally oriented ways of thinking about writing there are also some important overlaps, and it is perhaps in these overlaps where new knowledge about writing and its processes is increasingly to be found. Robust psychological-neuroscientific and socio-cultural theories can take us a long way towards better understanding of writing, but for many people their interest is also in the practice and craft of writing, and how people can be educated to write more effectively. The philosophy of pragmatism includes attention to educative processes as central to understandings of human culture and behaviour. And effectiveness of teaching and learning is the prime concern of the academic discipline and field of education.

Three overarching developments are addressed in this chapter and the one that follows: (1) Societal changes from oral language only, to oral and written

[1] Havelock, *The Muse Learns to Write*.

[2] Philosophers, however, also continue to address the ontology of mind, rather than the cognitive aspects of the brain.

language; (2) the idea of spoken language as the preeminent language form, with writing initially not deemed to be particularly important; (3) recognition of writing as a distinct symbolic form of language, and an essential element in metalinguistic thinking.[3] This chapter reviews philosophical, cognitive, and socio-cultural theories in order to better understand the processes of writing but also to initiate some key themes for the book as a whole. The first section, The Emergence of Written Language, begins by examining some of the profound changes in thinking in ancient Greece that the emergence of written language led to. Next, in The Clothes of Language, I home in on one of the most important philosophical contributions to the understanding of writing: the idea that language is a different object to the thoughts that precede the writing.

The second half of the chapter addresses more recent theories of writing, derived from psychological-neuroscientific and socio-cultural theories. In Writing and the Individual, cognitive models are addressed. This is followed by Mediation and Multimodality in which socio-cultural theories of *sign* and *tool*, as part of *mediation*, explain how humans use objects and language in unique combinations to make meaning. The digital developments in writing are also addressed in relation to socio-cultural theory, focusing particularly on the concept of 'multimodality' that links with systemic functional linguistics. The chapter concludes, in The Meaning of Writing, with a return to philosophy, drawing new attention to the importance of language through Dewian Pragmatism, and in particular Dewey's theories of communication, as an important way to conceptualise how writing works.

The Emergence of Written Language

There are three significant problems with surveying ancient Greek philosophical thinking about writing. The first is that writing, as opposed to language more generally, was very rarely addressed. The second problem is that the evidence base for attribution of many philosophical ideas is often poor, and what evidence there is is located in second-hand accounts by philosophers other than those who it is assumed established the ideas in the first place. The third problem is that philosophy of language was usually secondary to different philosophical concerns that were the primary focus in a given text, such as, what truth is.[4] Acknowledging these problems, I restrict my attention to ancient Greek philosophy in this section as much as possible to examples where writing is the focus.

The main ideas about writing, as for so many topics, are most evident in the thinking of Plato, Socrates, and Aristotle. Other schools of philosophy did

[3] Olson, *The Mind on Paper.* [4] Castagnoli and Di Lasco. 'Ancient Philosophy of Language'.

address language but are subject to the caveats raised above. The Sophists shared an interest in language, speech, and argument as *logos* but also offered teaching on diction (probably in relation to poetry), and the correctness of words (including quasi-synonyms, understanding of ambiguity, and convention and signification). Similar to the problem with the evidence base for Sophists' views, there is very little evidence to confirm the attribution of ideas about language from the other major schools of the Hellenistic age: the Epicureans, Stoics, Academics, and Peripatetics apart from short surviving fragments.[5]

Concerns by Plato about writing were not limited to the role of the teachers. He described writing as inhuman; as a means to destroy memory (an interesting contention in the light of theories of sign and tool that I review later in the chapter); and non-responsive compared to someone you talk to.[6] In Plato's dialogue *Phaedrus*, Socrates recounts an ancient story. The king of Egypt was the god Thamus who was visited by the god Theuth, who wanted to show some of his new inventions, such as 'numbers and arithmetic and geometry and astronomy, also draughts and dice, and, most important of all, letters.'[7] Thamus discussed the merits of each of the inventions but was completely dismissive of the letters that make up writing:

> 'This invention, O king,' said Theuth, 'will make the Egyptians wiser and will improve their memories; for it is an elixir of memory and wisdom that I have discovered.'
>
> But Thamus replied, 'Most ingenious Theuth, one man has the ability to beget arts, but the ability to judge of their usefulness or harmfulness to their users belongs to another; and now you, who are the father of letters, have been led by your affection to ascribe to them a power the opposite of that which they really possess. For this invention will produce forgetfulness in the minds of those who learn to use it, because they will not practice their memory. Their trust in writing, produced by external characters which are no part of themselves, will discourage the use of their own memory within them. You have invented an elixir not of memory, but of reminding; and you offer your pupils the appearance of wisdom, not true wisdom, for they will read many things without instruction and will therefore seem to know many things, when they are for the most part ignorant and hard to get along with, since they are not wise, but only appear wise.'[8]

Thamus' point distinguishing the role of the writer (to beget arts) and the role of the reader (to judge usefulness) was an important early conception of the way that once writers, or other artists, 'publish' their texts they are no longer in sole control of the meaning because the readership for the writing will ultimately interpret its meaning and determine its qualities. The concern that reading 'many things without instruction' is insufficient for wisdom is also of particular interest to the concerns of this book. Although learning happens through reading, learning also happens as a social process that includes rehearsing new ideas in the company

[5] Castagnoli, L., and E. Di Lasco., 'Ancient Philosophy of Language'.
[6] Ong, *Orality and Literacy.* [7] Fowler, H. 'Plato, *Phaedrus*', 274.
[8] Fowler, H. 'Plato, *Phaedrus*', 274.

of others. In the extract then, we perhaps see the importance ascribed to what might be called a *dialogic* process of learning that requires the contribution of the teacher, and even education, not just the text.

In another of Plato's dialogues, Socrates has a discussion with his pupil Theaetetus. Consistent with the problem identified at the start of this section, in relation to language as a secondary focus to other primary philosophical topics, the dialogue is mainly about knowledge, and what knowledge really is. Part way through their dialogue Theaetetus and Socrates arrive at a preliminary definition of knowledge: 'true opinion accompanied by reason is knowledge.'[9] As part of their further exploration of knowledge, they then consider the addition of 'rational explanation' as part of 'true opinion'.

The first example chosen to test their new conception of knowledge was that of a wagon. Understanding of wagon, as an object, as a construction, and as a mental representation, leads them to agree that true knowledge requires not only understanding of what a wagon is as a whole, but also of its 'one hundred [wooden] parts'. They decide that it is only with the knowledge of the 100 parts that 'rational explanation' is achieved.

The second example chosen to test Socrates' and Theaetetus' theory is the writing of a person's name. Socrates and Theaetetus agree that syllables as part of words are not the same as letters, '**Socrates** ... Perhaps we ought to have said that the syllable is not the letters, but a single concept that has arisen from them, having a single form of its own, different from the letters.' Extending this they agree that explanation of things is not fully realised if elements such as letters and syllables are not considered in relation to each other: '**Socrates** ... there can be no rational explanation of the primary elements of which other things are composed, because each of them, when taken by itself, is not composite ... '. The discussion continued using the example of the writing of a person's name.

Socrates Take an example: When at such a stage in his progress a person in writing 'Theaetetus' thinks he ought to write, and actually does write, T H and E, and again in trying to write 'Theodorus' thinks he ought to write, and does write, T and E, shall we say that he knows the first syllable of your names?

Theaetetus No, we just now agreed that a person in such a condition has not yet gained knowledge.

The person has not yet gained knowledge because the first syllable of Theodorus has the letters T H E not T E. Knowledge has not been gained in this instance because full knowledge of the meaning of syllable, including its constituent parts and how these fit with the whole word, has not necessarily been understood. True knowledge about the meaning of a written text, similar

[9] The quotes in this section are from Fowler, 'Plato, *Theaetetus*'.

to true knowledge of anything, requires sufficient understanding of the whole text, including its purpose and readership. But true understanding also requires the necessary knowledge about the building blocks of the text, and how these enable precise meanings to be expressed.

As part of Socrates' and Theaetetus' more general argument about knowledge, it is made clear that even if accurate opinion is combined with rational explanation this still does not represent knowledge because knowledge requires understanding of the full range of meanings and implications of, for example, a wagon as a physical and mental reality, similarly a person's name in all its meanings and forms including when written down. It is also made clear that true knowledge of the syllable is only complete with accurate knowledge of the parts that make up the syllable, the letters. True knowledge of writing, similar to true knowledge of anything, requires full understanding of the whole, the parts, and how these are linked.

Aristotle's contribution to philosophy included some of the first thinking about language and writing. His early work examined the smaller elements of language; then much later Aristotle turned to rhetoric and style.[10] In *Categories* Aristotle begins his argument with an analysis of things and their names. This is followed by an explanation of forms of speech as either simple or composite. For example, the word 'man' on its own is simple whereas 'The man runs' is composite because the word 'man' is linked grammatically with running. In part four of the short text Aristotle goes on to explain further categories of language. Non-composite expressions are grouped into different categories of meaning. For example one category is 'quality', with examples of this category being 'white' or 'grammatical'.

Aristotle also addressed some of these themes in *On Interpretation*. The first sentence of *On Interpretation* is, 'First we must define the terms "noun" and "verb", then the terms "denial" and "affirmation", then "proposition" and "sentence".' Aristotle first establishes that a noun makes complete sense on its own, but also that no separate part of it makes complete sense on its own: 'In the noun "Fairsteed", the part "steed" has no significance in and by itself, as it does in the phrase "fair steed".' The importance of understanding the relationships between parts and wholes that make written meaning is emphasised.

In another significant contribution to language and writing the concept of words representing things was described as 'a convention' by Aristotle:

> The limitation 'by convention' was introduced because nothing is by nature a noun or name – it is only so when it becomes a symbol; inarticulate sounds, such as those which brutes produce, are significant, yet none of these constitutes a noun.[11]

[10] Assuming the assumptions about chronology in Immanuel Bekker's organisation of the *Corpus Aristotelicum*, in the nineteenth century are accurate.

[11] Edgehill, 'On Interpretation, by Aristotle'.

Aristotle's attention to grammar in his early work was followed much later by attention to the structures of language, and particularly his conception of rhetoric, the art of speaking persuasively. He argued that the sources of proof necessary for good rhetoric are important, but also that to be good rhetoric it had to be spoken in the most persuasive style. One aspect of Aristotle's theory of style was the components of volume, tone, and rhythm of the oral delivery, a clear link with music (as was his attention to the performance of poetry). He argued that different kinds of rhetoric[12] require different styles of delivery: Aristotle established that the preparation in writing of speeches by rhetoricians, if spoken, would sound authentic in a public debate but 'silly' if read aloud in a different context. Aspects such as the repetition of words is acceptable, and necessary, in public debate but not in other contexts for writing. In comparison, the writing of poets, if used in a public debate rather than in the context of performance of poetry, would similarly appear silly. Knowledge of rhetoric in writing and in oral delivery was required for effective communication in both contexts, and, 'The style of written compositions [poetry] is most precise, that of debate is most suitable for delivery.'[13] Aristotle emphasised that the style in which rhetoricians were to use oral language was inappropriate for writing, and that the way writers (by which Aristotle meant poets) used language was inappropriate for oral public debate. Aristotle also made distinctions between prose (by which he meant spoken prose) and poetry, and in so doing sowed the seeds for the modern concern with style, which as you will see in Chapter 3 continues to be of particular interest in the United States. The identification, by Aristotle, of genre and context as essential to understanding of language was striking.

Looking from the position of modern linguistic understanding, one of the problems with Aristotle's theory of language is the extent to which the distinction between oral language and written language is robust enough. An example from another late work, *Poetics*, is illustrative:

> Language in general includes the following parts: Letter, Syllable, Connecting Word, Noun, Verb, Inflection or Case, Sentence or Phrase. A Letter is an indivisible sound, yet not every such sound, but only one which can form part of a group of sounds. For even brutes utter indivisible sounds, none of which I call a letter. The sound I mean may be either a vowel, a semivowel, or a mute. A vowel is that which without impact of tongue or lip has an audible sound. A semivowel that which with such impact has an audible sound, as S and R. A mute, that which with such impact has by itself no sound, but joined to a vowel sound becomes audible, as G and D. These are distinguished according to the form assumed by the mouth and the place where they are produced; according as they are

[12] Or what we now call *genre*: see later in this chapter.

[13] Freese, J. 'Aristotle, Rhetoric', *Rhetoric* III, chapter 12, section 1.

aspirated or smooth, long or short; as they are acute, grave, or of an intermediate tone; which inquiry belongs in detail to the writers on meter.[14]

The point Aristotle makes about the difference between vocal sounds of the animal kind and sounds that are part of meaningful human language is accurate, and is another point that has continued to receive attention up to the present day. But Aristotle conflated the idea of 'letter', including further designation as vowel or consonant, with the vocal sounds that when added together in particular ways make up words. But a letter is a grapheme that signifies particular sounds, and so is not synonymous with sound. And in the English language, letters are usually associated with more than one sound dependent on their context in a word, and sometimes even dependent on their sentence context (e.g. the word 'read' as I explain in Chapter 6). There is also a lack of consideration of the difference between spoken linguistic sounds and musical sounds. The example, in the next chapter, of the first known written musical composition appears to shed some light on the reason for this weakness in Aristotle's explanation of sounds and symbols.

The ancient Greeks articulated new thinking related to understanding the differences between oral language and written language. This included attention to teaching and learning as an important focus for philosophical consideration. Conceptions of the writer to beget arts and the reader to judge usefulness can, as I show later in the chapter, be linked with modern pragmatist understandings of consummatory forms of language. Most important of all is the understanding of holism in written language: the importance of understanding the relations between the constituent parts of language and meanings. The concept of convention was also a revelation, as this became important in understanding the idea of standard language, including the related concepts of correctness and error. Together, these new understandings represented the beginnings of metacognitive understanding of written language, and, as David Olson argues, the development of writing became inseparable from the development of humans' rationality.[15]

The Clothes of Language

Since the origins of Western philosophy in ancient Greece, and the beginnings of writing and thinking about writing, language has continued to be one of the most important of philosophical topics. The continuing philosophical interest gave rise to 'the linguistic turn', a phenomenon that originated in the thinking of Gottlob Frege and other seminal thinking by Bertrand Russell and Ludwig Wittgenstein. Frege's placement of language at the heart of philosophical thinking

[14] Aristotle, *Poetics*, section XX. [15] Olson, *The Mind on Paper*.

was encapsulated in the 'context principle', in particular that words can only be understood in the context of a sentence.[16]

Russell's work as part of the linguistic turn in philosophy included a central focus on meaning and language.

> Words, spoken, heard, or written, differ from other classes of bodily movements, noises, or shapes, by having 'meaning'. Many words only have meaning in a suitable verbal context, such words as 'than', 'or', 'however', cannot stand alone. We cannot begin the explanation of meaning with such words since they presuppose other words. There are words, however including all those that a child learns first – that can be used in isolation: proper names, class-names of familiar kinds of animals, names of colours, and so on. These are what I call 'object-words', and they compose the 'object-language', as to which I shall have much to say in a later chapter. These words have various peculiarities. First: their meaning is learnt (or can be learnt) by confrontation with objects which are what they mean, or instances of what they mean. Second: they do not presuppose other words. Third: each of them, by itself, can express a whole proposition; you can exclaim 'fire!', but it would be pointless to exclaim 'than!' It is obvious with such words that any explanation of 'meaning' must begin; for 'meaning', like 'truth' and 'falsehood', has a hierarchy of meanings, corresponding to the hierarchy of languages.[17]

The distinction that Russell made between particular kinds of nouns that signify physical objects, and other words such as conjunctions is of enduring interest to philosophers and linguists. But the emphasis on *context* by Russell is fundamental to understanding how written language works. To give a single word example of the importance of context, the word 'present' cannot be fully known unless it appears in a sentence ('present' can be a noun, as in a birthday 'present'. It can also be a verb as in being 'presented', or 'the military sense of 'present arms'). Broadly speaking it is true, as Russell suggested, that the words of language have a special quality that is uniquely human, and that this quality of words is different from the ways that meanings are expressed in other human sounds, including music.

Russell also engaged with Wittgenstein's ideas about language, for example in Russell's introduction to Wittgenstein's *Tractatus Logico-Philosophicus*. Building on philosophical traditions, Wittgenstein's work addressed the relationships between words and things. More particularly it focused on the problems of using language to represent ideas. One of the most significant understandings that Wittgenstein established was that language is a different object to that which it describes; this was part of Wittgenstein's thinking on the grammar of language.

> 4 The thought is the significant proposition.
> 4.001[18] The totality of propositions is the language.

[16] Potter, 'Frege, Russell, and Wittgenstein', 852.

[17] Russell, *An Inquiry into Meaning and Truth*, 25.

[18] Wittgenstein used the hierarchy of his numbering of statements to indicate logical relationships.

> 4.002 Man possesses the capacity of constructing languages, in which every sense can be expressed, without having an idea how and what each word means – just as one speaks without knowing how the single sounds are produced. Colloquial language is a part of the human organism and is not less complicated than it.
> From it it is humanly impossible to gather immediately the logic of language.
> *Language disguises the thought; so that from the external form of the clothes one cannot infer the form of the thought they clothe, because the external form of the clothes is constructed with quite another object than to let the form of the body be recognized.*
> The silent adjustments to understand colloquial language are enormously complicated.[19]

In Wittgenstein's focus on logical propositions and oral language, he made clear that two symbols, a written sign and a sound sign, have the sign in common but they signify in different ways.

The extent to which Wittgenstein's thinking in the *Tractatus* was superseded by his other great work, *Philosophical Investigations*, is difficult to judge because of the complex process of completion of the manuscript by translators and editors from its inception, and continued in the fourth edition published in 2009 (in this regard the process shares in a small way something of the story of the completion of Mozart's *Requiem* that I alluded to in the introduction to this book). In *Philosophical Investigations* Wittgenstein returns to the importance of 'proposition' in language. The idea from *Tractatus* that language disguises the thought is confirmed in the argument that the essence of propositions 'lies *beneath* the surface' and '*is hidden from us*'[20]. But Wittgenstein extends his analysis to explain language as 'language games'. Language games are represented in the way young children are taught language, also in the activities of life, including the games that humans play: for example, games played with a ball. A group of people playing with a ball might engage in games with rules; some games might then not be finished; and playing with the ball might then become a more creative and spontaneous activity. An observer watching the group play with the ball sees 'rules' of ball games throughout the period of play, but the essence is hidden from the observer because she is not directly engaged in the games.

The *Tractatus* is particularly known for its picture theory of language, which Wittgenstein explained not only in relation to words on paper but also musical notes. The idea of text itself representing one reality, at the same time as communicating a different reality, was exemplified by Wittgenstein through comparison with music.

[19] Wittgenstein, *Tractatus Logico-Philosophicus*, section 4.002 (emphasis added).
[20] Wittgenstein, *Tractatus Logico-Philosophicus*, section 48e.

> 4.01 The proposition [thought] is a picture of reality.
> The proposition is a model of the reality as we think it is.
> 4.011 At the first glance the proposition – say as it stands printed on paper – does not seem to be a picture of the reality of which it treats. But nor does the musical score appear at first sight to be a picture of a musical piece; nor does our phonetic spelling (letters) seem to be a picture of our spoken language. And yet these symbolisms prove to be pictures – even in the ordinary sense of the word – of what they represent.
> 4.012 It is obvious that we perceive a proposition of the form *aRb*[21] as a picture. Here the sign is obviously a likeness of the signified.
> 4.013 And if we penetrate to the essence of this pictorial nature we see that this is not disturbed by apparent irregularities (like the use of ♯ and ♭ in the score). For these irregularities also picture what they are to express; only in another way.
> 4.014 The gramophone record, the musical thought, the score, the waves of sound, all stand to one another in that pictorial internal relation, which holds between language and the world. To all of them the logical structure is common. (Like the two youths, their two horses and their lilies in the story. They are all in a certain sense one.)[22]

Like Plato, Wittgenstein expressed the essence of communication as the overall logical structure (or perhaps form), with parts that are subservient to the whole. Although the sharp or flat in music changes the music, just as the use of different letters leads to different words, the holistic pictorial nature of score or text remains unaltered when viewed or heard as a whole.

The differences that Wittgenstein drew between the writing of a proposition (a thought) and the writing of a musical score are true up to a point. However, the representational aspects of the letters of the alphabet are in at least one way different from the representational aspects of musical notes and signs. A musical note such as *middle C* when performed will always produce a particular musical pitch (very close to 262 hertz: a measure of musical pitch subject only to human ability for correct intonation or the accuracy of tuning on a piano, for example).[23] Whereas the letter C will sometimes produce the hard C in carpet, the soft C in ceiling, or the /ch/ in church. Musical note C is different to the letter C because the letter C changes its meaning altogether in its different contexts of use. Wittgenstein referred explicitly to letters and to 'a picture of reality' in the following passage:

> 4.015 The possibility of all similes, of all the imagery of our language, rests on the logic of representation.

[21] *R* = a Relationship between the objects *a* and *b*.

[22] *The Gold Children* by the Brothers Grimm.

[23] Having said that, it is true that in the hands of a musical performer the way the middle C is played will differ at every performance. For example the pitch will differ by very small amounts. For players of string instruments, the variation can even be as a result of playing in different musical keys because of the location of C in relation to the musical scale, but this does not render the concept of the note completely different.

> 4.016 In order to understand the essence of the proposition, consider hieroglyphic writing, which pictures the facts it describes. And from it came the alphabet without the essence of the representation being lost.
> 4.02 This we see from the fact that we understand the sense of the propositional sign, without having had it explained to us.
> 4.021 The proposition is a picture of reality, for I know the state of affairs presented by it, if I understand the proposition. And I understand the proposition, without its sense having been explained to me.

Symbolic systems are fundamentally rooted in representation of meaning, or 'propositions' as Wittgenstein terms them. It is true that 'proposition' as a picture, in the sense of the whole musical score or written text, communicates meaning without the need for oral explanation. But the relationship between, for example, hieroglyphic writing and the development of the alphabet has generated considerable argument, as I show in the next chapter. It may be true that the essence of representation was not lost in the change from hieroglyphics to alphabet, but the alphabet brought the capacity for a much wider range of meanings, so in that sense the representations of hieroglyphics were radically changed.

In *Philosophical Investigations*, Wittgenstein continued to address the idea of proposition and the picture of a reality (or state of affairs). Linking language and music once again, he argued that understanding a spoken sentence is close to understanding a musical 'theme', although his use of the word *theme* in relation to music is not particularly clear. 'Melody' would perhaps have been more accurate. A sentence *can* be replaced by another sentence in order to communicate the same or very similar meaning. At the same time, the precise meanings change whenever such a change to the words of a sentence is made, so in this way it also *cannot* be replaced to retain the same meaning. A musical melody can also be similarly replaced, and not replaced. But the way that notes make musical meaning in a melody is not with the same precision of meaning that is possible with words. For example, an instruction to action cannot be given through musical notes (unless through words in song).

In another example in *Philosophical Investigations*, Wittgenstein compares the reinterpretation of facial expressions with chords in music. For example, a face can be described as courageous, but with no implication that courageous action by the person will follow. The modulation of a musical chord from one key to another is argued to be comparable. But a clearer example might be to take a face that looks sad. Music certainly has the capacity to portray sadness, for example in Edward Elgar's movement *Nimrod* in *The Enigma Variations*,[24] or in the slow movement of Brahms' third string quartet.[25] But this is achieved

[24] Which includes the language games of Elgar's friends secretly depicted in each of the movements.

[25] His own language games conjured his embarrassment with trying to imagine what it might be like trying to paint a picture of Goethe composing Beethoven's Ninth Symphony!

not only with chords: a very particular arrangement of harmony, melody, tempo, timbre, instrumentation, and rhythm is required. Related to this, in a point made later in the *Philosophical Investigations*, the musical concepts of major and minor do not to modern ears[26] 'have emotive value',[27] they have structural value. These harmonic and melodic structures can be used to create emotive effect only in combination with the other compositional elements listed above.

The main point that Wittgenstein makes is that language games explain the possibilities of different 'readings' of faces, of music, of language, of pictures, that are arbitrary and changing, and where the surface features reveal meanings that are the same, different, and related, to the below-the-surface meanings. In Wittgenstein's work, we see attention to the central place of meaning. Humans seek to use language, by which 'every sense can be expressed'. Humans are also able to reflect metacognitively on language because it is a different 'object' to our thoughts. Thoughts are the mental processes of the brain that we translate into language, and this prompts us to consider which elements of language must be sufficiently understood for effective expression of meaning in writing, and those which need not be.

It is possible to relate elements of Wittgenstein's theory of language more directly to written language, although distinctions between oral language and written language are not strongly accounted for in *Philosophical Investigations*. The 'clothes' of language could be seen as the visible features of written language, that is, layout and other structural features, sentences, words, and letters. The intention to communicate, and the crafting of meaning in writing, as quite another object but nevertheless related to the clothes. For example, writers do not need to know the technical definition of a *subordinate clause* in order to communicate efficiently in writing, but they do need to develop an 'ear' for grammar that can effectively facilitate the expression of meaning in the ways intended. The ear of the writer once again links the writing of words with music, akin to the distinction between hearing versus listening, or as Wittgenstein put it, 'Speech with and without thought is to be compared to playing a piece of music with and without thought.'[28] The metalanguage of grammar, represented by terms such as 'subordinate clause', is a different knowledge to the holistic knowledge of letters and words and their meaning-making qualities.

As I have begun to explore, one of the essential elements of understanding writing is understanding the way it differs from oral language yet with which it is also strongly related. Gayatri Spivak, in the introduction to Derrida's *Of*

[26] Irrespective of the historic origins of the words major and minor.
[27] Wittgenstein, *Philosophical Investigations*, 220e.
[28] Wittgenstein, *Philosophical Investigations*, 116e.

Grammatology, summarised how Derrida overturned the prevailing view established by the linguist Ferdinand de Saussure that linguistics was and should be the study of speech because writing was essentially the same. Saussure's linguistics was built on his particular conception of the two-sided linguistic entity that he called the *linguistic sign*. Take for example the linguistic sign that is the written word 'viola'. The word represents both a concept and a sound pattern. The concept is a musical instrument (or the name of a person or a flower). The sound pattern is the articulation /v/ /ee/ /oh/ /l/ /a/ (sound pattern in Saussure's terms included all physical aspects needed to speak the word). Saussure called the concept *signification*, and the sound pattern *signal*; hence he said that, 'The linguistic sign thus defined has two fundamental characteristics [signification and signal]. In specifying them, we shall lay down the principles governing all studies in this domain.'[29] The translator of Saussure's *Course in General Linguistics*, a collection of his main ideas published in a book after his death, clearly identified the importance of Saussure's contribution:

> The revolution Saussure ushered in has rightly been described as 'Copernican'. For instead of men's words being seen as peripheral to men's understanding of reality, men's understanding of reality came to be seen as revolving about their social use of verbal signs. In the *Cours de linguistique générale* we see this new approach clearly articulated for the first time. Words are not vocal labels which have come to be attached to things and qualities already given in advance by Nature, or to ideas already grasped independently by the human mind. On the contrary languages themselves, collective products of social interaction, supply the essential conceptual frameworks for men's analysis of reality and, simultaneously, the verbal equipment for their description of it. The concepts we use are creations of the language we speak.

Derrida's critique of Saussure complained of a phonocentrism that promoted speech, and relegated writing as identical in meaning to speech that was just represented in a different form. As part of the *deconstruction* of the idea that speech and writing were so similar Derrida made a distinction between colloquial understanding of the term 'writing' by establishing a different word, 'arche-writing (*archi-écriture*)'[30], Derrida argued that in order to deconstruct the idea that writing has a straightforward signification of meaning, that is the same as oral language, then even the word itself is a problem because 'the proper name has never been, as the unique appellation reserved for the presence of a unique being, anything but the original myth of a transparent legibility present under the obliteration'.[31] Consistent with the concept and method of deconstruction, throughout *Of Grammatology* Derrida replaces arche-writing

[29] Saussure, *General Linguistics*. [30] Derrida, *Of Grammatology*, 14.
[31] Derrida, *Of Grammatology*, 160.

with 'trace' and 'difference' and other words to describe writing. Derrida identified some of the profound differences between speech and writing (which provides a rationale for the study of writing in its own right as an important part of language) including the use of signifiers (letters) that are also nonsignifying if there are no rules governing the ways they communicate meaning.

> Access to phonetic writing constitutes at once a supplementary degree of representativity and a total revolution in the structure of representation. Direct or hieroglyphic pictography represents the thing or the signified. The ideo-phonogram already represents a mixture of signifier and signified. It already paints language. It is the moment located by all historians of writing as the birth of phoneticization, through, for example, the picture puzzle [*rebus à transfer*]; a sign representing a thing named in its concept ceases to refer to the concept and keeps only the value of a phonic signifier. Its signified is no longer anything but a phoneme deprived by itself of all meaning. But before this decomposition and in spite of the 'twofold convention', representation is reproduction; it repeats the signifying and signified masses en bloc and without analysis. This synthetic character of representation is the pictographic residue of the ideo-phonogram that 'paints voices'. Phonetic writing works to reduce it. Instead of using signifiers immediately related to a conceptual signified, it uses, through the analysis of sounds, signifiers that are in some way nonsignifying. Letters, which have no meaning by themselves, signify only the elementary phonic signifiers that make sense only when they are put together according to certain rules.[32]

Derrida's recognition of the pivotal moment of the birth of the alphabet reminds us of its influence in ancient Greece recorded by philosophers, and signals its importance in the historical development of language, but also prefigures the greater attention to the concept of the phoneme that psychological and neuroscientific studies of cognition would come to focus on (see Chapter 6). However, Derrida's ultimate contribution was to attack structuralism and propose deconstruction, which in particular urged readers to critique binary opposites. This contribution was built on his advances in thinking about writing as a form of language important in its own right.

Thinking about writing progressed from the uncertainty of the impact of the invention of alphabetic writing, reflected upon by ancient Greeks philosophers, to sustained attention to how the signs of writing have signification and how this is related to oral language. One aspect of signification is the nature of the links between the author's or composer's intent to communicate, the specific written language used to establish meaning, and the meanings inscribed by recipients, readers, and audiences. Other more recent developments include the attention to the way the mind and brain operate in relation to the social context of language production, areas which are the subject of the next sections in this chapter.

[32] Derrida, *Of Grammatology*, 299.

Writing and the Individual

Psychologically oriented work on writing has been characterised by experimental research that uses multiple tests of the individual writers involved in experiments to determine their cognitive processes. In the last decade, this has been augmented by work in neuroscience, so much so that psychology is considered by some to be synonymous with neuroscience. One influential cognitive perspective on writing is that by Hayes (2006). Hayes proposed that the two key components of writing are the individual writer and the environment for their writing (Figure 1.1).

Individuals and their writing are characterised by the cognitive functions of working memory, which is the writer's short-term memory; long-term memory; and the writer's motivations and affect. The writer's motivation is subdivided into goals, predispositions, beliefs and attitudes, and cost-benefit estimates. Let's take an example. A writer has set the goal of writing a novel. She is predisposed to have many aims in her life which she frequently doesn't realise because she lacks the determination to apply herself to the hard work that is often involved. The writer believes that she can write a novel that will change the world. She envisages very little cost in terms of the amount of work she will have to do, but huge financial benefits when she sells millions of copies of her novel. It is unlikely that the novel will get written!

The writing process, it is argued by Hayes, like all mental processes is driven by *working memory*. Unlike the Hayes model of writing, the original concept of working memory also includes the *central executive*, a component of the brain that orchestrates the other elements of working memory, although research evidence to support this theory is not conclusive. Phonological memory allows the writer to convert spoken language into written language, and vice versa. The visuospatial sketchpad deals with information that is visual or spatial in character. For example, conceptions of the physical environment for a character in a novel require processing that might include the visuospatial sketch pad. What Hayes calls semantic memory is not usually described as part of working memory. However, attention to semantics is a vital part of the writing process. Semantics, or meaning, exists at many levels, from the overall intention that underlies a text, to the inferences that readers make, to the smaller details of the literal meanings of sentences, phrases, and words.

Cognitive processes, in Hayes's model, include text interpretation. The writing process requires the continual interpretation and re-interpretation of what the writer has already written in order to know how to continue writing, which is the text production. Writing also requires use of the *long-term memory*. In a way, *task schemas* reflect one of the central concerns of this book. Task schemas are established ways of thinking about a task. Within the task schema of writing, the writer has to be cognoscente of what the audience

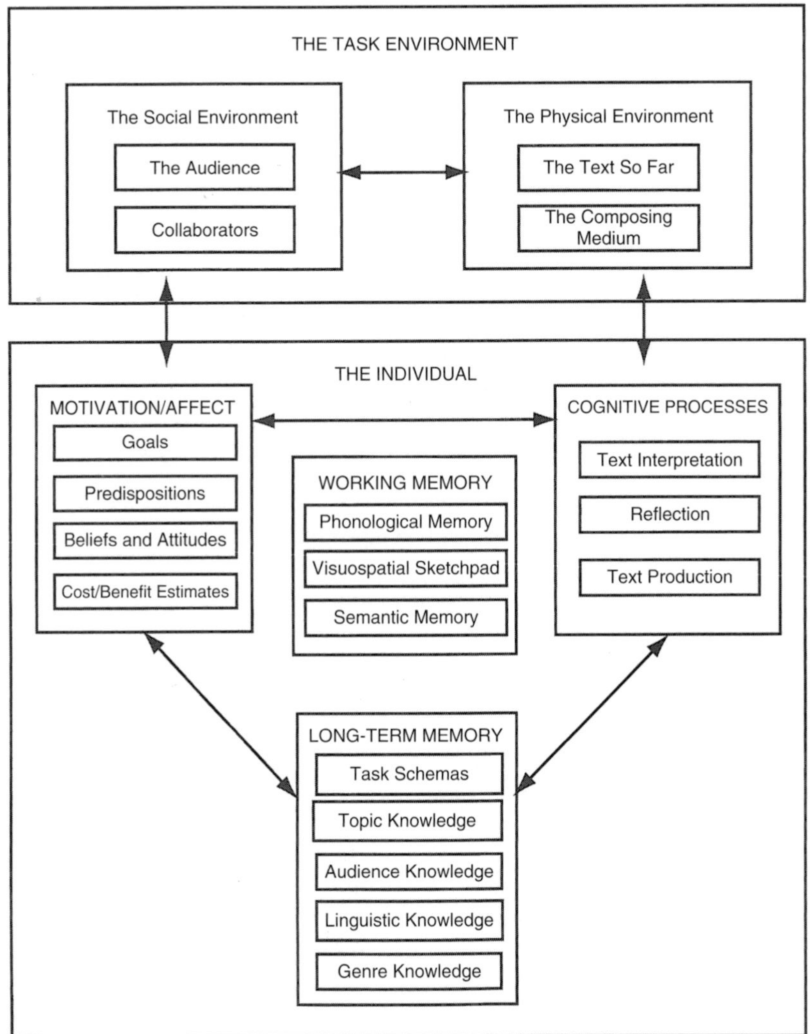

Figure 1.1 Cognitive perspective on writing proceses. Figure taken with permission from Hayes, J. R. 'New Directions in Writing Theory'. In C. MacArthur, S. Graham, & J. Fitzgerald (Eds.), *Handbook of Writing Research* (28–40). New York: The Guilford Press, 2006.

for the writing might expect. For any writing, there is a need to express thoughts in relation to a particular topic, something that requires *topic knowledge*. For non-fiction writing, the use of research material is part of this, but also the knowledge the writer has more generally about the topic. For the fiction writer, the topic is bound to the overall concept of the story and its realisation through the characters in it. Genre knowledge[33] is knowledge of the particular conventions that are required for an effective piece of writing in a particular genre.

The environment, or *task environment*, is subdivided into the social environment and the physical environment. A key component of the social environment is the actual audience for the writing (rather than simply knowledge about audience in more general terms). This will be a known audience if for example writing a letter to a particular person, or unknown/anticipated audience if for example writing a novel. Collaborators may be a part of the social environment for writing. For example, writers often have preferred readers for early drafts. Later drafts may need to be shown to editors, including copy-editors, and proofreaders. *The physical environment* includes the composing medium, for example pen and paper, or word processor. Any text, notes, stimuli for writing are part of *the text so far.*

In order to test psychological models, neuroscience has offered new empirical methods. There is a range of neuroscientific brain imaging tools, each of which assesses different aspects of brain function and structure.[34] One way of measuring the activity of the brain is electroencephalography (EEF), which involves recording voltage changes in the neurons of the brain through electrodes that are placed in a net on the scalp. In relation to language and literacy research, a method that has produced promising results involves measuring the brain's response following a language stimulus. In particular, understanding of meaning, or semantics, has been investigated through the use of experiments that involve language 'events' that are likely to be expected or not. So, a stimulus that is unexpected produces an electronic wave that has a greater amplitude than a stimulus that is expected. This electronic wave, associated with semantics, is known as the N400 because the wave occurs at about 400 milliseconds (msec) after the stimulus.

Examples of stimuli that produce the greater amplitude wave in adults are *pseudowords* (nonsense words that obey some rules of the language such as *vank*). Brain response to pseudowords has been compared to the response to *nonwords* (nonsense words that break the rules of language such as *sxoq*). One study found that the brain activity of children as young as 19 months showed that they had some awareness of semantic aspects of word meanings. Words of different kinds were said slowly aloud to the young children. The N400 showed that the pseudowords triggered a response, but the nonwords did not.[35]

33 Genre in this case does not simply refer to the genres of novels, such as science fiction, historical fiction etc., but refers to different forms of writing such as newspaper front page, dictionary entry, shopping list, poem, etc. and other elements – covered later in this chapter.

34 James, Jao & Berninger, 'The Development of Multileveled Writing Systems of the Brain'.

35 Friedrich, and Friederici, 'Phonotactic Knowledge and Lexical-Semantic Processing in One-Year-Olds'.

Although we have a measure that may indicate semantic awareness, it is difficult to identify brain mechanisms involved in the creation of meaning in writing. There is some evidence that learning to write is dependent on ability to translate cognitive impulses to meaningful linguistic units through use of working memory components, and that this may relate to ideas such as the Language Acquisition Device (LAD) proposed by Chomsky.[36] Building on Chomsky's work, the idea that humans have a genetic capacity for language was developed by Steven Pinker.[37] However, Chomsky's theory of the LAD has been critiqued as part of a general reaction against 'grand theories' in favour of more nuanced understandings from multiple perspectives. Another key criticism was the lack of sufficient consideration of social and cultural factors in language acquisition. As another polymath, Jerome Bruner, observed:

> The infant's Language Acquisition Device could not function without the aid given by an adult who enters with him into a transactional format. That format, initially under the control of the adult, provides a Language Acquisition Support System (LASS). It frames or structures the input of language and interaction to the child's Language Acquisition Device in a manner to 'make the system function'. In a word, it is the interaction between the LAD and the LASS that makes it possible for the infant to enter the linguistic community – and, at the same time, the culture to which the language gives access.[38]

The evidence on cognition supports understanding writing as a system where multiple cognitive components, language systems, and levels of language interact in the brain to support the different composition and transcription aspects of the processes of writing. The multiple components of the working memory system work at the levels of subword, word, syntax, and text. This is seen in 'the higher-order executive functions that support the bidirectional cognitive-linguistic translation process'.[39] The language systems involved in writing include ear, mouth, eye, and hand. The links between writing and sound (including music) and multiple language modes (including digital modes) are part of these interacting cognitive systems.

Neuroscientific evidence linking language and music suggests the important place of the communication of, and response to, *emotion* in both language and music: 'It is proposed here that the culturally-shaped melodic, rhythmic behaviours that we call music, and semantic, lexical linguistic abilities, later emerged as specialised behaviours building upon the foundations of this system of vocal and kinaesthetic communication of emotion.'[40] Like the physical apparatus of the airways, larynx, and mouth used for speech, another aspect

[36] Chomsky, *Syntactic Structures*. [37] Pinker, *The Language Instinct*.
[38] Bruner, *Child's Talk*, 19.
[39] James, Jao, and Berninger, 'The Development of Multileveled Writing Systems of the Brain', 116.
[40] Morley, ' Multi-Disciplinary Approach to the Origins of Music', 167.

shared between music and language is the ability of the brain to discriminate intonation patterns. This discrimination is more refined for music than that required for speech. Overall, it appears that although there are some linked mental processes and shared physical apparatus, the semantic elements of speech draw upon specialised areas of the brain different from some of those drawn on for music.

Mediation and Multimodality

Psychological and neuroscientific theory has provided multiple insights into language, both oral and written. But the main frames of reference for this work, as we have seen, are individuals and their cognition (accepting that areas such as social psychology are part of the tradition). Socio-cultural thinking has argued that any action undertaken by an individual has to be seen in a holistic context that links the individual's thinking with social and cultural influences.

If we return to Hayes's psychological model (Figure 1.1), consistent with many psychological models a clear separation is made between the individual and the wider social environment. Even the use of the word 'task' in relation to the environment is indicative of a way of thinking. A socio-cultural perspective does not see the environment, or context for writing, as a task. Writing, like most processes that require higher-order thinking, is part of a continual process of human development. At any time when the activity of writing takes place, it does so in the context of the history of the writer and the physical, social, and cultural factors that intertwine to form the context for writing.

Although the two-way arrows between the individual and the task environment in Figure 1.1 suggest the links between these domains, a socio-cultural perspective sees them as completely interconnected. For example, the motivation for whether to write or not derives from both personal motivation and social drivers. Even for simple everyday examples of writing, this is the case. The writing of a shopping list is driven by the need to buy food to live; the limitations of memory for items in a list, the inconvenience of having to return to the shop if something is forgotten, requests by family for particular items, for some people an interest in cooking, and the division of labour in a household which comes through constant social negotiations. The writing of a shopping list is not usually a one-off event carried out by the lone writer. It may be started on one day then continued as the various social influences interact. It may be written by more than one person, and certainly is likely to be influenced by more than one person. The control of the shopping list by parents is important in relation to young children's health, a topic that is of major national and international concern, and this entails control of the written form, which generates questions about use of power and control in relation to writing. Who decides which foods are to be bought and why?

The most influential thinker in the socio-cultural tradition is the Russian Lev Vygotsky. In fact the very frequent, and sometimes too frequent and inaccurate, citations of his work by others in the socio-cultural tradition attest to Vygotsky as a founding figure of socio-cultural thinking. At first glance, Vygotsky's expertise as a psychologist may seem paradoxical in relation to his influence on socio-cultural thinking. But what is more important, beyond the disciplinary label of psychology, is the breadth of Vygotsky's scholarship, and the particular ways he thought about human activity. Vygotsky's subjects of investigation were culture and consciousness, as the editor's introduction to one of his most well-known books explains:

> Vygotsky argued that psychology cannot limit itself to direct evidence, be it observable behaviour or accounts of introspection. Psychological inquiry is *investigation*, and like the criminal investigator, the psychologist must take into account indirect evidence and circumstantial clues – which in practice means that works of art, philosophical arguments, and anthropological data are no less important for psychology than direct evidence.[41]

Vygotsky's contribution to the understanding of the development of higher psychological processes in humans includes his important concept of 'indirect (mediated) activity', consisting of an interplay between *sign* and *tool*. In explaining mediation Vygotsky drew on Karl Marx's idea of the tool as an instrument of labour. The tool, as a physical entity, is used by humans to 'make other substances subservient to his aims';[42] implements for food preparation, and weapons, being two examples from the dawn of human beings. Vygotsky and Marx cited Hegel's broader general idea that the exercise of reason (the mental capacity) is a mediational tool that results in objects acting and reacting without direct interference in the process by the person doing the reasoning.

Vygotsky's proposition was that the tool is involved in externally oriented activity that leads to changes in objects and hence allows humans to control nature. Whereas the sign is internally oriented allowing a human to control themselves through their behaviour. As Vygotsky said:

> The very essence of human memory consists in the fact that human beings actively remember with the help of signs. It may be said that the basic characteristic of human behaviour in general is that humans personally influence their relations with the environment and through that environment personally change their behaviour, subjugating it to their control. It has been remarked that the very essence of civilization consists of purposely building monuments so as not to forget. In both the knot [as an aid to memory] and the monument we have manifestations of the most fundamental and characteristic feature distinguishing human from animal memory.[43]

[41] Vygotsky, *Thought and Language*, xvi. [42] Marx, *Capital*, 128.
[43] Vygotsky, *Thought and Language*, 51.

Although tool and sign are different, their use is linked as mediated activity. For Vygotsky, writing as *sign* was seen first in the marks made by early human beings: for example, carvings on sticks to represent meaning. One example he gave was of early humans in Borneo developing a particular kind of stick for digging or hoeing. The bottom part of the stick for Vygotsky represented tool (literally and metaphorically). The top part of the stick had an additional small stick attached that made a sound that acted as a call to work.

> This intertwining of sign and tool which found its concrete symbolic expression in a primitive hoeing stick shows how early the sign (and later, its highest form, the word) begins to participate in the use of tools by man, and how early it begins to fulfil a highly specific function, to be compared with nothing else in the general structure of these operations that stand at the very beginning of the development of human labour. This stick is fundamentally different from that used by apes, although without doubt they are related to each other genetically.[44]

The function of the small stick was therefore seen as sign because it acted as a form of communication.

The presentation of sign and tool as part of mediation in Vygotsky's more popular book *Mind in Society: The Development of Higher Psychological Processes* has been made clearer as a result of further study and clarifications: for example, as a result of correcting mistranslations and erroneous edits. Explicit recognition that words are a form of sign was part of a section of Vygotsky's earlier work omitted in the English edition of *Tool and Sign in Child Development* which should have included the following text:

> the functional use of sign *(the word)* as a means of directing attention, abstracting, establishing connections, generalizing and other operations which form part of this function, is the necessary and central section of the entire process of the appearance of new concepts.[45]

Vygotsky's theory of the mediational function of words as signs helps understanding about writing as a cognitively *and* socially derived impulse that requires the control of tools and signs.[46] Close attention to Vygotsky's work is an important corrective to some post-Vygotskian scholarship, which has moved too far beyond Vygotsky's original thinking. Vygotsky was clear that concepts were established through the holistic connections and relations of dialectical logic and synthesised though mediation in words.[47] Tools include the implements and devices necessary for production of written language. The

44 Vygotsky, and Luria, 'Tool and Symbol in Child Development', 56.

45 Kellog, and Yasnitsky, 'The Differences between the Russian and English Texts', 109. Italics added.

46 Chapter 6 includes further reference to Vygotsky's work, on creativity.

47 As Jan Derry makes clear, by building on the work of the pragmatist philosopher Robert Brandon: Derry, 'Abstract Rationality in Education', 49–62.

tools can on occasion be used simply for making marks without linguistic meaning. But if used to write meaningful words, these tools create signs, and hence tool is intertwined with sign. To Vygotsky, the application of these concepts to human development meant that evidence of children's first use of tools and signs was such that naïve notions of predetermined organic sequences of behaviour had to be rejected because the mediated activity 'broadens the range of activities within which the new psychological functions may operate'.[48] In consequence the use of tool and sign was described as part of the development of *higher psychological function*, something unique to humans.

Semiotics and Digital Tools

One interesting very recent extension of socio-cultural mediation is the concept of *multimodality*. Multimodality extends the understanding of sign and tool to modes of representation of meaning that include image, sound, gesture, gaze, and body posture. Multimodality can be seen as part of socio-cultural thinking particularly in its idea of *affordance* which is described as follows: 'Attention to sign-making and sign in a multimodal perspective foregrounds the agentive work of the sign-maker and the importance of their social, historical and cultural location.'[49] For example, a *tweet* posted on Twitter can be under the full control, or agency, of someone when posted through a personal account (within the bounds of legally acceptable language). But a person's agency to control the message through a work-based Twitter account is more constrained by the policies of the workplace. Personal and institutional dimensions like these are part of the cultural location of the tweet. Similarly, the ethnic origin of the person sending the tweet may result in particular ways of using language and the selection of topic to tweet about. The topic will also to some degree be part of a history of tweets, and history of other modes of communication.

Although multimodality is socio-cultural in character, it draws its theoretical inspiration from the linguistics of Michael Halliday. Some of Halliday's main ideas have clear links with the themes of this chapter. First and foremost, Halliday saw meaning as the central concern of language. His strong emphasis on semiotics (the study of signs and symbols and their use) was not on the signs and symbols per se but more on language as a systemic resource for meaning. Like Vygotsky he saw language as intimately related to the social. Language was not in Halliday's terms simply a reflection of social structure but more an integral part that could modify the social, not just reflect it.

[48] Vygotsky, *Mind in Society*, 55.
[49] Jewitt, and Kress, 'Multimodality, Literacy and School English', 343.

Halliday's theories of Systemic Functional Linguistics (SFL) have influenced another aspect of writing that has not yet been considered in this chapter, the overall structure of written texts. *Genre theory* seeks to specify the structures and purposes of different texts. The word *genre* in this case does not apply simply to the more commonly understood genres of narrative fiction, such as science fiction, chick lit, detective fiction, and so on. Genre, in this case, is the particular structural features of texts, and in some variants includes oral language events. For example, we could say that the newspaper genre, in printed form, includes an overall political orientation perceived by its readers and wider society; a main purpose to entertain or to probe in depth; the vital feature of the front page that has to attract possible readers; and the variety of other formatting features such as the main headline, main story, picture relevant to the main story with heading and caption; at least one other news story with smaller headline and picture(s).

In the late 1970s a new variant of genre theory emerged from a group of academics and educationalists based in Sydney, Australia. They hypothesised that if the features of different genres could be identified in a range of texts, then people could be better taught to write these texts.[50] The genre theorists made particular distinctions between fiction and non-fiction genres. Furthermore they identified a specific number of particular non-fiction genres that were described as follows: recount; instruction; report; procedure; explanation; discussion; persuasion. A very recent update to the work suggests that over the intervening thirty years these categories have only had minor modifications. The categories are now seen as stories, factual texts, and, unusually, a separate category for 'Arguments'. Story genres are subdivided into recount (purpose: recounting events) and narrative (resolving a complication); factual texts into description (describing specific things); report (classifying and describing general things); explanation (explaining sequences of events); and procedure (how to do an activity).[51]

The work of the linguist Michael Halliday is cited as the derivation of the genre theory that emerged out of Australia. But a close reading of Halliday's seminal book, *An Introduction to Functional Grammar*, reveals a disjuncture between the genre theorists' advocacy of the teaching of elements of written text forms to help the learning of writing, and Halliday's theory. Halliday's functional grammar has little overall to say about the elements of text structures. Consistent with other comprehensive grammars of the English language, the overwhelming focus of his book is at the sentence level and below. However, the most significant attention to whole texts (with text very broadly defined as 'any instance of language, in any medium, that makes sense to someone who knows the language')[52] by Halliday was in the concept of

[50] Kress, *Learning to Write*.
[51] Rose, 'New Developments in Genre-Based Literacy Pedagogy'.
[52] Halliday and Matthiessen, *An Introduction to Functional Grammar*, 3. Underline added.

instantiation: 'the system of language is instantiated in the form of a text'.[53] This entails two main linguistic perspectives: language as system and language as text. The system is the potential of language as a meaning-making resource. And with regard to text types:

> When we study this sample of texts, we can identify patterns that they all share ... *However, research has shown that texts vary systematically according to contextual values; texts vary according to the nature of the contexts they are used in*. Thus recipes, weather forecasts, stock market reports, rental agreements, e-mail messages, inaugural speeches, service encounters in the local deli, new bulletins, media interviews, tutorial sessions, walking tours in a guide book, gossip during a team break, advertisements, bedtime stories and all the other innumerable text types we meet in life are all ways of using language in different contexts.[54]

Another part of SFL, within which Halliday's concept of *ideation* is situated, is the idea that language is driven by two fundamental aspects: humans making sense of their experience and humans acting out social relationships. In this, there lies clear linguistic support for the psycho social and pragmatic model of language and writing that informs this book. And equally important is that functional grammar is derived not from hypothetical examples and logic but through systematic analysis of corpora of real examples of language in use.

As interesting as the accounts that argue for limited numbers of text types and predictable text structures are, the problem with the argument is that the features of texts that might align them with particular categories of text are less important than the features that render them different from a particular category. Even more important is the way in which so many texts show characteristics of more than one category. Accounts of text archetypes are also subject to the natural human capacity for bias: to notice patterns but then continue to seek confirmation of the patterns more than seek divergences from categories.

Multimodality is informed by the Hallidayan inspired metafunctions of *ideational meaning, interpersonal meaning*, and *textual meaning.*[55] My colleagues Carey Jewitt and Gunther Kress argue that through the grammar of a language, ideational meaning is the expression of events and states of affairs in the world. Interpersonal meaning is the way people are positioned in relation to other people, and textual meaning is bound up in the creation of coherent texts (in the broadest sense to include the different modes according to multimodality theory).

[53] Halliday and Matthiessen, *An Introduction to Functional Grammar.*
[54] Halliday and Matthiessen, *An Introduction to Functional Grammar*, 27 (emphasis added).
[55] Jewitt and Kress, 'Multimodality, Literacy and School English'.

A social semiotic approach is consistent with the historical trajectory of thinking that eventually made clear distinctions between speech and writing, but the advent of multimodality has added theorisation of gesture, touch, and sound. For example, an emphasis on the temporality of sound and the *spaciality* of image.[56] The social semiotic approach is also consistent with my concern with meaning as the central and driving force of written language, as Gunther Kress shows:

> A multimodal ensemble – a designed complex of different modes – can be seen either as a sign-complex or as text. Seen as the former, the emphasis is on its modal composition; seen as the latter, the emphasis is on the function of the object, usually in an interaction: as a 'message', for instance. The maker has brought together signs in different modes into a semiotically coherent entity. Each of the signs (in its specific mode) plays a part in constituting the meaning of the ensemble, from the maker's perspective. That is, the meaning of the whole arises out of the contribution of each part in its interaction with all other parts. The complex modal ensemble is the result of the semiotic work of design by its initial maker. As message, it becomes subject to the subsequent semiotic work of interpretation-as-redesign, by the person who engages with the message/ensemble. Given that the overall meaning (both for the initial maker and for the subsequent re-maker) depends on all parts of the ensemble/text considered, it is evident that the contribution of each element separately – of each sign in each mode – provides a part only of the meaning of the whole. That is, each mode's contribution to the meaning of the whole is partial.[57]

However, while multimodality is undoubtedly present in the growth of digital forms of meaning-making the contribution that theories of multimodality might make to understanding of writing processes are only in their infancy, with disagreements in relation to multimodality as a theory, a phenomenon, a domain for social-semiotic action, and/or an approach.[58]

Psychological thinking and socio-cultural thinking have produced important insights into understanding the processes of writing. However, the context for these insights has often been from disciplinary silos. Psychologists and neuroscientists have their own university departments, ways of thinking, and specialist journals and book publishers. Socio-cultural thinking has been more dispersed because it has been found in a range of social science disciplines, including education, philosophy, history, social geography, sociology, cultural studies, and so on, but the thinking rarely penetrates the discipline of psychology, still less the natural sciences. Such differences represent epistemological positions that have been the cause of intense philosophical argument and debate over many hundreds of years.

56 Kress, 'Applied Linguistics and a Social Semiotic Account of Multimodality'.
57 Kress, 'Applied Linguistics and a Social Semiotic Account of Multimodality', 57.
58 Kress, 'Applied Linguistics and a Social Semiotic Account of Multimodality'.

The Meaning of Writing

Having explored some key ideas emanating from ancient and more recent philosophy – along with perspectives from cognitive-neuroscientific, socio-cultural and multimodality theory – I turn finally in this chapter back to philosophy. Building on some of the themes addressed so far, I additionally frame writing in pragmatism and education, and particularly through John Dewey's philosophy of language.

The pragmatism of John Dewey addressed many of the classic topics that had their origins in ancient Greek philosophy. An important element of his work, in relation to the aims of this book, was Dewey's explicit and direct attention to education and educative processes. But just as important was the philosophical attention that Dewey gave to language and the nature of meaning. Dewey regarded communication, language, and discourse as a natural bridge between existence and essence.[59] The importance of Dewian philosophy to my thinking also lies in his explicit attention to, and 'coordination', as he put it, of both psychological and social factors.

As we saw earlier in the chapter, the ancient Greek's discovery of discourse was conceptualised through grammar and rhetoric. But the strong and tidy alignment between representation and an ideal discourse omitted the idea that things, including physical things, assume different forms as *part o*f discourse, a problem that was the stimulus for the linguistic turn in philosophy. Correspondence between things and meanings is not present a priori but in fact only exists when the things become the subjects of discourse: as objects: physically, grammatically, and ultimately metaphorically.

One of the simple but memorable examples that Dewey uses is a scene where one person (described by Dewey as 'A') points to a flower and asks another person ('B') to bring him the flower. Animals respond in general to movements, but humans recognise pointing not just as a general movement but as a particular meaning: in this case the meaning of 'please bring me the flower'. B not only responds to the request physically but also, crucially, by taking into account A's likely perspectives, which Dewey saw as an actual and potential 'relationship' between person A and the flower (the thing). The significance of the example for Dewey was that the thing becomes common to A and B, and hence the thing changes. Understanding of the meaning of discourse is therefore centrally about shared referents 'and in a common, inclusive, undertaking'.[60] This is perhaps in essence a much clearer example of the concept of mediation, where the flower represents a tool, and the gesture and language of the discussants represents signs, and the tool is changed, through the use of signs, when it is

[59] My account of Dewian philosophy of language is informed by his book *Experience and Nature*, particularly the chapter, 'Nature, Communication and Meaning'.

[60] Ibid., 55.

an integral part of the meanings inherent in the discourse. Vygotsky claimed that Dewey asserted the 'tongue' as the tool of tools and hence accused Dewey of not maintaining the appropriate distinction between tool and sign. In fact, Dewey described 'language' as the tool of tools, meaning: 'As to be a tool, or to be used as means for consequences, is to have and to endow with meaning, language, being the tool of tools, is the cherishing mother of all significance.'[61] Like Vygotsky, Dewey also described the example of a stick used as a primitive form of plough, but argued that the stick returns to being simply a stick unless language is used socially to register the new use and institutionalise this.

Dewey was critical of more modern philosophies of language. He recognised that personal inner experience was a phenomenon of human brains and thinking, but he criticised 'the moderns' failure to recognise the links between inner experience and the social nature of language. According to Dewey, language doesn't just *enable* inner experience, it *is* inner experience, and it *is* social interaction. This philosophical distinction between language enabling versus language *as* inner experience can be seen mirrored in the different ways that much psychological and neuroscientific work conceives language compared with socio-cultural conceptions. For example, the social and cultural are not simply contextual to processes of writing; they are an intrinsic part, and to neglect this relationship is to fail to fully understand writing and its elements.

Dewey's sense of meaning as a preeminent aspect of language not only encapsulates simple instrumental meanings, meanings created through the mediation of tools and signs, but also through the potentiality of meaning: 'The quality of meaning thus introduced is extended and transferred, actually and potentially, from sounds, gestures and marks, to all other things to be enjoyed and administered, precisely as are song, fiction, oratory, the giving of advice and instruction.'[62] When Dewey offered the example of opera, that integrates movement, language, and music, as the 'consummatory': 'the dance is accompanied by song and becomes the drama', it was part of Dewey's analysis of discourse as both instrumental and consummatory. The instrumental part of language can be seen in its capacity to get things done, and the consummatory in its capacity for endless invention and creativity, 'at first with direct participation of an audience; and then, as literary forms develop, through imaginative identification'.[63]

Dewey extended the link made between the instrumental and consummatory aspects of literary forms to argue that a form such as poetry supplies oral and written meanings at a societal level so that the standards of appreciation that all art forms engender are an essential part of how human life is judged:[64]

[61] Ibid., 58. [62] Ibid., 53. [63] Ibid., 57.

[64] And in so doing implicitly linked with Aristotle's concerns with the rhetoric of poets and debates in Greek society.

> Here, as in so many other things, the great evil lies in separating instrumental and final functions. Intelligence is partial and specialized, because communication and participation are limited, sectarian, provincial, confined to class, party, professional group … When the instrumental and final functions of communication live together in experience, there exists an intelligence which is the method and reward of the common life, and a society worthy to command affection, admiration, and loyalty.[65]

The non-routine processes of making meaning in oral language and in written language are subject to the 'surprise' they engender in the speaker or writer. This is why in the end writing is not a simple rule-bound process. If there are rules, they are of logical order and consistency of ideas, economy and efficiency of expression: these are rules of experimentation because they involve a degree of spontaneity (even in writing which on re-reading contains surprises for the author). And music is never far away from experimentation:

> In trying new combinations of meanings, satisfactory consequences of new meanings are hit upon; then they may be arranged in a system. The expert in thought is one who has skill in making experiments to introduce an old meaning into different situations and *who has a sensitive ear for detecting resultant harmonies and discords*. The most 'deductive' thought in actual occurrence is a series of trials, observations and selections (my italics).[66]

At the more general philosophical level Dewey's emphasis on communication as a metaphysics of existence is ground breaking because it starts from a *process* as a philosophical origin rather than a substance as an origin.[67] However, while Dewey's emphasis on participation as a defining feature of communication is important in relation to education, and in relation to understanding writing, it is the concept of deconstructive pragmatism inspired by Derrida that, it has been argued, acts as a corrective to Dewey's theory.[68] This corrective is the recognition that the inherently social aspect of communication means that Dewey's philosophy will necessarily be challenged as a result of the social consequences of its dissemination. I accept the Dewian 'offer' to collaboratively make meaning by using his ideas, and other ideas, to explore writing, as I seek to build new knowledge through a pragmatic multi-disciplinary framework.

*

The profound influence on society that was the result of the invention of alphabetic writing, in particular the influence on the educative contexts where writing is learned and taught, is a primary concern that underpins this book. Within this social context, sophisticated understanding of the differences between the larger aspects of writing, such as communicative intent and

[65] Dewey, 'Nature, Communication and Meaning', 65.
[66] Dewey, 'Nature, Communication and Meaning', 61.
[67] Biesta, *Beautiful Risk of Education*. [68] Biesta, *Beautiful Risk of Education*.

establishment of meaning, and the ways in which the building blocks of writing, such as words and letters, interact, is vital. The recognition that writers' thoughts are in important ways both clearly linked to the task of writing, but also composed of words that express meanings that are not ultimately under the exclusive control of the writer (not least because readers determine meanings as well), is central to our task of understanding writing. Ancient philosophy also introduced the paramount idea of 'convention'. Understanding language as conventions, as distinct from language as strict 'rules', is an idea that is built on in other chapters.

At the level of the individual writer's cognition, evidence has grown about the importance of working memory, in particular, the phenomenon of continual reinterpretation that is part of writing processes. But the idea that mental processes are crudely 'left brain–right brain' is no longer tenable on the basis of neuroscientific advances, although thoughtful and provocative ideas about the different sides of the brain have continued to be published, even the claim that a link can be made between 'the making of the western world' and divisions in the brain (the attention to both music and language in Ian McGilchrist's book is another example of music as an important comparator).[69] Humans' development of written language has been central, and some argue uniquely aligned with, their development of thinking and rationality.[70]

In a challenge to limited conceptions of social factors as part of writing processes, prevalent in some work on cognition, our understanding of the place of the social and the cultural in writing, its processes, and its development (historically and as part of individuals' cognitive development), is fundamental. Mediation, through tools and signs as part of language events, is a central feature of socio-cultural knowledge and has direct application in understanding human higher psychological development. Digital tools are also implicated in socio-cultural understanding through nascent theories of multimodality.

The Dewian idea of language as inner experience and social interaction suggests the need for attention to individuals' intentions and associated social structures and artefacts. The history of writing presents one important social context for writing, as do the experiences of writers, and the individuals and groups who seek to prescribe writing through rules and conventions. The instrumental and consummatory aspects of writing are always in play, for novice writers, including young children, and for expert writers, including Nobel laureates. And the processes of judgement that are part of human life are an essential element of understanding how writing works, including in defining creativity in writing.

In the next chapter, I continue my multidisciplinary pragmatist exploration with a history of writing that provides some more of the cultural and social

[69] McGilchrist, *The Master and His Emissary*. [70] Olson, *The Mind on Paper*.

factors that accompany the theories addressed in this chapter. The philosophers' attention to the birth of the alphabet suggested the need to examine this history but also some of the precursors, from the first recorded marks made by humans. The focus on the English language in this book (not least as a means to restrict its scope) also necessitates a brief account of historical developments in the language. But it is with the earliest historical evidence of human language and mark-making that I begin.

2 A History of Writing

Fossil records suggest that 500,000 years ago (at the least) humans' ancestors had developed the vocal anatomy and neurological control necessary for language.[1] It is theorised that the vocal sounds made by our ancestors became important in evolutionary terms because of their role in the establishment and maintenance of social relationships. These pre-linguistic sounds included singing and 'duetting'. The loud, long bouts of sounds made by mated pairs of gibbons (the arboreal apes living in the tropical rain forests of south-east Asia) possibly represented 'songs' that were the substrate from which human singing ultimately emerged.[2] The use of pre-linguistic sounds to aid communication eventually evolved into the words of language.

This chapter explores the processes of writing with a particular focus on three key developments in the history of language. The first is the development of the alphabet, one of humans' most significant inventions. As a precursor to this section, I review some of the important changes that began with cave pictures and ended with writing. One precursor is exemplified in the story of the decipherment of the Rosetta Stone, which was important for so many reasons in relation to understanding the development of writing. A comparison is also made with the first known writing of music. The second key development in the chapter is the advent of the printing press, a new technology that revolutionised access to written language. And the third key development is the point at which digital text became a reality in many millions of people's lives.

Until recently it was theorised that the Aurinacian deposits (from the Aurignac area in France) of engraved and painted materials, which were composed in the period between 25,000 BC and 10,000 BC in the late Old Stone Age, were the oldest examples of art.[3] These beginnings coincided with the time that humans became the dominant hominid species. The larger brain size that humans had compared to other animals was linked to dominance of their habitat. Big brains may also have been a causal factor in the emergence of

[1] Morley, 'A Multi-Disciplinary Approach to the Origins of Music', 147–177.
[2] Geissmann, 'Gibbon Songs and Human Music from an Evolutionary Perspective'.
[3] Goody, *Interface between the Written and the Oral.*

language. But in 2014 a new discovery was made that upturned the idea that cave paintings started in Europe, something that had puzzled scientists in view of the known spread of humans out of Africa. On the Island of Sulawesi, in Wallacea, a zone of oceanic islands between continental Asia and Australia, the oldest known hand stencil (created by blowing paint around hands pressed to cave walls), and the oldest figurative depiction of an animal (a babirusa or 'pig-deer') in the world was found. It is assumed that the painting of the wild endemic dwarfed bovid, found only in Sulawesi, was probably hunted by humans. This finding showed that 'humans were producing rock art by 40,000 years ago.'[4] The oldest known musical instrument, found in a cave in Germany, is a flute made out of mammoth ivory and is dated at about 35,000 years old. The flute's three holes for the fingers enabled five notes of a scale to be played.[5]

The significance of the paintings as some of the earliest forms of scribed communication includes questions about the kind of communication that was taking place. For example, to what extent were these graphic entities *expressive* and/or *communicative*? A defining characteristic of the expressive is the more general meanings that are expressed, and hence less specificity in the message: for example, the depiction of familiar animals to be worshipped and/or hunted. But communication has a more specific intent to transmit a particular message, to a particular person or group of people, with narrower meaning. The expressive nature of the first paintings and hand prints was an important precursor to human's development of written language.

Evidence of the use of tallies, a form of *proto-writing*, has been dated to 13,500 BC: for example, as notches on an eagle bone to record phases of the moon as a form of calendar.[6] Around 4000 BC the use of clay tablets to replace tokens increased.[7] An interesting aspect of clay tokens was the earliest known development of educational exercise tablets (see Figure 2.1), showing that students practiced copying the letters of the cuneiform script, and the work of advanced students who copied more elaborate texts.[8] The important idea of moving from the physical representation of one-to-one correspondence between token and object, to multiple objects imprinted, for example, as signs on wet clay was an important development towards greater abstraction of meaning, and towards more efficient means of communication.

4 Aubert, Brumm, Ramli, et al. 'Pleistocene Cave Art from Sulawesi, Indonesia', 227

5 Smithsonian National Museum of Natural History. 'Mammoth Ivory Flute'. Washington, DC: Smithsonian Museum of Natural History, 2016.

6 Robinson, *The Story of Writing*.

7 The range of the years for possible date for objects were sometimes as wide as 25,000 years. A visit to the Washington National Museum of Natural History revealed the difficulties inherent in dating the marks on clay tablets, in addition to dating the clay material, even with carbon dating.

8 Exhibits seen in a visit to the Royal Ontario Museum, Canada. When I asked, at the information desk of the museum, where the exhibits about 'writing' were, the answer was that there weren't any, because the exhibits were regarded as 'language'.

Figure 2.1 Front side of clay tablet with character exercises. Unfired clay inscribed with cuneiform, year-date unknown, Old Babylonian period. Mesopotamia (Iraq). With permission of the Royal Ontario Museum © ROM.

The moves towards greater abstraction in written marks made another important leap forward around 3100 BC. A slate palette known as the Narmer Palette from Egypt is one of the first known examples of the use of the *rebus* technique in written language[9] (a rebus uses pictures or symbols to suggest the sounds of syllables or words). Palettes were originally used for grinding cosmetics but later became ceremonial decorative pieces only. The ceremonial Narmer Palette's pictures contain a range of significant meanings including on one side mixed human/cow heads depicting the setting as the world or cosmos; King Narmer depicted in god-like form about to smite his enemy, who are represented as a figure on its knees; and a falcon (a representation of the god Horus) sitting on a rebus meaning defeated country, with a rope to hold a prisoner.[10]

Far from being writing in the modern sense, the Narmer Palette combines graphic forms and pictures to express its meanings. The images in the top rows of both sides of the palette, in the middle, are a phonetic representation of Narmer's name. The way each of the images represents meaning uses the rebus, where pictures represent spoken sounds: the picture of a catfish to represent the syllable /Nar/ and the chisel to represent /mer/. The phoneme links are technically to /nr/ and /mr/ which were separated by a guttural sound found in Semitic languages.[11]

[9] The Narmer Palette can be seen at https://commons.wikimedia.org/wiki/File:Narmer_Palette.jpg.
[10] Baines, *Visual and Written Culture in Ancient Egypt*, 268.
[11] Robinson, *The Story of Writing*.

This beautiful object shows the beginnings of the more abstract representation of spoken language in writing through the important technique of the rebus. In such objects we see a moment in humans' gradual movement from pictures only, towards the full complexities of alphabetic writing. As Baines points out, 'It is as if the originators of the mixed Egyptian system were the first semioticians: the system seems to be designed with the maximum emphasis on differentiation and meaning.'[12]

We would not fully understand Egyptian hieroglyphics if it were not for the decipherment of the texts on the *Rosetta Stone*. The story of the Rosetta Stone is important for three reasons: (1) It enabled understandings of 3,000 years of human history[13]; (2) it reveals some key aspects of the development of alphabetic writing; and (3) its decipherment is in itself an important story partly about writing and its processes. The decipherment of the texts on the Rosetta Stone, 'brought about a revolution in our knowledge of how writing works, and its origins',[14] and enabled the birth of Egyptology and the recovery of the identity of a civilisation and its people. The quests to decipher the languages of the Rosetta Stone ultimately uncovered the literal meaning of the stone, and unlocked the written history of ancient Egypt. Before the decipherment of the Rosetta Stone most of what was conjectured about Egypt was wrong.[15]

The Rosetta Stone lay for centuries in the ruins of a temple, probably in the Nile delta. It was reused as building material and may not have reached the Egyptian town of Rashid, also known as Rosetta, until the latter part of the fifteenth century. It wasn't rediscovered until 1799, when an invasion by the French resulted in some rebuilding work to secure the coast militarily. The French generals were persuaded, by the savants, of the potential importance of the stone. One of the savants, Vivant Denon (1747–1825), published what was effectively an anthropology of Egypt that included details of every temple, wall, and hieroglyph including the Rosetta Stone. The work was called *Voyage dans la basse et la haute Égypt* (Travels in Lower and Upper Egypt), which became a sensation when it appeared in 1802. The further nine volumes of text, and eleven of illustrations, are known as the *Description de l'Égypt.*

The powerful human instinct to engage with meaning and texts is exemplified in many ways in the story of the decipherment of the Rosetta Stone. First and foremost was the drive to understand the literal meaning of the texts on the stone. The texts of the Rosetta Stone are in three languages: ancient Egyptian hieroglyphics; demotic script (a cursive form of Egyptian hieroglyphics); and ancient Greek. The instinct for the decipherment was so powerful that it drove a succession of people, who were some of the most brilliant thinkers of the

[12] Baines, *Visual and Written Culture in Ancient Egypt*, 283. [13] Parkinson, *The Rosetta Stone.*
[14] Ray, *The Rosetta Stone*, 7.
[15] The points made in relation to the Rosetta Stone are informed by Parkinson, *The Rosetta Stone* and by Ray, *The Rosetta Stone*.

Enlightenment, to devote large parts of their working lives to the project. Another layer of the power of meaning in writing was the belief by some that understanding this kind of early writing could directly reveal the hand of God.

The first small step towards understanding the languages of the Rosetta Stone was the clergyman Edward Stillingfleete's idea that the ancient Egyptians must have had many important things to say in writing. In other words, he hypothesised that the hieroglyphs were not simply decorative, they represented meaning. This line of thinking was augmented by another clergyman, William Warburton, who theorised that the development of writing began with pictures but then moved to figurative ideas, such as a picture of an eye to represent divine omniscience. Warburton's key contribution was the idea of figurative meaning in symbols.

The major breakthrough prior to the final decipherment was the work of Thomas Young (1773–1829). Young was a brilliant scientist who, amongst his many discoveries, identified the way the human eye perceives colour. He focused his attention on the demotic script of the stone. Young's achievement was to identify the equivalents between 218 demotic words and 200 hieroglyphic groups, and ancient Greek.

In the end, though, it was not Young who finally deciphered hieroglyphics but Jean-François Champollion (1790–1832) who became regarded as the founding father of Egyptology as a result of his discoveries. Champollion built on Young's approach by starting with people's names as a key. He also became aware of a repeating pattern of four signs that appeared on cartouches on the walls and columns of a temple at Karnak. The repeated pattern was likely to be a king's name, but Champollion had to work out which king. His knowledge of Coptic helped him identify 'Ramesses' as the meaning of one of the patterns. Rather pertinently the second repeated pattern group Champollion's deciphered was an Egyptian god of writing, and wisdom: Thoth or Thot.

Coptic gave Champollion the clue to the links between sound, symbol, and ideogram that were the basis of hieroglyphics' meanings. As part of the decipherment one of his key discoveries was that hieroglyphics also relied on determinatives, symbols which were not sounded but used to make the grammatical forms of words clear.

The meaning of the Rosetta Stone's text was a decree by King Ptolemy V dated in the text as 196 BC.

> [King Ptolemy] has created temples, shrines and altars once more for the gods; he has put other things in order, since he is at heart a god pious towards the gods. He has sought after the glories of the temples, to make them new again in his time as Pharaoh, as is fitting. In exchange for this the gods have granted him might, victory and triumph, prosperity and health, and all other blessings for his reign as Pharaoh are secured for him, together with his children.[16]

[16] Ray, *The Rosetta Stone*, 132.

The decree represents an agreement made by a synod of Egyptian priests. Egyptologists tend to describe most Egyptian texts as 'literature', and the typical inclusion of somewhat fictional aspects, even in texts such as decrees, renders the term *literature* not completely without merit. The ownership of the text by a king, and the nature of the text as a decree, reveal another aspect of the power of written language, and the way power can be expressed, both of which are enduring features that continue to be relevant to understanding writing:

> ancient texts are not just windows on the past: in ancient Egypt, literacy was very restricted and so all texts are elite products. As such they embody a particular world-view developed by a small percentage of the population and only describe certain aspects of their world. The Rosetta Stone, with its hierarchy of different scripts and languages, embodies this aspect of written records, as well as being the key to deciphering them.[17]

Around the world, writing systems continued to make progress at different rates. Pictures and rebuses were also extended in Zapotek, an ancient writing system that used *hieroglyphs*. Zapotek was the oldest language of four that emerged in Mesoamerica, one of six areas in the region from Mexico to the south-east of modern South America. Zapotek appeared in the Oaxaca Valley (located within the modern-day State of Oaxaca in southern Mexico) as early as 600 BC.[18] Another example was Aramaic that became a dominant language, as a result of the choices made by the empires that ruled Mesopotamia, during the first millennium BC. Aramaic finally gave way to Iranian languages.[19]

Although pictographic, rebus-based, and hieroglyphic forms of writing had much greater capacity to communicate meaning than paintings could alone, this capacity was limited. It was not possible to efficiently represent the complexities of meaning in written language when there were so many separate graphical signs to represent words or syllables.[20] The organic nature of language development was reflected in humans' continuing search for more efficient systems of written language, ones that could use fewer symbols to represent a greater number of words.

The Invention of the Alphabet

The most momentous development, and perhaps the greatest invention of all time (across all domains of human invention), was the alphabet, because this opened the doorway to an explosion of writing that would lead ultimately to the written forms of the digital age, including the use of the English language.

[17] Parkinson, *The Rosetta Stone*, 54. [18] Goody, *Interface between the Written and the Oral*.
[19] Daniels, 'Grammatology'.
[20] Even the characters of modern Chinese scripts do not all have unique meanings, and many can represent more than one meaning.

Research currently dates the origins of alphabetic writing to between 2000 BC and 1500 BC in Egypt. As carvings in rock have revealed, early alphabetic signs were derived from hieratic and hieroglyphic Egyptian writing.[21] However the first known alphabet, which was an alphabet of consonants, was the Phoenician/Proto-Canaanite script. This was adapted by the Greeks, from the eighth century BC onwards, who added their own five characters to represent vowels.[22] The development of the modern alphabet came from both Greek script and the Roman alphabet, and can be seen in the use of the Latinised form of the first two letters of the Greek alphabet in the word itself, 'alphabet'. Alpha was derived from the Semitic 'aleph' and 'beta' from 'beth'.[23]

The earliest example of Greek alphabetic writing found so far is *Nestor's Cup*[24]. The script written on the cup means:

> Nestor's cup is good to drink from;
> but he who drinks from this cup, forthwith him
> will seize desire of fair-garlanded Aphrodite.[25]

The addition of the written text transformed the cup from a functional object only, to one that also communicates the power and potential of the supernatural and the power of love.

Ancient Greece also provides the first examples of the writing of music although the separation of written music and language that is so distinct in modern times was not so at the inception of notated music in Greece. The earliest musical notation is in fragments: such as The *First Delphic Hymn* – late second century BC; the *Second Delphic Hymn* – 128–127 BC.[14] The first example of a complete whole written musical composition in the world is the *Epitaph of Seikilos*[26] (Figures 2.2 and 2.3), which it has been suggested is from the first century AD.[27]

On the stone there are 12 lines of text (the thirteenth line was ground off so that the object could serve as a pedestal for a vase). The first five lines explain the purpose of the object: 'I am a tombstone, an image. Seikilos placed me here as an everlasting sign of deathless remembrance.' The next seven lines are the words of a song of which the approximate translation is:

21 Darnell, Dobbs-Allsopp, Lundberg, et al., Two Early Alphabetic Inscriptions from the Wadi el-Ḥôl, 63–124.

22 Goody, *Interface between the Written and the Oral*.

23 Goody, and Watt, 'The Consequences of Literacy', 304–345.

24 Images of Nestor's cup can be seen here: https://commons.wikimedia.org/wiki/File:Coppa_di_Nestore.png.

25 Watkins, C., 'Observations on the "Nestor's Cup" Inscription', 25–40.

26 Images can be seen here: https://commons.wikimedia.org/wiki/File:Seikilos1.tif.

27 Mathiesen, T. *Appollo's Lyre*.

Figure 2.2 The Seikilos stelae. The Seikilos stelae: CC-BY-SA Lennart Larsen, The National Museum of Denmark.

> As long as you live, shine
> Grieve you not at all
> Life is of brief duration
> Time demands its end.[28]

One of the reasons the Epitaph of Seikilos is so significant is that it contains written language and musical notation. The musical 'notes' appear between the lines of text. The notes are symbols (which to modern readers of English could almost be letters of the English alphabet) from the Ionian alphabet that was used to represent the notes in vocal music. Instrumental music had a different notation for musical notes.[29] The rhythms of the notes are marked similar to the modern western musical notation, for example, a dot to indicate a longer note like a dotted crotchet, and slurs to indicate moving note patterns while syllables are held by the singer.

[28] Mathiesen, T. *Appollo's Lyre*, 150. [29] Cosgrove, *An Ancient Christian Hymn*.

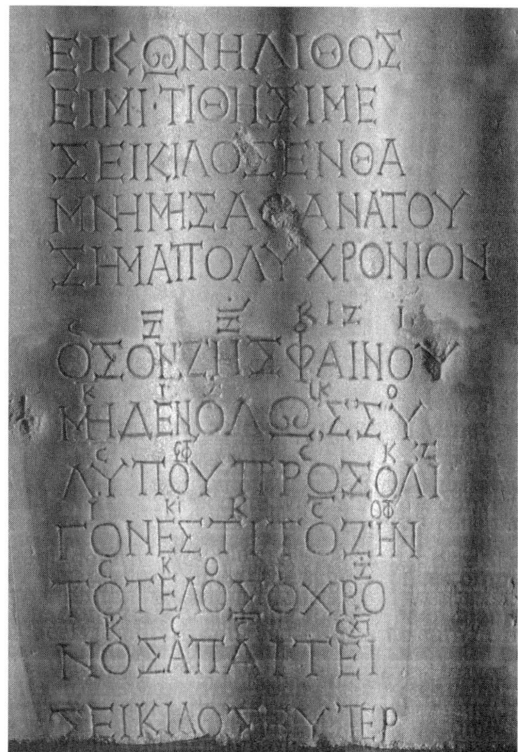

Figure 2.3 The Seikilos stelae. The National Museum of Denmark.

The use of written letter-like symbols for music was a major deviation from the use of letters as representing oral speech sounds. The idea that letters when combined as in the word 'ace' represent the meaning of the number one in a deck of cards (or high achievement) is radically different from the three musical notes A C and E played, for example, in sequence as part of a melody, or played together as the most basic musical chord, C Major in western music. The emergence of musical notation based on philosophical theories represented in texts, and the derivation in the Ionian alphabet, shows the original close links between written language and music.

Another of the interesting connections between text and music is that the inclusion of the music on the Epitaph allows us to understand aspects such as the length of pronunciation of spoken syllables at the time because of the information implied by the rhythms of the musical notes. The character of the music, including its musical range of an octave, and emphases on the notes 'e' and 'a', seems appropriate to the contemplative nature of the text.

There are many sources of information about language, and music, in ancient Greece including accounts by philosophers but also depictions through stories such as *The Iliad* and *The Odyssey.* The works include depictions of music and text. For example in *The Iliad*, Hephaestus' creations include a wedding accompanied by pipes and lyres: a very early juxtaposition of musical meaning and the meaning of words in a hymn. Later in the same section we read that 'a godlike singer of tales sang with them to the lyre, while a couple of solo dancers led off and spun round among the people.'[30] Evidence of the semantic importance of music also came from the philosophers:

> Plato's remarks underscore the fact that the practical manifestations of music form only one part of the Greek concept of *mousikē*: music occupied a prominent place in everyday life not only because it was amusing and socially valuable but also because it embodied universal principles *and was a vehicle for higher understanding.*[31]

Although many fragments of music notation have been found, there are no surviving treatises (theories) contemporary with the fragments, leading to the suggestion that 'it is not unreasonable to assume that musical notation was largely the province of the practising musician rather than the theorist and came to be recorded in later theory only as a way of preserving (or recovering) a dying tradition.'[32] The Epitaph of Seikilos uses the composition of writing enhanced by the composition of music to express, in multiple meanings, powerful aspects of the human condition.

The use of the alphabet in ancient Greece was remarkable historically not only for its own sake but also because of the unique context of its emergence. Havelock[33] identified five things that made the context for the creation of the alphabet unique:

1. Greek society was free from contact with any other literature culture.
2. Political and social autonomy meant a firm consciousness of its own identity.
3. Maintaining a record of this identity was exclusively oral until the advent of the alphabet.
4. The invention of the alphabet was made by the speakers of the language.
5. The application of the alphabet was controlled by Greek speakers.

No other instance of transition from orality to literacy (e.g. Scottish; African) can meet all these five requirements. Another unique feature of the alphabet was the completeness of the record that it enabled, and the complete visibility of language. This was not the case for the Sumerian or Babylonian scripts, such

[30] Homer, *The Iliad*, 335.
[31] Mathiesen, Conomos, Leotsakos, et al., 'Greece', Section 4 (italics added).
[32] Mathiesen, Conomos, Leotsakos, et al., 'Greece'.
[33] Havelock, *The Muse Learns to Write*, 86.

as the epic story *Gilgamesh* which included economisation of details because they were intended to be read aloud (and perhaps intoned), not just read in their written form.

Historically, the alphabet has been at the heart of some of the most enduring debates about the development of written communication, for example whether the alphabet simply emerged from logographic or pictographic forms (the alphabet at the heart of debate in modern times can be seen in Chapter 7). In Richard Harris's examination of the origins of writing,[34] he called this particular idea of emergence an evolutionary fallacy, arguing that the alphabet was 'the great invention' because unlike logos or pictographs its graphic signs have almost no limitations for human communication. David Olson thoroughly reviews the arguments about historical developments and concludes that,

> the history of scripts . . . is the by-product of attempts to use a script for a language for which it is ill-suited . . . the models of language provided by our scripts are both what is acquired in the process of learning to read and write and which is employed in thinking about language, writing is in principle meta-linguistics.[35]

The ancient Greeks' development of the alphabet enabled the expression of an infinite number of meanings through the most efficient means. Its development was the catalyst for a process of linguistic change that continues to the present day.

The Emergence of English

The invention of the alphabet paved the way for writing in many languages, not least the English language, which was to become the world's most used. The earliest indigenous writing found in England was a runic inscription known as the Caistor rune (from the name of the town Caistor-by-Norwich) dated from 400 AD. The origin of the word 'rune' is secret or mystery. The shape of the rune 'H' suggests that the runes were carved by someone originally from Scandinavia who was living in East Anglia, considerably before the date usually given for the arrival of Anglo-Saxons.[36]

The Caistor runes were written on the ankle bone of a roe deer. The meaning of the runes is *raihan* an early form of the Old English word *raha* that probably meant 'from a roe'. The bone could have been one of the pieces for a game. The identification of the source of the object (the roe) as the meaning of writing was common at the time. The runes, derived from an ancient Germanic alphabet (that grew out of a Roman alphabet), were used by Scandinavians and Anglo-Saxons. At the time of their use in England, there were only 24 graphemes

[34] Harris, *The Origin of Writing*. [35] Olson, *The World on Paper*, 89.
[36] Crystal, *Evolving English*.

(letter symbols) to represent 40 phonemes (sounds). Later 'i' and 'j', 'u', and 'v' were changed from being interchangeable to having distinct functions, and 'w' was added, but many sounds still had to be signalled by combinations of letters.

From AD 450 to 480 in England the first Old English was being written. The Undley bracteate (a gold medallion) includes the earliest example of Old English found so far. The bracteate was found in 1982 in the county of Suffolk. A translation of the runes on the Undley bracteate (which surround the helmeted head, and a she-wolf suckling in the centre of the bracteate) that read 'gægogæ mægæ medu' is 'this she-wolf is a reward to my kinsman'.[37]

The few texts that have survived from the period AD 675 to 975 are in four main dialects: West Saxon, Kentish, Mercian, and Northumbrian. The last two are sometimes grouped together and called Anglian. West Saxon became the standard dialect at the time but is not the direct ancestor of modern Standard English, which is mainly derived from an Anglian dialect.[38] If you take the modern word 'cold' as an example, the Anglian 'cald' is a stronger influence than the West Saxon version, 'ceald'.

The period from William the Conqueror in 1066 to the death of Edward I in 1307 marked a dramatic increase in the amount of writing in England.[39] The quantitative evidence for this increase is in the growth from 2,000 charters and writs in Anglo-Saxon England to tens of thousands that survive from thirteenth-century England. The quick increase in the number of texts from the Middle English period can also be seen in a study of medical texts written in English: 20 medical texts in the thirteenth century; 140 in the fourteenth century, and 872 in the fifteenth century.[40] The spread of documents such as charters to convey property meant that the main authorship of documents by royalty and other elites, in major urban settlements, adjusted so that literacy spread to rural areas. An important part of this spread was the development in the practice of signing a name. 'In Edward the Confessor's reign only the king is known to have possessed [a seal or *signum*] for authenticating documents, whereas in Edward I's reign even serfs were required by statute to have them.'[41] One of Clanchy's cautions is that we should not conceive causal connections between literacy and an approbatory sense of *civilisation*. More controversial is the claim that supporting evidence for this lack of causal connection is that only a minority of people can be proven to benefit in economic or cultural terms from literacy teaching at state schooling. There is now robust evidence, for example from cross-sectional analyses, of education as a causal factor in people's life time earnings[42]. It is true that beyond the literal meaning of the word 'literacy'

[37] Crystal, *Evolving English*, 12. [38] Barber, *The English Language*.
[39] Clanchy, *From Memory to Written Record*. [40] Crystal, *The Stories of English*.
[41] Clanchy, *From Memory to Written Record*, 2.
[42] Hermannsson. 'Economic Impact of Education'.

there lie cultural assumptions and value judgements, and as I show in chapter 6, the role of the state in influencing literacy in national curricula remains contentious.

The very first concepts related to the idea of standardising language were seen in the ancient Greek philosophers' explanation of signification as *convention*. The conventions that ultimately led to the modern idea of standard English began as early as the fourteenth century. The interaction of people with shared interests, such as those in *guilds*, was an example of social and cultural influences on the development of a standard language. For example, as early as 1373 the *Writers of Court Letters* was established as a guild for *scriveners*. In addition to the importance of lawyers, and the scriveners who worked for them, influencing the development of a standard English, other professional groups developed writing for their own purposes. The social contact of these groups accelerated the drive towards agreed conventions and hence standard forms.[43]

The influence on standardisation of English by people in southern parts of England, particularly East Anglia, the south-east of England, and London was strongly linked to trade. In the late fourteenth century Norwich was the second-largest city in England, in part because of the concentration of cloth manufacturers who supplied the continent. However, as the century progressed people moved to London, a journey made easier by the Great North Road (now the A1 M Motorway in England) and Watling Street. The influence of the East Midlands accent on London became significant, as a result of population movements, and high-status institutions such as the University of Cambridge. As Crystal makes clear,

> An area of relatively high population, the practical needs of commerce in the Norfolk area may well have fostered the replacement of Latin and French by English much earlier than in other parts of the country. In 1388–9, for example, Norfolk was the only place outside London to have its guild certificates written in English.[44]

As I have shown, much more common use of written English had been well established by the early part of the fourteenth century, for example as a result of charters and writs documenting property transactions. More consistent processes and hence the development of shared conventions of English were emerging as a result of the social interaction of individuals and groups. These were the beginnings of a standard English. But the English language was to continue to be subject to dramatic changes, more than any other major European language.[45] The development of printing resulted in another large expansion of writing and reading.

[43] Crystal, *The Stories of English*. [44] Crystal, *The Stories of English*, 245.
[45] Milroy, 'The History of English'.

The Advent of Printing

From the fifth century BC to the fifteenth century AD the role of scribes was the dominant one in production of books.

> Out of the entire production of books till 1500, amounting to fifteen to twenty million copies of 30,000 to 35,000 separate publications, by far the greatest proportion, seventy-seven per cent, are in Latin. But just as the printed book had routed the manuscript between 1500 and 1510, so the vernacular was soon to supersede Latin.[46]

McLuhan claimed that in the middle ages scholars were largely indifferent to the identity of the authors whose books they studied. The writers did not see the need to give citations of authors of the quotes they took from other books. They were even indifferent to putting a signature to their own work. Also there was no reading public in the modern sense because in the world of manuscripts an author could not have a public. But all of this was to change when a revolution of the magnitude of the invention of the alphabet was to take place, the development of the printing press.

In 878 AD, the Chinese printed the earliest known book, *The Diamond Sutra*, using inked wooden relief blocks. By the beginning of the fifteenth century the printing process had developed in Korea to the extent that printers were manufacturing bronze type sets of 100,000 pieces. In the West, Johannes Gutenberg (1390s–1468) is credited with the development of moveable metal type in association with a hand-operated printing press.[47] Printing in Europe from the fifteenth century onwards was a combination of technologies: wine/oil press; chemistry of ink; metallurgy of casting; and the goldsmiths' ability to make the tiny elements of type sets.[48]

In England it was William Caxton (1422–1491) who produced the first printed book in English which was, *The Recuyell of the Historyes of Troy* [The compilation of the histories of Troy]. Ironically Caxton's, and England's, first book was translated from French. It was started when Caxton was living in France, continued when he moved to Ghent, then finished by him in Cologne on 9 September 1471. The French original by Raoul Lefèvre was a collection of popular stories very loosely based on the tales of the Trojan Wars.[49] In the prefaces to the books that Caxton printed he included his own reflections on the book:

> Here begineth the volume entitled and named the recuyell of the historyes of Troye / composed and drawn out of diverse books of latyn in to french by the right venerable person and worshipful man. Raoul l Ffeure. priest and chaplain unto the right noble glorious and mighty prince in his time Phillip Duke of Burgundy of Braband etc. In the

[46] McLuhan, *The Gutenberg Galaxy*, 207.
[47] Crystal, *The Cambridge Encyclopedia of Language*. [48] Daniels, 'Grammatology'.
[49] British Library. 'First book printed in English', *Learning English Timeline*.

year of the incarnation of our lord god a thousand four hundred sixty and four / And translated and drawn out of French into English by William Caxton mercer of ye city of London / at the commandment of the right high mighty and vertuous Princess his redoubted lady. Margarete by the grace of god. Duchesse of Burgundy of Lotryk of Braband etc. / Which said translation and work was begun in Bruges in the County of Flanders the first day of march the year of the incarnation of our said lord god a thousand four hundred sixty and eight / and ended and finished in the holy city of Cologne the 19th day of September the year of our said lord god a thousand four hundred sixty and eleven etc.[50]

The printing process involved estimating the number of lines per page (casting off), making up a page by 'composing' the metal type into a holding frame (a forme), then making textual corrections. A book was broken down into sections called *signatures*. Each section would be *composed* and printed. Then the type would be removed from the forme and recomposed for a different section. Several people would work at the same time on each signature so it is easy to see how personal preferences over things such as spelling could emerge, hence a need for standardisation. Use of foreign compositors meant introduction of influences of other languages, and lack of full understanding of the emerging standard of English. For example, they may have assumed that some silent letters were random rather than standard, such as 'e' at the end of some words, and as a result did things such as add an extra letter at the end of a line to fill the type line.[51]

The advent of printing was a highly significant acceleration of the standardisation of written English, not least because it stimulated the first books that aimed to prescribe and/or describe the English language and hence seek to contribute to a standard form. One of the first printed educational guides written in English, about English, was by Richard Mulcaster a teacher and headmaster of Merchant Taylors' School in London[52]. It was called, *THE FIRST PART OF THE ELEMENTARIE WHICH ENTREATETH CHEFELIE OF THE right writing of our English tung, set furth by RICHARD MULCASTER*. Mulcaster explained that the purpose of the Elementarie was to help teachers working in elementary schools, and parents, to help young children learn by providing elementary educational principles:

The thinges be fiue in number, infinite in vse, principles in place, and these in name, *reading, writing, drawing, singing*, and *playing*. Why & wherefor these fiue be so profitable and so fit for this place, it shall appear hereafter, when their vse shall com in question. In the mean while this is most trew, that in the right course of best education to learning and knowledge, all these, & onelie these be Elementarie principles, and most necessarie to be delt with all. Whatsoeuer else besides these is required in that age, either

[50] Crystal, *Evolving English*, 32. [51] Crystal, *The Stories of English*, 257–258.

[52] Mulcaster also published what may be the first theory of primary education: Mulcaster, *The Educational Writings*.

to strengthen their bodies, or to quiken their wits, that is rather incident to exercise for helth, then to Elementarie for knowledge. Thus I haue shewed both why I begin at the Elementarie, and wherein it consisteth.[53]

Beyond the importance of helping young children learn Mulcaster argued that the principles of the Elementarie needed to be warranted 'by generall autoritie of all the grauest writers'.[54] He reminds the reader that Plato stressed the importance of gymnastic for the body and Music for the mind, noting that music was considered much more important in Plato's time than Mulcaster perceived it to be in the school curriculum of his own time. Plato saw music, and comprehension in reading and writing, as important to support speech. He also emphasised singing and playing for the utterance of harmony. Other ancient writers are also cited in the Elementarie: for example, Pamphilus on drawing as part of liberal science; and Quintilian's mastery of rhetoric in support of reading, writing and music. Mulcaster's main purposes or principles for his Elementarie are summarised as follows:

1.3 The Elementarie is designed to develop people who are good people and who make a positive contribution to society. Learning is for all people not just elites.
1.4 The principles are based on logical reasoning and evidential proof.
1.5 The Elementarie consists of a curriculum which is the best for young children (or much more colourfully in Mulcaster's language: 'seasoneth the young mindes with the verie best, and swetest liquor'). The Christian religion was a strong driver for the five areas of Mulcaster's curriculum. Consistent with school curriculum for hundreds of years to follow, reading was regarded as the most important curriculum area. Writing was mainly seen to serve reading although the place of memory and handwriting, beautifying the mind, and the link with drawing is interesting. Music is a central part of the Elementarie's purpose. The role of Grammar is to support the understanding and enactment of the broader principles:

> When the childe shall haue the matter of his *Reading*, which is his first principle so well proined and so pikked, as it shall catechise him in relligion trewlie, frame him in opinion rightlie, fashion him in behauiour ciuillie, and withall contain in som few leaues the greatest varieties of most syllabs, the chefe difference of most words, the sundrie pronouncing of all parts, and branches of euerie period, doth not *Reading* then which is the first principle seme to season verie sure? enriching the minde with so precious matter, and furnishing the tung with so perfit an vtterance? When the argument of the childs *Copie*, and

[53] University of Oxford, 'The First Part of the Elementarie', section 1.1.
[54] University of Oxford, 'The First Part of the Elementarie', section 1.2.

the direction of his hand, whereby he learns to write shalbe answerable to his reading, for chocie of good matter, and reuerence to young yeares, neither shall offer anie thing to the eie, but that maie beawtifie the minde, and will deserue memorie, will not *writing* season well, which so vseth the hand, as it helpeth to all good? When the *pen* and *pencill* shalbe restrained to those draughts, which serue for present semelinesse, and more cunning to com on, for the verie necessarie vses of all our hole life, doth not that same liquor, wherewith theie draw so, deserue verie good liking, which will not draw at all but where vertew bids draw? When *Musik* shall teach nothing, but honest for delite, and pleasant for note, comlie for the place, and semelie for the person, sutable to the thing, and seruiceable to circumstance, can that humor corrupt, which bredeth such delite, being so eueriewhere armd against iust chalenge, of either blame or misliking? For the principle of *Grammer*, I will not tuch it here, bycause I entend not to deall with it here, but wheresoeuer I shall tuch it, I will tuch it so, as it shall answer to the rest in all kinds of good. In the mean time till the grammer principle do com to light, that *Reading* shalbe so relligious, *Writing* so warie, *Drawing* so dangerlesse, *Singing* so semelie, *plaing* so praise-worthie, the euent shall giue euidence, and the relice it self shall set furth the seasoning.

1.6 The Elementarie ensures that children learn well.
1.7 The Elementarie reflects children's natural learning.
1.8 Future learning should be made easier as a result of the Elementarie
1.9 Ignorance will be avoided.
1.10 Learning about language, and therefore grammar, is the height of the Elementarie.

Mulcaster was the first to put forward the case for sticking with the long established alphabet and emerging spelling, rather than creating any kind of new or simplified system. In general, spelling reforms, such as new symbols and conventions, were not taken up apart from the vowel 'i' distinguished from the consonant 'j', and 'u' from 'v'.[55] Linguistic descriptivism is seen in Mulcaster's attention to language being used, linked to his enlightened views about young children's learning, although his drive for correct language use is also clear: 'is it not a verie necessarie labor to set the writing certain, that the reading maie be sure?'[56]

At first the development of standard English was not due to high-prestige institutions and individuals, but was more a result of multiple influences including population movements, trade, and social groupings. Much later in

[55] Crystal, *The Stories of English*, 268. [56] Mulcaster, *Elementarie*, 61.

the eighteenth century, more systematic attempts were made to standardise the language. In my introduction, I drew attention to John Walker's book, planned in 1774 then finally published in 1791, which focused on pronunciation (his theory of inflections), but one of the first most influential guides was Robert Lowth's *A Short Introduction to English Grammar with Critical Notes*, first published in 1762.

The book begins with a preface which contains Lowth's arguments for why his book was needed (consistent with printing practice at the time there is, incidentally, no contents page for the book). Lowth begins his preface by acknowledging the development of the English language over the preceding two hundred years. He noted the great enlargement of the language, and that its energy, variety, and richness had been proved in verse and in prose, in all subjects, and styles. Like so many prescriptivists who would come after him, he notes with admiration the writing of an earlier period, in particular the writings of Richard Hooker (the priest and theologian). Jonathan Swift is also noted as 'one of the most correct, and perhaps the best, of our prose writers', not least because of his knowledge of Swift's famous letter on the same topic: *A Proposal for Correcting, Improving and Ascertaining the English Tongue in a Letter to the Most Honourable Earl of Oxford and Mortimer, Lord High Treasurer of Great Britain*. Lowth puts forward his major criticism: 'whatever other improvements it may have received, it [the English language] hath made no advances in Grammatical Accuracy'.[57] The specifics of Lowth's argument were that even the most recognised authors, and the 'politest part of the nation … often offends against every part of grammar'.[58] He goes on to say that this is no fault of the language itself, because it was in Lowth's opinion the simplest of all European languages. His evidence for this point is based on grammatical aspects such as the very few nouns (what Lowth calls 'substantives') in English that have different forms according to case or gender. Ironically Lowth's view of the main reason for poor grammar seems to be a rather good account of the way in which meaning is at the heart of language use, and how we don't actually need rules because people are able to communicate without knowing prescriptive 'rules':

> Were the language less easy and simple, we should find ourselves under a necessity of studying it with more care and attention. But as it is, we take it for granted, that we have a competent knowledge and skill, and are able to aquit ourselves properly, in our own native tongue: a faculty, solely acquired by use, conducted by habit, and tried by the ear, carries us on without reflection; we meet with no rubs or difficulties in our way, or we do not perceive them; we find ourselves able to go on without rules, and we do not so much as suspect, that we stand in need of them.[59]

[57] Lowth, *A Short Introduction to English Grammar*, iii.
[58] Lowth, *A Short Introduction to English Grammar*, v.
[59] Lowth, *A Short Introduction to English Grammar*, iv.

A rather more convincing point that Lowth made was his view that even the experts in language from a previous time, for example experts in ancient languages and ancient authors, had not, or were not able to analyse language of 'ordinary use and common construction in [the] VERNACULAR IDIOM'.[60] Lowth did attempt to apply his rules to examples of language in use, although these were of written language not spoken language.

The understanding of language in the context of education is seen in Lowth's argument that the investigation of the principles of language, and the study of grammar, should be expected of 'every person in a liberal education, and it is indispensably required of every one who undertakes to inform or entertain the public, that he should be able to express himself with propriety and accuracy'.[61] He then goes on to accuse the best authors of the day of 'gross mistakes' because of their poor knowledge of English grammar. Lowth admits that his examples of authors' poor grammar were simply ones that he came across in his own reading. Like so many who have followed in Lowth's footsteps he confused the communication of meaning with correctness:

> The principle design of a Grammar of any Language is to teach us to express ourselves with propriety in that Language; and to enable us to judge of every phrase and form of construction, *'whether it be right or not.'*[62]

Lowth then went on to suggest a secondary use of his grammar, its application to the learning of other languages. The use of grammatical knowledge to inform the learning of other languages may have been more accurate than some of his other points. However he saw the practical outcome of this foreign language learning as school children using his grammar in order to learn Latin. Unfortunately the closing remarks of Lowth's preface make clear that he preferred 'easiness and perspicuity' to 'logical exactness', and 'All disquisitions, which appeared to have more of subtlety than of usefulness in them, have been avoided. In a word, it [Lowth's grammar] was calculated for the use of the learner, even of the lowest class.'[63] And so the links between identity (e.g. social class) and standards of language ('politeness') at this time were clear. The negative portrayal of almost all language users (apart from Lowth himself) is another common element of prescriptivist approaches to language.

Lowth's list of poor users of language was pretty impressive: Swift, Dryden, Bolingbroke, Bentley, and Pope! Lowth consistently confuses description of the language with prescription about how he thinks others should use the language. So with regard to verbs we see Lowth's not unreasonable ideas about a relationship between verbs and prepositions, and the way that changes

[60] Lowth, *A Short Introduction to English Grammar*, ix (capitals in original text).
[61] Lowth, *A Short Introduction to English Grammar*, x.
[62] Lowth, *A Short Introduction to English Grammar*, xi (italics added).
[63] Lowth, *A Short Introduction to English Grammar*, xiv.

in placement of grammatical forms will affect meaning. But in his extensive footnotes, which are often longer than the main text, he attack's Swift's use of language; the language that Swift used in his own letter about the English language. Lowth claims that Swift's use of,

'Your character, which I, or any other writer, may now value ourselves *by* drawing'

Should be,

'Your character, which I, or any other writer, may now value ourselves *upon* drawing.'

And hence, according to Lowth, Swift's use of language is wrong, or at least showed 'impropriety'.

The links between language and music are wonderfully and very specifically recorded by Lowth in the section on punctuation:

> The proportional quantity, or time, of the points, with respect to one another, is determined by the following general rule: The Period is a pause in quantity or duration double of the Colon; the Colon is double of the Semicolon; and the Semicolon is double of the Comma. So that they are in the same proportion to one another, as the Semibref [semibreve], the Minim, the Crotchet, and the Quaver in Music. The precise quantity, or duration, of each Pause or Note cannot be defined; for that varies with the Time; and both in Discourse and Music the same Composition may be rehearsed in a quicker or a slower Time: but in Music the proportion between the Notes remains ever the same; and in Discourse, if the doctrine of Punctuation were exact, the proportion between the Pauses would be ever invariable.

Lowth also gives an account of the way in which punctuation is linked to his view of grammar, for example the particular ways in which he sees sentences demarcated by imperfect phrases, simple sentences and compounded [*sic*] sentences. But what he fails to do is identify the main role of punctuation, for example commas, in making clear the meaning, and helping to avoid ambiguity; the kind of ambiguity captured memorably in *Eats, Shoots & Leaves.*[64] Since the time of Lowth's book the idea of punctuation demarcating pauses, a remnant of Roman oratory, has become less and less tenable because punctuation's functions are closely tied to sentence structure.

In 1755 the book that would have one of the most profound impacts of any book on the standardisation of the English language was published: Samuel Johnson's dictionary. Although the dictionary wasn't the very first, it was unique because of Johnson's linguistically rigorous approach. It was more comprehensive than any that had gone before: '42,773 entries in the first edition, with 140,871 definitions and 222,114 quotations'.[65] His approach was comprehensive, so included attention to orthography (letters and their sounds), pronunciation, etymology (derivation of words), analogy, morphology (the

[64] Truss, *Eats, Shoots & Leaves*. [65] Crystal, *The Stories of English*, 382.

forms of word e.g. singular/plural), syntax, phraseology (collocation: the juxtaposition of one word with another word); distribution (usage, such as the concept of 'obsolete'). The overall keys to Johnson's impressive contribution were firstly his recognition that all language is of value, and worthy of study for that reason. And secondly that some variants of a language carry particular prestige in the eyes of some in society.

The dictionary as style guide raises questions of identity, authority, elitism, and democracy that are part of the consideration of language. Johnson's accurate linguistic approach to his subject should have established the path for all who followed. For some it did, but for others, who perhaps saw Johnson's recognition of the equality of language as a threat, the grammar wars had started:

> This is the real harm that the prescriptivism of the mid eighteenth century did to English. It prevented the next ten generations from appreciating the richness of their language's expressive capabilities, and inculcated an inferiority complex about everyday usage which crushed the linguistic confidence of millions. We have begun to emerge, at the beginning of the twenty-first century, from the linguistic black hole, notwithstanding the purist temperaments which continually try to suck us back into it.[66]

The gradual emergence of linguistically informed standardisation was accompanied by the dramatic impact of printing. McLuhan's *Gutenberg Galaxy* was built on the idea that the study of form had been neglected by historians. A consequence of the printing press was to remove many of the technical causes of anonymity, and at the same time, in this the Renaissance period, new ideas of literary fame and intellectual property were building. The printing press resulted in a new kind of consumer world. As McLuhan made clear, the entire production of books up to 1500 AD was 15 to 20 million copies representing 30,000 to 35,000 separate publications. The majority of these publications were in Latin. Just as the printed book revolutionised manuscripts so the vernacular language superseded Latin. As part of this process, print contributed to the standardisation of language. Prior to the printing press a Latin dictionary would have been impossible as medieval authors changed definitions according to the context of their thinking.

And while McLuhan was right that the medium has a profound social impact its function is always to serve the message rather be the message. His suggestion that the changes in humans' senses, that result from technology extending the physical reach of the human body, are 'comparable to what happens when a new note is added to a melody'[67] was not fully explained. Nevertheless the failure to understand the profound connections between medium *and* message is at the heart of many modern problems with writing.

[66] Crystal, *The Stories of English*, 386. [67] McLuhan, *Gutenberg Galaxy*, 41.

Somewhat like the dramatic rise in written texts that began around 1066, the advent of printing gave access to texts to vastly increased numbers of people. This enabled them to access a much greater range of meanings, including in the form of stories written down. The result of building a reading public challenged writers to write for this new 'audience'. The need for standardisation of language became more pressing, both from the ground up as people's need for unambiguous messages increased but also from the top down from those who wished to impose order and control language.

The Digital Age

The advances in writing that came as a result of the alphabet and the printing press are now seen from a considerable distance in time. There have only been a limited number of accounts of such developments written by people who lived through such revolutions. But for the final revolution covered in this chapter, the issue of documenting change at the time of the change itself is currently more straightforward, for myself as a writer and for all, because we live in the digital age.

During the late twentieth century the invention of personal computers, and crucially, the development of the internet were to be even more profound than the development of the printing press. Understanding the influence of digital developments on writing is necessarily a work in progress. The importance of studying the digital world, by using 'media archaeology', is perhaps more important than ever, as electronic interfaces both provide access to previously unimaginable sources of information and opportunities for writing online. These interfaces also conceal more, partly as a result of the growth of the user-friendliness and affordances of touch screen technology and apps.[68]

The internet as we know it today emerged from a series of technological breakthroughs. One of the first electronic networks was the Advanced Research Projects Agency Network or ARPANET developed in 1969. Len Kleinrock's group at the University of California, Los Angeles (UCLA) first tried to log on to a computer at the Stanford Research Institute. Kleinrock described what happened:

> We set up a telephone connection between us and the guys at SRI . . .
> We typed the L and we asked on the phone, 'Do you see the L?'
> 'Yes, we see the L,' came the response.
> We typed the O, and we asked, 'Do you see the O?'
> 'Yes, we see the O.'
> Then we typed the G, and the system crashed . . .
> Yet a revolution had begun . . .[69]

[68] Emerson, *Reading Writing Interfaces*, xii.
[69] MIT OpenCourseWare, 'A Brief History of the Internet'.

How familiar the idea of a computer system crashing still is to many of us! But also how exciting technological discoveries can be when people have the vision to accurately predict their potential.

The invention of the internet was made possible by discoveries in computer science laboratories. For example the idea of *packet switching* is essential to the channels of communication that make up the internet. Packet switching is a method of structuring digital data into blocks called packets that are suitable for communication across digital networks. The structure of packets is a system of seven layers called Open Systems Interconnection (OSI). The simplest way to understand packets and OSI is to think of them as analogous sending a letter. The letter writer has a message to send to a particular person. OSI layer 7 (the application layer) opens the channel for the communication.[70] This is equivalent to the structure of a postal service including post offices, addresses of houses, and letter boxes. The actual words of the letter have to be translated in various ways into appropriate digital formats, ultimately into binary code (OSI layers 6 to 2). Finally OSI layer 1 conveys the message in its final physical form in electrical, optical, or radio form through hardware.

The ARPANET was only the first of many network methods developed internationally. In time it was realised that these multiple methods needed to be unified. The beginnings of the internet were seen in the first internet protocol, the unglamorously named text called *RFC 675 – Specification of Internet Transmission Control Program* developed in December 1974.[71] This is regarded as the first use of the term *internet* which at that time was used as an adjective unlike its use as a noun now.

Development of an internet paved the way for the World Wide Web (WWW) which provides access to text globally, and which enables people to communicate through the development of web pages and formats such as *blogs*. The WWW was invented by the British scientist Tim Berners-Lee who wrote his proposal for an information management system on 12 March 1989.[72] The description by Berners-Lee and colleagues in their later formal document the *Architecture of the World Wide Web* provides a very useful definition:

> The ***World Wide Web*** (***WWW***, or simply ***Web***) is an information space in which the items of interest, referred to as resources, are identified by global identifiers called Uniform Resource Identifiers (***URI***).
>
> Examples such as the following travel scenario are used throughout this document to illustrate typical behavior of ***Web agents*** – people or software acting on this information space. A ***user agent*** acts on behalf of a user. Software agents include servers, proxies, spiders, browsers, and multimedia players.

70 Kroon, D. 'Osi Reference Model (Open Systems Interconnection)'. ND.

71 Cerf, V., Y. Dalal, C. Sunshine, and Network Working Group. 'Specification of Internet Transmission Control Program December 1974 Version', 1974.

72 Wikipedia, 'World Wide Web'.

Story While planning a trip to Mexico, Nadia reads 'Oaxaca weather information: 'http://weather.example.com/oaxaca' in a glossy travel magazine. Nadia has enough experience with the Web to recognize that 'http://weather.example.com/oaxaca' is a URI and that she is likely to be able to retrieve associated information with her Web browser. When Nadia enters the URI into her browser:

1 The browser recognises that what Nadia typed is a URI.
2 The browser performs an information retrieval action in accordance with its configured behavior for resources identified via the 'http' URI scheme.
3 The authority responsible for 'weather.example.com' provides information in a response to the retrieval request.
4 The browser interprets the response, identified as XHTML by the server, and performs additional retrieval actions for inline graphics and other content as necessary.

The browser displays the retrieved information, which includes hypertext links to other information. Nadia can follow these hypertext links to retrieve additional information. (W3 C, 2004, http://www.w3.org/TR/webarch/)

As part of opening up the world to electronic communications the development of the World Wide Web and the internet have had implications for language spread. The most powerful evidence that the desire to express meaning drives language change can be seen in the way languages spread globally. In a world of international communications through the internet, and a world of international trade, one language shared by all would be very convenient. This phenomenon appears to be happening in the form of the English language, which it is argued has become a *world lingua franca* (WLF). The expression lingua franca is defined by the OED as 'Any language that is used by speakers of different languages as a common medium of communication; a common language.' For example in some African countries Swahili is used as a common language in the context of many different tribal languages. However, my interest is with the idea of a world lingua franca rather than a regional lingua franca.

To be described as a WLF the language concerned must have a reasonable claim to have the highest number of speakers globally, and to have very wide geographical spread. Arriving at accurate figures is complicated as Crystal explains.[73] The first problem is the world population growth of about 1.2% per annum, which means that figures for numbers of speakers in less-developed nations in particular will change rapidly because it is in these countries that population growth is at its most rapid. Even in more stable populations, acquiring information is difficult. The most extensive information comes from a census because these are completed by nearly every member of a

[73] Crystal, D. *The Cambridge Encyclopedia of Language* (3rd ed.). Cambridge: Cambridge University Press, 2010.

population. But most census questionnaires do not include questions about linguistic background. Even if you can ask people about their language(s), there are difficulties. For example, it is difficult to establish the extent of language proficiency. Only being able to speak a few words and phrases perhaps would not count as speaking a language. Ability to write a language is subject to similar problems of level of use, and particular difficulties for surveying use of writing and skill levels. Also, if a language has particularly high status in a country, survey respondents may feel obliged to exaggerate their familiarity with the language. Allowing for these caveats Crystal estimated that the figures for the languages spoken by the largest numbers of speakers globally were as follows:

English, in countries where people are regularly exposed to English, including learning English in school 2,902,853,000
English, second language speakers 1,800,000,000
Chinese, mother tongue, all languages 1,071,000,000
Mandarin Chinese, mother tongue 726,000,000
English, mother tongue, 427,000,000[74]

A further problem for estimating the growing use of English is that there are no figures available for people who have learned English as a foreign language in countries where English does not have special status (including in China where anecdotal accounts suggest that numbers of people learning English continues to grow dramatically).

Technological inventions by scientists in English-speaking nations, such as the internet and the World Wide Web, have also resulted in infrastructure and prototypes being based on English. The USA's continuing dominance in world markets is now linked with global digital communications as companies such as Apple Computers; Microsoft, IBM, and so on continue to dominate world markets. The links between global commerce, digital communication, and language are to some an example of a new form of imperialism.[75] It is certainly true that *one* of the reasons for the spread of English round the world is as a result of the British Empire and the imposition of English in countries such as India, Tanzania, or the 58 countries where English is an official language.[76] It is also pointed out that such developments can be linked with the extinction of some languages, which again is seen by some as a form of imperialism because of the close links between language, identity, emancipation, and democracy. Yet while all these factors are real, although the extent of an active form of imperialism is a moot point, language spread is driven primarily as a result of people's desire, enthusiasm, curiosity, and need to communicate, hence my

[74] Crystal, D. *The Cambridge Encyclopedia of Language* (3rd ed.).
[75] O'Regan, 'English as a Lingua Franca: An Immanent Critique', 533–552.
[76] Wikipedia, 'List of Territorial Entities Where English Is an Official Language'.

description of language spread as organic. Language spread brings with it the twin phenomena of variation in language, and in a seeming contradiction, standardisation of language. Variation in language arises because the geographical spread results in people who use a range of other languages and dialects altering the new language to fit their own needs for expression. Linked to this, the pressures towards standardisation come from two sources: (1) efficiency and clarity of communication that requires the reduction of ambiguity though standardisation; (2) as a result of the first factor guides to standard language use, of a wide range of kinds, are established.

Consistent with other social science research, the digital world, and its affordances, is now being studied through large-scale quantitative work and in-depth qualitative work. For example, the use of *big data* supported by the use of *supercomputers* has enabled a new approach called *Culturomics*. In one study, more than five million books, approximately 4% of all books ever published, were analysed. The units of analysis in this study were the *1-gram* and *n-gram*. The 1-gram is a meaningful sequence of characters not separated by a space that includes words, part-words (such as SCUBA), numbers, and typos (such as 'excesss').[77] The analyses revealed significant results in relation to the ways in which the English language continues to change. At the time the study was published the size of the language had increased by more than 70% in the past 50 years, adding about 8500 words per year. An analysis of irregular verbs showed much stability over a period of 200 years but also that 16% went through change of grammatical regularisation:

> These changes occurred slowly: It took 200 years for our fastest-moving verb ('chide') to go from 10% to 90% [regular]. Otherwise, each trajectory was sui generis; we observed no characteristic shape. For instance, a few verbs, such as 'spill', regularized at a constant speed, but others, such as 'thrive' and 'dig', transitioned in fits and starts (7). In some cases, the trajectory suggested a reason for the trend. For example, with 'sped/speeded' the shift in meaning from 'to move rapidly' and toward 'to exceed the legal limit' appears to have been the driving cause.[78]

Writing Computer Language

Parallel to the development of the internet, computers and computer languages were also developing. The term 'language' in relation to computer language prompts reflection on the similarities and differences with the language of writing that is the subject of this book. For some people a computer language

[77] Michel, Shen, Aiden, et al., 'Quantitative Analysis of Culture Using Millions of Digitized Books', 176–182.

[78] Michel, Shen, Aiden, et al., 'Quantitative Analysis of Culture Using Millions of Digitized Books', 177.

is perhaps seen purely as a technological phenomenon unrelated to the meaning-making of human interaction. Yet these languages not only facilitate the human interaction through computers but increasingly engage with humans *using* their language, for example, Apple Computer's *Siri* which can understand simple oral commands to launch applications and find information. Some scholars have emphasised the need to understand computer languages like any other important human tool and sign system: the computer programme can be seen 'as a distinct cultural artefact, but it also serves as a grain of sand from which entire worlds become visible; as a Rosetta Stone that yields important access to the phenomenon of creative computing and the way computer programs exist in culture.'[79]

The vital place of both instrumental and consummatory (creative) meanings as part of the process of programming has been powerfully evident since the development of the very first 'high-level computing language' in the 1950s. High-level computing languages are those languages that allow programmers to be able to read and understand the meaning of the language in a more straightforward way than working with the computer's first language known as 'machine code' (or mother tongue perhaps), the mathematical language of *binary*: zeros and ones that relate to electronic micro switches that are either on (one) or off (zero).

The first high-level computer language was *Fortran*, which stands for 'Formula Translation' because Fortran included a 'compiler', part of the programme that translated the meaning of Fortran language into the meaning of machine code.[80] The Oxford University–educated scientist Barbara Alexander, who worked with machine code prior to the invention of Fortran, described Fortran as 'absolute bliss' compared to working with machine code. Alexander worked at the Harwell Atomic Energy Research establishment, in Oxfordshire, England, which included what is now the world's oldest original working computer, the Harwell Dekatron that, like most early systems, filled a whole room with its 738 Dekatron electronic tubes.[81] The invention of Fortran enabled computing tasks that would have taken one year to be done in about two weeks. One of Fortran's most important features was that it was more meaningful to the programmer, so it could be read more efficiently.

Questions about standards, power, and identity are a feature of all languages, and computer languages are no exception. Fortran was, and still is, a language for the elite. At the time of its invention, programmers used to compete, shown for example in the idea that 'real programmers don't use Pascal they use Fortran' (admittedly a joke for computer scientists!).[82] Fortran was a language

[79] Montfort, Baudoin, Bell, et al., *10 PRINT CHR$(205.5+RND(1)); : GOTO 10.*
[80] BBC Radio 4 (2015, 6 April), *Codes That Changed the World: Fortran.*
[81] The National Museum of Computing, 'First generation – WITCH & EDSAC'.
[82] Pascal was a programming language that came after Fortran.

developed and used initially by the gifted elite mathematicians and scientists from US and UK universities. It was invented by the Columbia University graduate John Backus with help from his team at IBM. Fortran was used to develop nuclear weapons and NASA space exploration, and in other research such as survey work that contributed to establishing the links between smoking and cancer.[83] Fortran is still used today, and is a requirement if you want to be an astronomer. It is unsurpassed if raw power for mathematical calculations is what is needed.

The story of Fortran includes a moment when the links between the smallest elements of language, such as particular symbols, are linked directly with meaning, with profound consequences for society. The space shuttle disaster that I described in the opening chapter shares some similarities with what happened in relation to the *Mariner 1* spacecraft although fortunately no lives were lost. *Mariner 1* was designed by NASA as part of its programme to explore planets in our solar system such as Mars, Venus, and Mercury.[84] Unfortunately only a few minutes into its first launch it veered dangerously off course, and so a self-destruct instruction was issued by the Range Safety Officer.

The problem has been attributed to the omission of an 'overscore' line above the dot in the extract of computer code (see below) in the course of transferring the handwritten code to computer.

$$\overline{\dot{R}}_n$$

The science fiction writer Arthur C. Clark called this, 'the most expensive hyphen in history' because the crash cost something in the region of $1,017,000 at today's values. Although the error was not a hyphen (it was an overscore), the media were attracted to the more widely understandable imagery of the hyphen. And even some official reports attributed the failure to a hyphen.[85]

The elitist nature of computer programming was to be comprehensively routed by a new language called BASIC (Beginner's All-purpose Symbolic Instruction Code), which as you saw in the first chapter drew me into computing when younger. The rationale for the study of BASIC by Nick Montfort and colleagues,[86] whose work I build on here, was that computer languages are a cultural resource, complete with both machine and human meanings, that should be studied just as other cultural resources are. In contrast to the quantitative analysis of big data, an alternative approach is great depth of analysis of one particular phenomenon. The extreme depth of their approach is reflected in their analysis of just one line of BASIC programme code that also

[83] BBC Radio 4, *Codes That Changed the World: Fortran*. [84] Wikipedia, 'Mariner 1'.
[85] Neuman, 'Mariner I – No Holds Barred'.
[86] Montfort, Baudoin, Bell, et al., *10 PRINT CHR$(205.5+RND(1)); : GOTO 10*.

is the title of their book. The line of code was regarded as important partly because it represents a complete computer programme in one line. As Montfort and his colleagues explain,

> code is a cultural resource, not trivial and only instrumental, but bound up in social change, aesthetic projects, and the relationship of people to computers. Instead of being dismissed as cryptic and irrelevant to human concerns such as art and user experience, code should be valued as text with machine and human meanings, something produced and operating within culture.
>
> 10 PRINT CHR$(205.5+RND(1)); : GOTO 10
>
> The pattern produced by this program is represented on the endpapers of this book. When the program runs, the characters appear one at a time, left to right and then top to bottom, and the image scrolls up by two lines each time the screen is filled. It takes about fifteen seconds for the maze to fill the screen when the program is first run; it takes a bit more than a second for each two-line jump to happen as the maze scrolls upward.[87]

The first example of an emphasis on cultural resource, in studying computer programming, in their book can be seen in the authors' attention to history, including the beginnings of programming. Many regard Ada Byron (1815–1852) as the first computer programmer. Ironically Ada's mother's encouragement for her to understand mathematics and logic was a reaction against following the route of Ada's father, Lord Byron, into the writing of poetry.

Education is also part of the story of BASIC. BASIC was developed by John Kemeny and Thomas Kurtz, who in 1964 shared a working version for all who were interested. By 1971 90% of students at Dartmouth College received computer training. It was also shared with other colleges and with high schools. Kemeny's liberal approach to computing, in what was a liberal arts college (a significantly different location to the most typical emergence from science institutes) had other highly significant results:

> Kemeny presided over Dartmouth's conversion to a coeducational campus, removed the 'Indian' as the college's mascot, and encouraged the recruitment of minority students. On his final day as president, he gave a commencement address that warned students, including those involved in the recently founded conservative Dartmouth Review, against the impulse that 'tries to divide us by setting whites against blacks, by setting Christians against Jews, by setting men against women. And if it succeeds in dividing us from our fellow beings, it will impose its evil will upon a fragmented society' (Faison 1992).

Another aspect of BASIC's success was its link with Microsoft. In 1975 Paul Allen saw the *Popular Electronics* advert for the 'Altair 8800: The most powerful minicomputer project ever presented – can be build for under $400.'[88] He showed it to his friend Bill Gates who was at Harvard University. Allen's and Gates's software interpreter (of the original BASIC) was licensed by *MITS (Micro*

[87] Montfort, Baudoin, Bell, et al., *10 PRINT CHR$(205.5+RND(1)); : GOTO 10*, 8.
[88] Montfort, Baudoin, Bell, et al., *10 PRINT CHR$(205.5+RND(1)); : GOTO 10*, 170.

Instrumentation and Telemetry Systems), and hence Microsoft was up and running. The key changes to the software that Allen, Gates, and their collaborator Monte Davidoff made were crucial for use of home computers and would have made little sense in relation to the original 'time-sharing' use of computers at Dartmouth College. The changes included the introduction of the statements called PEEK and POKE. In the introduction to this book a POKE command was included in the extract of basic programming language. In my extract the function of POKE was to prompt the amplifier to make a sound to confirm the correct selection of the number for a particular bell in the change sequence.

The new field of media research called *platform studies*, which can be seen as connected to the methodology of *media archeology*, makes clear the importance of social and cultural developments in computing. A significant example that linked language, technology, creativity, and education was the BBC Micro Computer that 'became a machine of many possibilities rather than one directed solely at education'.[89] Seen by some simply as a hardware development, Alison Gazzard makes it clear that the Computer Literacy Project (which contextualised the hardware of the BBC Micro) linked broadcast media (television and teletext: CEEFAX; radio); print media (books, software, and magazines); and education and society (schools, colleges, and government departments for education). The idea of computer programming as a language, and something to be understood as part of wider understanding of written language, continues to be important as this quote from the originators from MIT of a current simple programming language attest:

> With Scratch, you can program your own interactive stories, games, and animations – and share your creations with others in the online community.
>
> Scratch helps young people learn to think creatively, reason systematically, and work collaboratively – essential skills for life in the 21st century.[90]

Meanings in Digital Media

So far in this section of the chapter, I have looked at some underlying processes, including technical ones, that have allowed digital communication to flourish. These tools are, of course, there to facilitate the generation of meanings through text and images. So now I turn briefly to an example of the kinds of meanings that are being expressed, in one of the most popular new forms of communication. If *blogging* facilitated ease of publication of written text and still images then *vlogging* has facilitated video production and consumption. At the time of writing the first draft of this section of the chapter, the most subscribed vlog by

[89] Gazzard, *Now the Chips Are Down: The BBC Micro*, 13.
[90] Lifelong Kindergarten Group at the MIT Media Lab, 'About Scratch'.

highest number of subscribers was 'BF vs GF' (Boyfriend vs. Girlfriend) at 5,501,357 subscribers according to the VidStatsX website. Only about one year later (October 2016), the subscribers had increased to 9,164,902 subscribers. But the site had also been relegated to number two in the one hundred most subscribed list because *Good Mythical Morning* had replaced it, with 11,299,723 subscribers.[91]

The numbers of subscribers to such sites are one example of the scale of the composition, production, and publication of meaning that is available to be written and read in the twenty-first century. The affordances of these new digital forms of authorship include the combination of multiple modes. BF vs. GF features two young people who record light-hearted videos that feature 'challenges'. For example, the 'Touch my body challenge' required one partner to take the blindfolded partner's finger and touch a part of the non-blindfolded partner's body which the blindfolded partner has to guess. The 'set' for this YouTube video was an expensive-looking apartment. A cat wandered around in the background and sometimes became part of the story of the Vlog. The 'challenge' might be described as a party game, something that has in the past been described in traditional print magazines. But the video format, of course, offers direct physical representation of any bodily movements required for a game, the non-verbal aspects such as laughter while playing the game, physical appearances of the vloggers (young, American, and photogenic in this case), and over time an understanding of the on-screen personalities of the vloggers.

The close links between printed text and image that have been part of written composition for hundreds of years are also part of digital video, but with enhancements. The YouTube site that hosts the BF vs. GF vlog also features text-based comments from viewers. When the video is not playing, the YouTube site is packed with a mixture of text, images, and icons many with hyperlinks. Adverts constantly appear on top of the videos. BF and GF also have Twitter accounts where they maintain communication with their followers. Jeanna@PhillyChic5 (GF) had 583,000 'followers' when I viewed the Twitter site. One of her tweets ('Took the Christmas tree down today. Boy that was a lot of work.' [icon of xmas tree and hand]) was directly related to one of the BF GF videos called 'Upside down Christmas Tree' that included taking down a Christmas tree. During the video they decide that they wanted to watch a movie. GF says that she tweeted her followers to ask what they should watch ('I wanna watch a movie. Any recommendations?'). BF played with Siri on his Apple IPhone and was amused by Siri saying 'Brrr' in relation to the outside temperature. This particular Vlog ended with GF saying they had fallen out.

[91] VidStatsX. 'One Hundred Most Subscribed People & Vlogs Channel Rankings List by Subscribers'.

The most popular Bloggers are making significant sums of money that are paid to them by YouTube, and by advertisers who they agree to work with (under rather different production control conditions compared to old media television advertising).[92] The links with older forms of communication are also evident in the opportunities to, for example, publish books as a result of the fame that the Vloggers have attracted.

One indication of the scale of change that digitisation has brought can be seen in statistics on worldwide usage. Rather disconcertingly these statistics can be seen changing before our very eyes. The *internet live* statistics site has changing counts which use robust data sources as the basis for models which inform the estimates. For example, the changing count of numbers of 'Internet users in the world' was increasing at a rate of approximately 500 users per minute. In September 2016, at the time of writing, the estimated population of the world was 7,457,904,000 people and constantly increasing at a rate of about 3 births per second.[93] For July 2016, the total number of internet users was fixed at 46.1% (3,424,971,237 users). Only 14 years earlier, in 2000, the estimate of internet users was 5.9% of the population. The percentage of growth between 2000 and 2014 is estimated at 741.0%. However, these internet figures hide enormous regional disparities. For example as of July 2013 the region with the highest number of internet users was Asia with 87.7%. The lowest was Oceania with 0.9% followed by Africa with 9.8%.

The global nature of growth in social media use including across multiple *apps* used for information, entertainment, and intimacy is clear, as an in-depth anthropological approach comparing social media use in different countries of the world has shown.[94] This is an area where research struggles to keep up. For example although the phenomenon of Facebook, with its 1.25 billion users, has attracted research, the Chinese sites QQ (820 million users), QZone (625 million), and WeChat (355 million) had not been mentioned in any published research publications listed in a well-regarded research bibliography. Much of the use of new social media across the world is by young people. Research on young people's education in relation to 'media literacy' is regarded as exemplary research, which most of all has shown the need to equip young people with the skills to both produce meaning through new media, in other words to actively author and compose texts, but also to be critical consumers. And the most important tool worldwide, including low-income countries, is the mobile phone. This is the personal computer that allows composition in multiple modes, including composition of text, music, and image across multiple apps and platforms, from just one small device.

[92] BBC Radio 4, 'Meet the Vloggers'. [93] Worldometers, 'Current World Population', 2016.
[94] Miller, Costa, Haynes, et al., *How the World Changed Social Media*.

The medium perhaps never was the message because, 'It is the content rather than the platform that is most significant when it comes to why social media matters.'[95] This is why a focus on the processes of meaning-making in composition is so important. The signs of digital language are facilitated by the technological tools of language, and these tools are nothing more nor less than tools. The writer's task is to select and use tools to serve her intent to create meaning, and to beware the potential distraction that misplaced focus on the software and hardware, for their own sake, presents.

*

This brief selective history of writing has shown some of the ways that efficiency of communication, minimisation of ambiguity, and constant growth in speed and range of communication have driven the development of writing in an organic way. Over many hundreds of years, periods of incremental change are disrupted by profound developments, paradigm shifts, that result in significant increases in the numbers of writers and readers. The solving of the mystery of the Rosetta Stone typified the ways in which meaning is a driving force in human endeavours. It also helped us understand much more about some of the ways in which language developed from signs on clay to the infinite abstraction of the 26 letters of the alphabet.

The development of the alphabet had two overarching consequences for humans. Prior to the detailed meanings available from advanced writing systems, oral language was the only way to communicate complex meanings. Hence human culture as an oral culture was transformed to an oral *and* written culture, although it would be many hundreds of years before the distinctions between oral language and written language would be better understood. For the first time, meaning became something that was not only an instantaneous sharing with another human, within earshot, but something that could be crafted, reflected on, and communicated to a human at a distance. The new kinds of meanings this facilitated also had a reverse effect: expression of meaning through writing influenced oral expression of meanings, and enabled metacognitive thinking. The second overarching consequence was to change ideas about teacher and learner, teaching and education. Knowledge was increasingly to move from the preserve of the elite teacher to be accessible by a wider range of learners without the direct intervention of a teacher.

The invention of the alphabet paved the way for English as a language. Language is an inherently social phenomenon, and the emergence of English in the East Anglian region of England, in close proximity to London, brought new structures to the social nature of language. The idea of a standard language was born, and with it the first instructional books to attempt to prescribe a standard

[95] Miller, Costa, Haynes, et al., *How the World Changed Social Media*, 1.

English. The debates about standards of language have raged ever since. The writer's challenge is to develop appropriate levels of understanding of the significance of both stability and change in the social context where their writing is enacted.

The advent of printing at a much larger scale than had previously been possible created a new reading public who required more writers. Caxton's role in the printing press is perhaps better known than his engagement with the whole process of writing, including his role in the first book in England. Accompanying the change in scale of writing was a renewed need to maintain and establish standards of language. And here, through new books, the educators made their presence known, as some of the first self-appointed guardians of the English language.

The speed of digital technological change is concurrent with the stability of other aspects of language. New forms of social media still rely heavily on the alphabetic language of English. And new developments such as emoticons and images have been reunited with written language perhaps as an echo of the hieroglyphic past. At the same time the global spread of language, and particularly the English language, as a result of the internet, including in juxtaposition with still and moving images, music and sound, is on a quite extraordinary scale. The extent to which English establishes itself as a digital lingua franca remains an open question. One trend that we can be sure of is the debates about what standard written language is, and should be, will continue. But I hope that the debates may move away from repetitive complaints about 'right' and 'wrong' use of language towards 'effective' and 'ineffective'. So it is to these debates, as represented in modern guides to writing, that I turn next.

3 Writing Guidance

The development of the English language, from its early forms (including Germanic runic inscriptions) towards the beginnings of standardisation of the language as a result of the interactions between professional and other tradespeople, reached an important point in the eighteenth century. New attempts were made to prescribe 'correct' forms of English, for example, for the benefit of people from other countries who wanted to learn English. These attempts resulted in the first very popular books that took a prescriptive approach to the grammar and other elements of the English language, such as the books by Walker, Louth, and Mulcaster.

The growth of English has included an increase in the number and range of books and other texts intended as guides to the use of the English language. These texts vary in their priorities, from those that aim to maintain and document the conventions of the language, to those that seek to prescribe, to others whose main purpose is to entertain. These texts provide another source for analysis about how writing works or how it should work, as they reveal authors', and in some ways societies', perceptions of language. Hence this chapter is focused on a selection of writing guidance from the twentieth century to the present. I am interested not only in the types of such guides and their specific guidance but also some of the assumptions or fundamental rationales that underpin them.

The texts selected for analysis in this chapter (including digital sources) were a mixture of ones that I was already familiar with (as a result of research over many years) and texts new to me that I located as a result of a range of searches, and through recommendations from colleagues and friends. The final selection of texts for analysis for this chapter was 23 well-regarded, influential, relatively recently published texts. The selection process took account of aspects such as authors' background and knowledge; the type of text, including general to more specific language orientation; the apparent approach of the author to language and writing; evidence of impact such as high sales, high citations, and multiple editions; but also my intent to survey a wide variety of guides. The starting point for the analyses was to establish categories that describe the main orientation or type of the texts. The categories of texts, which are used to organise the sections in the chapter are as follows:

a) Media and journalism
b) General and popular texts
c) University teaching perspectives
d) Fiction writing perspectives

Inevitably the categories are a compromise between an analytical and organisational structure for the chapter and the reality that some of the texts featured could fit within more than one category.

For each of the sections of the chapter, some reflections on the general issues and implications are included as well as at least one additional in-depth exploration of a notable text. The final section of this chapter features books that have been written by writers of fiction about writing. This section acts in part as introductory to the chapter that follows in which I report a systematic analysis of expert writers' views and understandings, expressed in formal interviews, of the processes of writing that they engage in.

Media and Journalism

Perspectives on language and standards of language have a long tradition of debate in the media. Historically, this has been published in print media, but digitisation has brought additional ways for media organisations and their journalists to seek to comment on and influence language standards. To sum up a long tradition of argument, views about language can usually be summarised linguistically as either *descriptive* or *prescriptive*, although there is some evidence of a post-modern sensibility, with prescription and description being mixed depending on the context of authorship and production.

Descriptive views characterise language as conventions rather than rules. The idea that effective writing requires adherence to rules, particularly those based on outdated ideas of the links between the English language and Latin, is rejected in favour of analyses based on understanding of language in use including its changing conventions. The concept of error is weighed carefully in descriptive accounts, and hence descriptions of language as correct or incorrect are often deemed inappropriate. Written language is seen either to communicate the intended meaning efficiently and effectively, or not.[1] Prescriptive views are based mainly on seeing effective writing as requiring the adherence to rules of written language that are fixed. Therefore writing can be correct or incorrect.

[1] For a persuasive chapter about the concept of error in writing, see Kress, *Learning to Write*.

A headline in the *MailOnline* in 2014 was typical of prescriptive views of language, and the way in which standards of language are often represented in the media.

Don't rely on us for good grammar, says the BBC: Broadcaster is no longer the bastion of correct English, its 'style chief' admits

- Thousands now complain to the corporation every year over grammar
- Ian Jolly, who is the BBC newsroom's 'style editor', conceded his presenters and reporters repeatedly make basic errors
- They often confuse the words 'historic' with 'historical' and use the term 'chair' when they mean 'chairman' or 'chairwoman'[2]

On reading the article it is made clear that it was a BBC (British Broadcasting Company) listener who complained about the use of the words 'historic' and 'historical'; no examples are given of the presenters and reporters who apparently misuse these words. On the basis of etymology, the OED says that either historic or historical can be used interchangeably: '**1**. Relating to history; concerned with past events; = historical *adj.* 2'.

The complaint about the use of 'chair' in the MailOnline article is also interesting. The OED records that the word 'chair' is used in relation to a person presiding at a meeting:

b. Often put for the occupant of the chair, the chairman, as invested with its dignity (as *the throne* is for the sovereign), *e.g.* in the cry *Chair! Chair!* when the authority of the chairman is appealed to, or not duly regarded; ***to address the chair, support the chair***, etc. Now also used as an alternative for 'chairman' or 'chairwoman', esp. deliberately so as not to imply a particular sex.

The first use, in writing, of chair in the sense above (as invested with its dignity) was listed in the OED as coming from 1659. And the link with authority occurs in a number of the other definitions of chair including in 1392 as 'place or situation of authority, etc.' So although the use of 'chair' in a consciously gender neutral way, perhaps first used in the 1970s, is new, the overall meaning of the single entity in relation to authority is more than 600 years old. Language stability and language change seem to be combined in this example.

A different media organisation position on the use of the word chair in this context, and consistent to some degree with OED, is seen in the *guardianonline* writing style guide for journalists:

chair

acceptable in place of chairman or chairwoman, being nowadays widely used in the public sector and by organisations such as the Labour party and trade unions (though not

[2] Glennie, 'Don't Rely on Us for Good Grammar'.

the Conservative party, which had a 'chairman' in kitten heels); if it seems inappropriate for a particular body, use a different construction ('the meeting was chaired by Ian' or 'Kath was in the chair').[3]

Consistent with its political remit and characterisation as a politically left-leaning media organisation, the *Guardian* draws attention to the links between politics and standards of English. The reference to 'kitten heels' is to a remark that Teresa May MP made in 2003. When asked what kind of shoes best represented the Conservative (Tory) Party she said 'leopard-print kitten heels', defending this choice because '*I* am the party *chairman*.'[4] The suggestion by the guardianonline to avoid use of the word in place of 'a different construction' is also interesting as this suggests a sensitivity to language use, language change, and context of use. However the date of the Teresa May comment, and the claim about public sector organisations using 'chair' more than the Conservative Party, does raise a question about evidence for this claim, of which none is presented. An interview with David Marsh, one of the editors of the *Guardian and Observer Style Guide* makes clear his descriptive orientation to language.[5]

Other issues raised by the MailOnline piece are the idea of the British Broadcasting Corporation no longer being a 'bastion of correct English' because of the alleged errors (a clear suggestion of a gatekeeper role, and one to uphold standards of English). The BBC newsroom's style editor who is featured in the piece says that 'political correctness' was the influence on the use of the word 'chair' in place of 'chairman' or 'chairwoman'. The *evidence* of longstanding use of the word 'chair', in the OED, suggests a more nuanced picture. There is also, in my view, a serious point related to stereotypical assumptions about men taking up roles of authority needing to be challenged, including through reflection on careful use of words. The deployment of the phrase 'political correctness' is used by some as a device to denigrate the importance of equality by equating care with language as a politically motivated 'fad' rather than a topic worthy of serious consideration.

An even more contentious criticism in the MailOnline piece is noted: 'Last month, the BBC was criticised by the Queen's English Society for allowing presenters including Sara Cox and Radio 1 DJ Nick Grimshaw to say "haitch" instead of "aitch" when referring to the letter "H".' The lack of rigorous understanding of the differences between spoken and written forms of language is evident in this criticism. The BBC style editor reasonably defends difference in pronunciation on the basis that live broadcast presentation should be subject to 'leeway', as opposed to writing, but he did not go so far as to say that the way people speak is strongly linked to their identity, and because of this any direct

[3] Guardian and Observer Style Guide: C.
[4] Mann, 'Thoughts of Chairman May', (italics added).
[5] Freeman, 'Webchat: David Marsh Answers Your Questions about Grammar'.

criticism of the way someone speaks is at the least insensitive. The more linguistically informed interpretation is that the pronunciation would not lead to any ambiguity in what was meant. What's more, given that Radio 1's target audience is young people, the young radio presenters' pronunciation, and oral language in general, is likely to resonate and connect more effectively with their target radio audience if it shares some of their audiences' ways of using language.

The example I have described shows some of the ways that media organisations have a role, and are assumed to have a role, in the maintenance of standard English, and standards of English. The examples are also interesting in that they have moved, from what once would have been in-house printed guides, to online representation including the *Guardian's* updateable digital resource accessible by journalists and the general public alike. The capacity for online resources to be updated to reflect language change is one important development in language. However, the rigour of the evidence supporting views on language use remains an issue, for example, the speed and frequency with which updates are made in relation to rigorous checking against evidence. In this regard an interesting study found a variety of errors in both the online *Wikipedia* and the print form *Encyclopaedia Britannica* but no statistically significant difference overall in the accuracy of information in relation to a selection of science topics, as judged in a blind peer-reviewed exercise by science experts commenting on science entries in the encyclopaedias.[6]

It is rare to find guides that mix prescriptivism with descriptivism within the same source, partly because the two positions encapsulate some quite pronounced theoretical, cultural, and historical ways of thinking. However one book, published by a journalist, did this very memorably. *Eats Shoots & Leaves*, or if you prefer *Eats, Shoots & Leaves*, was first published in 2003, and in November 2016 was still number 26 in the language category of the Amazon Best Sellers.[7] Its success at publication was portrayed as something of a surprise because of its topic of punctuation. The success of this book is not so much its knowledge base, although it is on the whole an intelligent well informed popular account, but more that it is so engagingly written, not least the clever use of humour. The book mixes a declared prescriptivism with some descriptive analyses.

The subtitle of the book is 'The zero tolerance approach to punctuation'. This deliberate reference to criminality, the field in which the idea of zero tolerance was known for, is designed to both attract readers but also signal a prescriptive approach to correct use of punctuation. Being a 'stickler' for punctuation is

6 Nature, 'Internet Encyclopaedias Go Head to Head', 900–901.

7 I acknowledge that this book could perhaps have been part of the general and popular sources, but its authorship by a journalist and its focus on a small part of language – punctuation – meant I thought it fitted better in the media and journalism category.

celebrated; as is the idea that appropriate punctuation is similar to 'good manners'. Reminiscent of other prescriptivists, it is claimed that standards of language were better in years gone by. For example Truss says that it was good that the national curriculum for schools was introduced in England[8] because it taught young children how to use commas but 'there remains the awful truth that, for over a quarter of a century, punctuation and English grammar were simply not taught in the majority of schools'.[9] No evidence is offered to support this assertion. If we assume that Truss refers to the period from 1963 to 1988, a contrary argument to Truss's is that the period was characterised by a rather enlightened and appropriate descriptive orientation to language and literacy in primary/elementary education. For example, a seminal government-commissioned enquiry into primary education in 1967 observed that in relation to writing, when inaccuracy impeded communication then steps should be taken to remedy deficiencies in punctuation and other technical aspects.[10] Truss's argument that punctuation and grammar were not taught is not logical, because young people would not have passed secondary school exams if they had not been taught punctuation, grammar, spelling, and all other elements of writing. They were simply taught in ways that Truss appears to dislike. Truss's book has no footnotes or citations in general in the book, so the only clue offered for the sources of evidence is a short bibliography.

Truss's strong prescriptive tone is deceptive because on closer reading a descriptive orientation in the book is also evident. A good example is a discussion about the apostrophe. Early in the book Truss considers 'right and wrong' in the use of the apostrophe, and makes fun of the *Grocer's apostrophe*. But later she considers the use of the apostrophe in relation to the possessive form when writing names that end in the letter 's'. Having reviewed this variation Truss concludes that 'these are matters of style and preference that are definitely not set in stone, and it's a good idea not to get fixated about them . . . Consulting a dozen or so recently published punctuation guides, I can report that they contain minor disagreements on virtually all aspects of the above.'[11] Truss's review of other work in the field, her consideration of real examples of language use, and the conclusion she comes to, is contrary to the declared prescriptivism. It is tempting to speculate that this unusual combination of viewpoints is another reason for the book's commercial success as it perhaps appeals to prescriptivists and descriptivists alike.

[8] England's curriculum for state schools introduced as part of the Education Reform Act 1988.
[9] Truss, *Eats, Shoots & Leaves*, 14.
[10] Wyse and Jones. *Teaching English, Language and Literacy.*
[11] Truss, *Eats, Shoots & Leaves*, 56–57.

General and Popular Texts

One of the difficulties in selecting texts as examples for general features of language is the very high numbers of published texts addressing the topic. For example, pupil books aimed to support exams in the subject of English for secondary school pupils, and books on learning to write for children aged from three years to five years, are some of the best-selling books.[12] However, for reasons of space, in this chapter I limit my attention to books aimed at adult language use.

One particularly popular general guide is *Fowler's Modern English Usage*, another example of a guide originally written by a school teacher. The career of the original author, Henry Watson Fowler, included 17 years teaching Classics and English in the beautiful setting of the Sedbergh independent school in Cumbria just on the boundary of the Yorkshire Dales National Park.[13] Fowler's original was very much a prescriptive approach based on the classics in two senses, influences of Latin and Greek but also influences of a canon of mainly English literature. However, he also drew on newspapers but often without citing which ones. Fowler was interested in the readership in England and so did not attend to varieties of English spoken in other countries.

In 1995 *Fowler* (as it is colloquially known) had a major new edition edited by Robert Birchfield. Although that third edition was based on evidence, not least because of Birchfield's expertise required for his work on supplementary publications of the OED such as the *New Zealand Pocket Oxford Dictionary*, it retained its traditional grammar perspective rather than basing the work on other forms such as generative grammar. For example, the classification system for the words in Fowler was: 'adjectives, adverbs, concord, gerunds, infinitives, nouns and articles, ordinaries (a convenient term for points of disputed usage), passives, pronouns, and subjunctives'. And the somewhat old-fashioned approach resulted in views such as, 'The ordinaries field contains, for example, a formidable array of controversial uses of *due to, like* used as a conjunction, *of* used by children and poorly educated people to mean "have"'. The conflation of language with poorly educated people and with children was particularly unfortunate, and by descriptive grammarian's standards missed the point that the non-standard use of 'of' is simply dialect use.

In 2015, Jeremy Butterfield edited a fourth edition which brought a much more up-to-date reading: (1) the robust evidence-base for usage is now the Oxford English Corpus; (2) new words that emerged as a result of the advent of the internet are included; (3) more attention to variants of words used in

[12] E.g. in the 'languages' category of the Amazon site's 'best sellers', these were the top two types of texts when accessed in October 2016.

[13] The information about Fowler is taken from the introduction by Burchfield to *The New Fowler's Modern English Usage*.

different countries (apparently 'educationalist' is more common in British English whereas 'educationist' is more common in Indian English); and (4) acknowledgement that some dubious views on some subjects in the third edition required modernisation of the tone of these entries, and the inclusion of 250 new entries related to equality.[14] The latest revisions to Fowler seem to suggest that the modern linguistic descriptive view of language is prevailing even in the context of what was a classic prescriptive account.

Dictionaries are seen by some as serving a specific and limited purpose, to define words, but their contribution to understanding written language, its development, and standards of language is profound, as Samuel Johnson's contribution made clear. Whereas Fowler has a clear intent to instruct, consistent with its attention to 'usage', the OED is very much a descriptive account that is constantly being updated. One example of an entry from the Oxford English Dictionary (OED) online provides a glimpse of the richness of its linguistic record and hence its descriptive contribution to standards and guidance.

The OED identifies four main versions of the word 'meaning': three as nouns and one as an adjective. The first version, as a noun, is related to the idea of moaning or lamentation, a definition described as obsolete. The third version, as a noun, is a rare technical term from astronomy: 'The motion of the sun in mean longitude (i.e. along the ecliptic)'. The fourth version, as an adjective, is 'Having an intention or purpose' for example: 'One of them . . . is . . . as little meaning of harm to any one as his mother.' But it is the second main version, as a noun, that is particularly relevant for my purposes: 2 (See Figure 3.1b). The sense or signification of a word, sentence, etc.

The complexity and richness of language is evident firstly in the six definitions of this second main version that are offered. And even within these six definitions there are often several categories of meaning. The etymological examples, another impressive and valuable feature, include a quote from Milton's *Paradise Regained* (from 1671): 'That I might learn In what degree or meaning thou art call'd the Son of God, which bears no single sence'. Another of the history of examples is of Bertrand Russell's book that I cited in Chapter 2: 'These are what I call "object-words" . . . Their meaning is learnt (or can be learnt) by confrontation with objects which are what they mean, or instances of what they mean.'

In addition to the meaning of the selected word described on the page online that presents the dictionary entry, there are a range of other parts of the main pane (see figure 3.1a). The entry begins with the word and its meaning version number. This is followed by guidance on pronunciation in British English and US English, including a link which allows people to hear the word spoken in a version 'in use among educated urban speakers of standard English in Britain and

[14] Butterfield, *Fowler's Dictionary of Modern English Usage* (4th ed.).

(a)

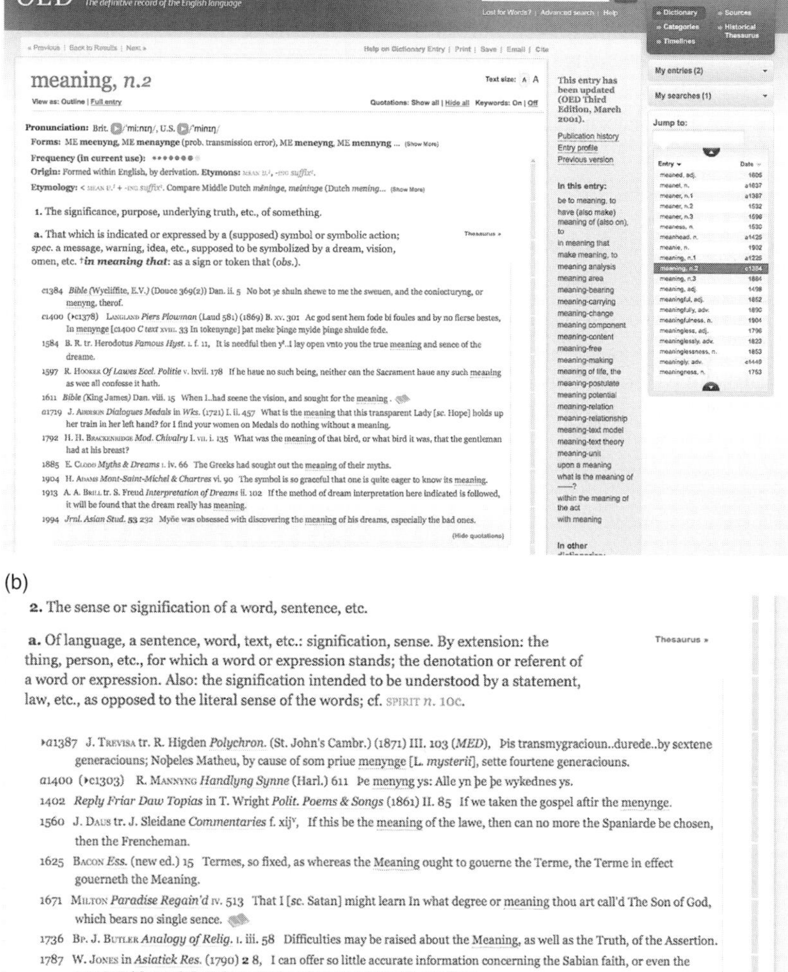

meaning, *n.2*

Pronunciation: Brit. /ˈmiːnɪŋ/, U.S. /ˈminɪŋ/
Forms: ME **meenyng**, ME **menaynge** (prob. transmission error), ME **meneyng**, ME **mennyng** ... (Show More)
Frequency (in current use): ●●●●●●●
Origin: Formed within English, by derivation. Etymons: MEAN *v.*[1], -ING *suffix*[1].
Etymology: < MEAN *v.*[1] + -ING *suffix*[1]. Compare Middle Dutch *mêninge, meininge* (Dutch *mening*... (Show More)

1. The significance, purpose, underlying truth, etc., of something.

a. That which is indicated or expressed by a (supposed) symbol or symbolic action; *spec.* a message, warning, idea, etc., supposed to be symbolized by a dream, vision, omen, etc. †***in meaning that***: as a sign or token that (*obs.*).

c1384 *Bible (Wycliffite, E.V.)* (Douce 369(2)) Dan. ii. 5 No bot ȝe shuln shewe to me the sweuen, and the coniecturyng, or menyng, therof.
c1400 (▸c1378) Langland *Piers Plowman* (Laud 581) (1869) B. xv. 301 Ac god sent hem fode bi foules and by no fierse bestes, In menynge [c1400 *C text* xviii. 33 In tokenynge] þat meke þinge mylde þinge shulde fede.
1584 B. R. tr. Herodotus *Famous Hyst.* i. f. 11, It is needful then y[t]..I lay open vnto you the true meaning and sence of the dreame.
1597 R. Hooker *Of Lawes Eccl. Politie* v. lxvii. 178 If he haue no such being, neither can the Sacrament haue any such meaning as wee all confesse it hath.
1611 *Bible (King James)* Dan. viii. 15 When I..had seene the vision, and sought for the meaning.
a1719 J. Addison *Dialogues Medals* in *Wks.* (1721) I. ii. 457 What is the meaning that this transparent Lady [sc. Hope] holds up her train in her left hand? for I find your women on Medals do nothing without a meaning.
1792 H. H. Brackenridge *Mod. Chivalry* I. vii. i. 135 What was the meaning of that bird, or what bird it was, that the gentleman had at his breast?
1885 E. Clodd *Myths & Dreams* i. iv. 66 The Greeks had sought out the meaning of their myths.
1904 H. Adams *Mont-Saint-Michel & Chartres* vi. 90 The symbol is so graceful that one is quite eager to know its meaning.
1913 A. A. Brill tr. S. Freud *Interpretation of Dreams* ii. 102 If the method of dream interpretation here indicated is followed, it will be found that the dream really has meaning.
1994 *Jrnl. Asian Stud.* **53** 232 Myōe was obsessed with discovering the meaning of his dreams, especially the bad ones.

(b)

2. The sense or signification of a word, sentence, etc.

a. Of language, a sentence, word, text, etc.: signification, sense. By extension: the thing, person, etc., for which a word or expression stands; the denotation or referent of a word or expression. Also: the signification intended to be understood by a statement, law, etc., as opposed to the literal sense of the words; cf. SPIRIT *n.* 10c.

▸a1387 J. Trevisa tr. R. Higden *Polychron.* (St. John's Cambr.) (1871) III. 103 (*MED*), Þis transmygracioun..durede..by sextene generacioun; Noþeles Matheu, by cause of som priue menynge [L. *mysterii*], sette fourtene generaciouns.
a1400 (▸c1303) R. Mannyng *Handlyng Synne* (Harl.) 611 Þe menyng ys: Alle yn þe þe wykednes ys.
1402 *Reply Friar Daw Topias* in T. Wright *Polit. Poems & Songs* (1861) II. 85 If we taken the gospel aftir the menynge.
1560 J. Daus tr. J. Sleidane *Commentaries* f. xij[v], If this be the meaning of the lawe, then can no more the Spaniarde be chosen, then the Frencheman.
1625 Bacon *Ess.* (new ed.) 15 Termes, so fixed, as whereas the Meaning ought to gouerne the Terme, the Terme in effect gouerneth the Meaning.
1671 Milton *Paradise Regain'd* iv. 513 That I [sc. Satan] might learn In what degree or meaning thou art call'd The Son of God, which bears no single sence.
1736 Bp. J. Butler *Analogy of Relig.* i. iii. 58 Difficulties may be raised about the Meaning, as well as the Truth, of the Assertion.
1787 W. Jones in *Asiatick Res.* (1790) **2** 8, I can offer so little accurate information concerning the Sabian faith, or even the meaning of the word, that I dare not yet speak on the subject with confidence.
1843 J. S. Mill *Syst. Logic* (ed. 3) II. iv. iv. §6. 225 It may be good to *alter* the meaning of a word, but it is bad to let any part of the meaning *drop*.
1876 W. S. Jevons *Logic Primer* 23 The confusion which arises between the different meanings of the same word.
1940 B. Russell *Inq. into Meaning & Truth* i. 25 These are what I call 'object-words'... Their meaning is learnt (or can be learnt) by confrontation with objects which are what they mean, or instances of what they mean.
1987 M. Collins *Angel* iv. 67 Every comment or question..began to hold in her eyes some hidden meaning.

(Hide quotations)

Figure 3.1 Extract from OED Online. Definition (screen-grab) of the word 'meaning'. By permission of Oxford University Press.

the United States . . . Words particularly associated with other parts of the English-speaking world are also given pronunciations in the appropriate global variety of English.' Next, the different forms of spelling are offered providing a very clear example of language change. In the case of the word 'meaning' the spelling changed from 'meenyng' in the fourteenth century to an eighteenth-century northern English variation of 'meanen'. After the frequency in current use indicator there is a line for 'origin', in this case 'formed within English'. But a link to the etymon, the verb 'Mean', provides a trail back to the history of the development of the English language in England, in particular the Germanic and Saxon influences:

> **Origin:** A word inherited from Germanic.
> **Etymology:** Cognate with Old Frisian *mēna* to signify, Middle Dutch *mēnen* to intend, signify, think, hold a good opinion of, love (Dutch *menen* to intend, think), Old Saxon *mēnian* to intend, signify, have in mind, mention (Middle Low German *mēnen, meinen* to intend, signify, hold an (especially good) opinion of, love, German regional (Low German) *menen* to intend, signify, be of the opinion, think), Old High German *meinen* to intend, signify, make known, mention, have in mind (Middle High German *meinen* to intend, signify, have in mind, hold an opinion of, love, German *meinen* to intend, have in mind, think, say, (poet.) love), all ultimately < a Germanic base cognate with Old Church Slavonic *měniti* to suppose, think, consider, have in mind, mention (this word exhibits an extraordinarily close parallelism of meaning with the Old English and Old Saxon verbs). The Scandinavian forms, Icelandic *meina*, Old Swedish *mena* (Swedish *mena*), Danish *mene*, all in sense 'to intend, signify, consider', are probably borrowings < Middle Low German. From the same Germanic base are derived the following nouns: Old Frisian *mēne* opinion, intention, Old High German *meina*, probably originally in sense 'opinion', but only attested in phrases (as *thia meina, bī thia meina* truly, really), and probably also (with a different ablaut grade) Old Frisian *minne*, Middle Dutch *minne* (Dutch *min*), Old Saxon *minnia, minnea* (Middle Low German *minne*), Old High German *minna* (Middle High German *minne*), all in sense 'love, affection, agreement'. The further etymology and the order of sense-development are uncertain (see also note below); probably < the Indo-European base of i-mene adj. (which might suggest the original sense 'to express opinions alternately or by turns'); a connection with the Indo-European base of mind n.1 has also been suggested, but this is difficult to explain phonologically.

Turning now to other layout features of the page online that presents the dictionary entry, there are two further columns to the right of the main pane for the definition information. The far right column is the 'browse' column. This includes four hyperlinks to significant sections, one of which is 'Sources'. Here we discover that the top five sources of texts to provide context for words in the OED are (1) The *Times* Newspaper; (2) William Shakespeare; (3) Walter Scott; (4) *Philosophical Transactions*; and (5) *Encyclopaedia Britannica*. The second additional column provides the date when the information about the word was last updated, and a link to the word's OED publication history. Below the publication history there is a list of phrases that include the word within them.

Taken as a whole, the wealth of information surrounding this example of 'meaning', and all entries in OED, renders the description 'dictionary definition' rather limited. The role of the OED in defining and maintaining standard language, including the decision to use the spoken English of urban educated speakers, is part of the long, ongoing debates about standards. The claim by the publishers that the OED is 'widely regarded as the *accepted authority* on the English language' (emphasis added) is indicative. One challenge to this claim is, which version of the English language is the OED the accepted authority?

American English includes its routes through America's most well-known first dictionary, written by Noah Webster, the rights to which subsequently were bought by what is now *Merriam Webster Incorporated*.[15] The format of the online version of the current Merriam Webster dictionary is radically different from OED, in particular the entries are very much shorter and simpler, although the presence of advertisements brings additional visual complexity to the pages. The comparative claim from Merriam-Webster is,

> For more than 150 years, in print and now online, Merriam-Webster has been America's leading and most-trusted provider of language information.
>
> Each month, our Web sites offer guidance to more than 40 million visitors. In print, our publications include Merriam-Webster's Collegiate Dictionary (among the best-selling books in American history) and newly published dictionaries for English-language learners.
>
> All Merriam-Webster products and services are backed by the largest team of professional dictionary editors and writers in America, and one of the largest in the world.[16]

The battle over who has the authority over language continues to be not only an epistemological one but also a competitive financial one.

Having acknowledged some very long-standing general texts that influence standards of language I turn now to a very recently published guide to writing: *The Sense of Style: The Thinking Person's Guide to Writing in the 21st Century* by Stephen Pinker. Stephen Pinker's contribution to language study over many years is a good enough reason for selection of his recent text as worthy of serious attention.[17] Pinker's earlier work is relevant to understanding some of the rationale for *The Sense of Style*. His seminal book was *The Language Instinct* in which the main argument was that:

> [Language] is a complex, specialized skill, which develops in the child spontaneously, without conscious effort or formal instruction, is deployed without awareness of its

[15] The location of Noah Webster's birth in Hartford, Connecticut, was a locus for nineteenth-century written language developments if taking into account Mark Twain's subsequent life there.

[16] Merriam Webster Incorporated. 'About Us'.

[17] He was also on the research team for the *big data* research on grammar I cited in Chapter 3.

underlying logic, is qualitatively the same in every individual, and is distinct from more general abilities to process information or behave intelligently.[18]

Pinker's key point was that language is an 'instinct', not 'a cultural artefact that we learn the way we learn to tell the time or how the federal government works. Instead it is a distinct piece of the biological make up of our brains.'[19] The book benefitted from a strong research base to its ideas, coming from a particular scientific perspective. Apart from Pinker's own research into cognition and language, the book drew heavily on Noam Chomsky's work (who at the time was a colleague of Pinker's at the Massachusetts Institute of Technology), particularly Chomsky's theory that humans are born with a Language Acquisition Device (LAD). An alternative perspective to Chomsky's LAD, also rooted in psychology, but more from social psychology, came from another renowned academic, Jerome Bruner:

> The infant's Language Acquisition Device could not function without the aid given by an adult who enters with him into a transactional format. That format, initially under the control of the adult, provides a Language Acquisition Support System (LASS). It frames or structures the input of language and interaction to the child's Language Acquisition Device in a manner to 'make the system function'. In a word, it is the interaction between the LAD and the LASS that makes it possible for the infant to enter the linguistic community – and, at the same time, the culture to which the language gives access.[20]

Subsequently cognitive neuroscience *and* socio-cultural work has shown the importance of the nature of the *interaction* between parents and children as a vital and indispensable part of language acquisition.[21] And in addition to the importance of parents supporting oral language development, there is now robust evidence of the importance of systematic teaching, usually at school, in supporting writing and reading.[22] Pinker's book *The language Instinct* was mainly about oral language, but as I have demonstrated throughout this book it is important to appreciate some of the relationships between oral language *and* written language in order to fully understand writing.

The main premise of Pinker's *The Sense of Style* is that, contrary to Oscar Wilde's remark that 'nothing that is worth knowing can be taught', which Pinker quotes (which appeared in *The Language Instinct* as well), 'many principles of style really can be taught'.[23] Of course, another of Wilde's aphorisms was, 'Psychology is in its infancy, as a science, I hope in the interests of Art, it will always remain so.'![24] Pinker's conception of teaching is not explicit teaching,

[18] Pinker, *The Language Instinct*, 18. [19] Pinker, *The Language Instinct*, 18.
[20] Bruner, *Child's Talk*, 19. [21] Kuhl, 'Early Language Acquisition', 831–843.
[22] Ziegler and Goswami, 'Reading Acquisition, Developmental Dyslexia and Skilled Reading across Languages', 3–29. Wyse and Goswami, 'Synthetic Phonics and the Teaching of Reading', 691–710.
[23] Pinker, *The Sense of Style*, 11 [24] Hart-Davis, *Selected Letters of Oscar Wilde*.

rather that the books that writers read can 'teach' them what Pinker describes as the elusive idea of style, and the 'ear' of a writer. This is not a new idea, as I show later in this chapter, nor is the idea of texts 'teaching' as the work of Margaret Meek the educator and scholar showed in relation to reading.[25]

Pinker argues that what he calls 'classic style' is the best way to think about writing, and he bases this view on the work of Francis-Noël Thomas and Mark Turner. The concept of 'style' in relation to writing has a particular resonance in the US as part of the history of writing guides, including the very popular *The Elements of Style* by William Strunk, which is a classic North American prescriptive approach.[26] Thomas and Turner begin with the classic prescriptive negative assertion that,

> THE TEACHING of writing in America is almost entirely controlled by the view that teaching writing is teaching verbal skills – from the placing of commas to the ordering of paragraphs. This has generated a tremendous industry, but the effect of this teaching is dubious. Why is American prose as bad as it is, even though we have more writing programmes than ever?[27]

Consistent with most prescriptivists who allege problems with language, no evidence is given by Thomas and Turner to support this assertion. More helpfully, they note that writing is not just a set of skills but is driven by thinking. Curiously, they draw inspiration from 'some of the outstanding French writers of the seventeenth century . . . that has no direct English or American equivalent'.[28] The subsequent, gentle implied criticism is that the diversity, of what they regard as outstanding writing by writers from England, is a reason for a lack of a more uniform classic style. A different interpretation is that diversity is what makes writing in English so versatile, powerful, and also demanding to learn, and hence adoption of a very different cultural model of language as the basis for advice on writing may not be the most appropriate.

According to Pinker, classic style is aristocratic not egalitarian. In support of this idea he offers an example that is left unexplained: 'The early bird gets the worm, for example, is plain. The early bird gets the worm, but the second mouse gets the cheese, is classic.'[29] But the ingenuity, attractiveness, and longevity of phrases like 'the early bird gets the worm' is surely their dual meanings, their *succinctness*, their rhythmic patterns, and the images they conjure. The literal meaning of birds and worms in nature (and the powerful instinct to survive) is juxtaposed metaphorically with the human who acts decisively, so succeeds where others do not. It is difficult to appreciate what

[25] Meek, *How Texts Teach What Readers Learn*.

[26] Although in editions that include E. B. White's contribution there is a very welcome descriptivism brought to bear that sets up a tension between the two parts.

[27] Thomas and Turner, *Clear and Simple as the Truth*, 3 (capital letters in original).

[28] Thomas and Turner, *Clear and Simple as the Truth*, 13.

[29] Pinker, *The Sense of Style*, 30.

Pinker's addition of the mouse and the cheese adds, and certainly why it might be classic style. Perhaps the first mouse is dead on the trap, and perhaps this addition makes the reader think more, but in my view it is less elegant than the traditional classic version. In fact the first part of the title of Pinker's book (*The Sense of Style*) is much more subtle, succinct, powerful, and attractive, including its dual, or perhaps triple, meaning of the word 'sense'.

Enjoyment of this kind of language play is why I have two particular favourite titles. The first is *Patient and Professional*, that was until 2006 the strapline of the West Yorkshire Metropolitan Ambulance Service, in the northern part of England. Perhaps even better was the oral play on words of *We Scan Do It*, the name of a photocopy and print shop I saw in Liverpool in the 1990s. You need to know that in Liverpool dialect 'youse' means 'you'. The aural similarity of We Scan Do It with the grammar 'wees can do it' (meaning 'we can do it') is an additional play on words. And a final meaning is the reminder of a music single record released by the Liverpool Football team in 1977 also called 'We Can Do It'. And, of course, the shop would have used scanners (We Scan) as part of its service (Do It).

The main approach taken by Pinker to understanding writing is to select some 'twenty-first-century prose', then to 'Think aloud as I attempt to understand what makes them work'.[30] His perceptive observations about the texts are thought-provoking, and this is an engaging approach. Richard Dawkins' writing is the book's first example presented. The opening sentence of Dawkins' book *Unweaving the Rainbow* ('We are going to die, and that makes us the lucky ones. Most people are never going to die because they are never going to be born.') is used to exemplify Pinker's first point that, 'Good writing starts strong. Not with a cliché ("Since the dawn of time"), not with a banality ("Recently, scholars have been increasingly concerned with the question of . . ."), but with a contentful observation that provokes curiosity.'[31] One of the most famous books about science ever written, Darwin's *On The Origin of Species* . . ., has this opening sentence:

> When on board H.M.S. 'Beagle,' as naturalist, I was much struck with certain facts in the distribution of the inhabitants of South America, and in the geological relations of the present to the past inhabitants of that continent.

This might fall into Pinker's banality category and could hardly be described as 'strong' in Pinker's terms. The problem with the advice, ironically, is language: 'good' and 'strong' fail to capture the complexity of the writing process. *Effective* writing of any kind engages the reader – a social function. Whether texts are effective, including the words and grammar of their opening sentences, is not sufficiently understood separately from the whole context. When the text was written, the overall vision and purpose of the text, the kind of text, the author's

[30] Pinker, *The Sense of Style*, 11. [31] Pinker, *The Sense of Style*, 12.

reputation, and particularly readers' perceptions (actual and anticipated) are all central to understanding the effectiveness of texts and their writing, all of which render definitive statements about what is 'good' about opening sentences naturally partial and subjective. And explicit acknowledgement of such subjectivity is another fundamental part of understanding writing.

Pinker's approach to studying writing begs some questions: for example, how and why were the writers selected? Was any kind of systematic approach taken to the selection of the writers, and the analysis of their writing? Dawkins is, like Pinker, another towering figure of non-fiction writing. However, Pinker's selection of Dawkins' work is as a result of the longstanding relationship they have through their work, rather than as a more objectively informed selection taking into account a range of other writers' work. The second writer Pinker chooses for an example is his wife. The writers who Pinker selected could instead have been chosen through more explicit and objective a priori criteria.

Pinker's 'think aloud' analysis of the chosen texts is his subjective opinion so not necessarily any more valid than any other expert 'thinking person' (as in the title of his book) who might read such texts. 'Think aloud protocols' are more often known as a technique used by some researchers to ask writers *themselves* to reflect aloud about the processes of their writing, at the time of writing. So a final problem in relation to Pinker's approach is that these are Pinker's words about how the writers' writing works, rather than the words of the writers themselves explaining how they wrote, and by implication how their texts might 'teach'.[32]

Pinker further reveals his underlying thinking about writing by referring to another scientist whose writing he particularly admires:

> It may not be a coincidence that Greene, like many scientists since Galileo, is a lucid expositor of difficult ideas, because the ideal of classic prose is congenial to the worldview of the scientist. Contrary to the common misunderstanding in which Einstein proved that everything is relative and Heisenberg proved that observers always affect what they observe, most scientists believe that there are objective truths about the world and they can be discovered by a disinterested observer.[33]

The idea that scientific worldview is correlated with more lucid exposition because scientists deal with objective truths discovered by a disinterested observer is challengeable on two grounds. Firstly there is a long-recognised problem in science that difficult ideas have not been lucidly communicated, and hence the modern attention to public engagement and communication of science as part of science research. Secondly the *positivist* perspective of objective truths and disinterested observers has repeatedly been challenged by philosophers, and through socio-cultural thinking, to show for example that what is 'true' is

[32] By contrast in Chapter 5 I report an analysis of writers' own views of their writing.
[33] Pinker, *The Sense of Style*, 35.

dependent on the many socio-cultural factors inherent in any written research publication or output, including scientific research papers and books.[34] So in my view, more effective writers demonstrate their awareness of these kinds of socio-cultural contexts in order to communicate more fully, more accurately, and more satisfactorily the intended meanings. Another part of the context for writing is that books like those authored by Greene are always collaborative to some degree, not least as a result of work by trusted readers of drafts, commissioning editors, copy-editors, and proof readers. Of course, I have to accept that my own worldview leads me to these observations, although in my defence I am genuinely interested in scientific *and* socio-cultural perspectives on knowledge as this book demonstrates.

Pinker goes on to poke fun at examples of writing that won a Bad Writing Contest.[35] And he concludes by identifying the culprits of bad writing, and their 'relativist academic ideologies such as postmodernism, poststructuralism, and literary Marxism'. This denigration of epistemological orientations that do not fit Pinker's worldview was already evident in *The Language Instinct*. For example, in the chapter on 'How Language Works', he presented a view of how language *doesn't* work: the idea of the 'Markov' model of language, or a word-chain device. Imagine three columns of words. A computer might select a word from each column, in order to create some kind of phrase. The phrase is not likely to make full sense, because it is random selection. So it is not hard to agree with Pinker (who again draws on Chomsky) that this Markov model is not sufficient. But Pinker then decides to have a bit of 'fun'. He presents his 'Social Science Jargon Generator' implying that social scientists simply randomly select words, from three columns, to create 'impressive sounding' terms. This is mildly amusing knock-about critique, but it is also revealing about Pinker's at times narrow theoretical perspectives on language, including written language.

Pinker's goal to add to knowledge of how writing works is one that I agree is vital. The promise of attention to the 'ear of the writer', and what I would call 'reading like a writer', was tantalising but in my view not in the end satisfactorily analysed and portrayed. His analysis of scholarly writing in popular book form and in more traditional university essay form is also important, but there is also well regarded research and scholarship *about* university and academic writing that would have been worthy of attention. As an example of what we might learn I address such work next.

[34] For an account of the way that one of the most reliable causal scientific findings, of the link between smoking and lung cancer, was subject to social and cultural factors that impeded government action for 40 years, see Oreskes, and Conway, *The Merchants of Doubt*.

[35] The examples of bad writing are taken from the 1990s, rather than from the twenty-first century, which would be comparable with his examples of exemplary writing.

University Teaching Perspectives

Academics who work in universities must 'publish or perish'. The writing that is done in universities, including the outputs of the research carried out there, is a significant aspect of writing worldwide. It is estimated that in 2016 there were 50 million research articles published, and that the prediction was that this number would double every twenty years.[36] However, there are also estimates that as many as 50% of articles are never read because the main audience for these articles, academics, have so little time to read! In this context the developments of digital technologies has resulted in *altmetrics*. Academics are relatively used to the idea that counts are made of the numbers of citations that articles receive, in other words when an article is cited by another academic in a journal that is included in the citation tables, the author's article receives one citation, which is recorded by computer-based systems. Altmetrics is a way of counting the attention that scholarly articles receive through different kinds of outlets: online through social media. In addition to academics' writing, nearly every published writer working outside of universities has studied at some point in their lives in a university and therefore had to write. I will turn to an example of the most demanding piece of writing that most students encounter, the *dissertation*, after a consideration of a range of successful texts about academic writing aimed at university students and some of the issues these texts raise.

The Open University in England has been a pioneer of work on university writing, in part because its student base has always been mainly at a distance rather than face-to-face, although digital developments have made synchronous online discussion feasible including in relatively large groups. As the students have less access to one-to-one face-to-face feedback the need for good quality guides to writing were perhaps even more pressing than at other universities that now all have departments devoted to supporting academic writing, particularly for students from abroad. One of the issues with academic writing is that it is almost like a different language for *all* students, not just for students for whom English is not their first language. The issues such as understanding how academic arguments are constructed, how evidence can be deployed how assertion and over-generalisation are dangers, and the ways in which careful citations and references are not only conventions but also intimately connected to the arguments made in the writing, are demanding areas of knowledge for all who write academically. An early successful text emerging from the Open University course materials was *Good Essay Writing: A Social Sciences Guide* by Peter Redman. As its title suggests, this book focuses on the main features of essays written for university assessments, and

[36] Robinson, 'Making an Impact: Authors, Articles, Almetrics'.

how the assessment systems in universities work. Another book emerging from research at the Open University is that by Phyllis Crème and Mary Lea called *Writing at University: A Guide for Students*. This book deals with the basic requirements of university writing assessments and is based on the authors' work researching the issues that university students face when encountering writing in the university.

More recently, work by Pat Thomson and co-author Barbara Kamler have provided a strong socio-cultural focus on writing in universities. Helping PhD students to appreciate the human cultural context for the ways in which researchers work; how to become part of the academic community or 'tribe'; and how to appropriately acknowledge and critique the work of other researchers are important aspects of Thomson and Kamler's book.[37] In more recent work that builds on classic work done in the USA, and taking account of some critiques of this work, Thomson has suggested three ways of thinking about structures of academic articles.[38] The first way of thinking about structure that Thompson suggests is 'Locate, Focus and Outline' as a 'three move' way to structure the vital introduction to a research paper: 'the Locate move is where the problem is put in context, delineated and justified . . . The Focus move is where the writer says exactly what they are going to do in the paper to address the topic . . . the Outline, shows the key steps that are to be taken to make the argument, and in what order.'[39]

The second way of thinking about introducing an academic paper is what Thompson calls 'the problematisation approach'. Building on the critique that the three move approach does not facilitate ground breaking work because writers are too restricted, the problematisation approach is characterised by more succinct introductory material (even one paragraph) then quick immersion in an extended critical appraisal of a particular topic.

The third way of thinking about structuring an introduction to a research paper is described by Thomson as 'a more literary style'. This is characterised by the use of first person narrative and the use of vignettes. So, for example, an academic doing qualitative research may start an article with an example, or what is sometimes described as a 'telling tale', which will be a significant moment very closely described, typically from the perspectives of the participants in the research.

Thompson summarises her chapter through the key argument that although the three ways of structuring the introduction to an academic paper appear to be different, they all do the work of Locate, Focus, and Outline: Thomson admits that this is classic *genre theory* (which I addressed in Chapter 2). The use of such genre structures for written texts raises the question: Are the deviations

[37] Kamler and Thomson, *Helping Doctoral Students to Write*.
[38] Thomson, 'Writing about Research'. [39] Thomson, 'Writing about Research'.

more significant than the aspects of compliance? It could be that it is both the understanding of classic structures combined with deviations from the structures that create memorable writing, and writing that gets read. Thompson's final idea in her chapter, that research can be disseminated in forms such as story, poetry, or play script, as part of the 'more literary style', is noted but unfortunately not developed.

Another way to think more about use of literary style as part of academic writing is through comparison with a very different tradition of university writing: creative writing courses. The pre-eminent place for university-based creative writing in the UK is located where the English language emerged, in East Anglia, and more particularly at the University of East Anglia. The authors Malcolm Bradbury and Sir Angus Wilson, established the UEA's creative writing course in 1970. The course is built on the idea that, contrary to some people's view, creative writing *can* be taught.[40] One part of the evidence that creative writing can be taught lies in the correlation between the many people who have done the course and those who have gone on to become successful professional writers.

There are two key ideas behind the pedagogy of the course and hence the course book: (1) It is not a professional training, it is an opportunity to reflect deeply on writing (which also leads to an academic qualification at undergraduate or master's level); (2) It is structured around workshop or seminar exercises designed to help students gain knowledge and experience of key techniques and ideas. The overall structure of the course, and hence its course book, is described as (1) Gathering, (2) Shaping, and (3) Finishing. Gathering, shaping, and finishing suggest work in motion, at play, responsive to change, hinting at never being finished. The gathering phase in non-fiction academic writing is the Locate, Focus, and Outline, which suggests systematicity, an additive process, and completion. Academics and researchers do gather evidence, shape their data, then work to finish publications, but a key difference between the creative writing structures and the traditional academic writing structures (evident right from the start – the gathering phase – of the UEA course) is the encouragement for students of creative writing to experiment: by writing every day; through the encouragement to first write about, or draw, everything and *anything* of interest; the need to read widely – 'everything and anything'; making long lists of words of interest; finding your own ways of writing including routines for writing. The relative lack of boundaries, in fact, the need to deliberately break through boundaries in this kind of writing is one of its hallmarks

[40] The information about the UEA course is taken from Bell and Magrs, *The Creative Writing Coursebook*.

The second chapter of the 'gathering' section is 'Training the Eye'. This is the attention to detail, the telling detail, and the ability to portray the detail in new ways. Sharp observation is also the skill of the academic ethnographer, and researchers doing other in-depth field work, but not with the prime purpose to create something completely new. For the ethnographer, the intent is to record objectively, as objectively as possible for a human researcher embedded in a social context who is inevitably biased by their subjective view. If done rigorously, there is an opportunity to contribute important knowledge, which should be original, but this is not the same as creating a new work of art to be judged as such.

The third chapter of the gathering section is titled 'Abstracts', a technical term that is also used in the writing of research. The abstract in a research paper is a succinct summary of the whole paper which hopefully will draw readers in to read the paper (abstracts are available free but whole papers require university subscriptions to publisher packages, or a cost to download a single paper). Other than superficial similarities, this seems very different from the idea of a fiction abstract that is the emotions and mental structures that drive narrative fiction, and poetry. A suggested exercise from the course book underlines the difference:

> Try this exercise: list abstract words and then describe them through the senses. What colour is love? What does it smell like? What does it taste like? What does it feel like? What does it sound like? One of my students said 'love tastes like Fizzy Chewits', another claimed it felt like 'watching the last-ever episode of *Dallas*'.[41]

The second strand of the course, after Gathering, is Shaping. It is here where the differences between academic writing and fiction and poetry writing seem most evident. Chapters on Characterisation, Setting, and Plotting and Shaping are evidence of distinctions between fiction and non-fiction writing. And yet the idea of text archetypes and text structures (which I address later in this chapter) is a consideration for both fiction and academic writing. The theoretical backdrop to the first chapter in this Shaping section is Aristotle's suggestion in *Poetics* that plot is a history of consequence which has a beginning, middle, and end. This is perhaps similar to the rather weak advice that in an essay students should (1) Say what they are going to say; (2) say it; (3) tell the reader what they have said!

In the second chapter in the Shaping section, creative writers are encouraged to consider the 'generic and conformist' structure of bestsellers; Courtroom Plots; Journey Plots; Moments in Time. The Western tradition 'paradigm narratives' of the Bible and Homer's narrative poems are said to give rise to either 'Siege Narratives' or 'Quest Narratives'. The writer of academic writing does not have these choices of genres, although the smaller but significant differences that reflect the writing of different academic disciplines might be

[41] Bell and Magrs, *The Creative Writing Coursebook*, 45.

seen as genre differences.[42] For example, the requirements from the discipline of natural science require some different conventions from those of the social scientist, but these are not the differences of siege or quest!

There are more similarities in the final stages of the writing processes of fiction and poetry with academic and wider non-fiction writing. The final section of the UEA course, called 'Finishing' is about the editing required and then the sharing with others. This section includes a chapter by David Lodge who was very well placed to think about the similarities and differences between fiction and academic non-fiction, as Lodge had written both fiction (about university life) and literary criticism in his role as a professor of English literature in a university. He talks about 'Reading Yourself', the ability to read your own writing as if you were your intended reader. I sometimes talk to students about wearing different hats, such as the authorial hat, the editorial hat, the professional educator hat, the researcher hat. Easy to say but difficult to successfully implement the necessary detachment from your writing. Lodge also notes the importance of understanding and working at 'cohesion': at the whole text level and at the level of words and sentences – something of fundamental importance to all writers. And he notes a link with music in his claim that narrative is even more universal than language itself, because literary stories can be translated into music or visual art, which are not verbal media.

These more abstract ideas are linked by Lodge with practical ways to 'defamiliarise' yourself with your writing: putting written drafts aside for a period of time; reading your writing aloud. Lodge also refers to Graham Greene's need to read aloud the 'cadence' of the sentence – another link with music through the harmonic and structural idea of musical cadence. Finally it is worth noting that the UEA course book deals head-on with the longstanding gulf between the work of writers and the work of literary criticism, and aims to bring these perspectives together within the course.

The Dissertation and Its Thesis

The final assessment of any course of study is the most demanding. Typically, assessments in university involve a strong emphasis on writing, to demonstrate knowledge, which is addressed in both traditional exams and/or course work assessment. Arts subjects often require both a piece of artistic writing, a performance, the creation of something such as a musical score or an exhibition of visual art, and extended critical commentary in writing. Natural science subjects often require not only the passing of traditional exams but also project

[42] For interesting research on disciplines and writing differences, see Tusting and Barton, 'Writing Disciplines', 15–34.

work and course work. For example the University of Cambridge final assessments for the physics programme has a course work element:

> The assessment of coursework includes oral assessment of a Research Review, Long Vacation Work or Physics Education reports (if offered), and may include oral assessment of a Computing Project report. It may also include up to two written tests on theoretical topics taken during the year, and oral assessment of up to two major experiments reports. Communication skills are appraised in all coursework assessments.[43]

For humanities and social sciences the final assessment is often a dissertation. The dissertation is demanding because it is the longest piece of writing that most students will ever have written. The word length of the dissertation in social science subjects increases from undergraduate, to Master's, and finally to PhD level where the maximum word-length in UK universities is usually 80,000 words.[44] The word count of a dissertation in humanities and social sciences is equivalent to a book, so one of the major challenges is how, for the first time, the student will control the overall structure and length of a long and complex document. A Master's dissertation prior to a PhD, which will have been an opportunity to engage with another long form of writing, will have been about 20,000 words, so the jump to PhD level is very challenging. Although a range of types of assessment is used in universities, including, for example, practical performances, creative outputs, presentations, and so on, the main way that students are awarded degrees is by demonstrating their knowledge through writing. The use of the written form for students is consistent with the idea of universities as places where knowledge is created and disseminated through writing including in digital forms. The achievement of a PhD (Doctor of Philosophy) is marked by the award that leads to a permanent change to someone's title from Mr/Ms/Mrs to Dr, unlike titles such as Professor that are only for the duration of the link with an institution.

A common misconception is the use of 'thesis' and 'dissertation' as synonymous. The dissertation is the written output, effectively a book, that is the student's work bound by a professional printer and placed on the university library shelves, as a contribution to knowledge. The thesis is the main line of argument pursued in the dissertation: 'A proposition laid down or stated, esp. as a theme to be discussed and proved, or to be maintained against attack . . .; a statement, assertion, tenet.'[45] Some of the important ideas in the definition include: propositions that are 'proved'; the roots of the definition in formal logic; and the striking idea of resisting attacks (from examiners for example!).

43 University of Cambridge, 'Natural Sciences Tripos: Physics', 2016.

44 Minimum lengths are not always specified, but the 'not more than 10% or less than 10% of the maximum wordcount' rule often applies.

45 OED, Online.

The etymology of the word, particularly from ancient times, is also interesting for its explicit link with music and with verse. The antithesis of thesis is arsis (and in passing I note the oppositional meaning of 'anti' and 'thesis': a strong thesis is able to anticipate and address opposing points of view). *Arsis* is defined as the strong syllable in the metre of English poetry. And,

1. Originally and properly, according to ancient writers, the setting down of the foot or lowering of the hand in beating time, and hence (as marked by this) the stress or *ictus*; the stressed syllable of a foot in a verse; a stressed note in music.

The most recent historical example recorded by the OED:

> 1891 *Thesis* . . . In musical rhythmics, a heavy accent, such as in beating time is marked by a down-beat.

As a conductor and orchestral musician myself, I know how important the conductor's downbeat (the first beat in any musical bar) is for ensuring the orchestra plays in time and together. The idea of a common purpose to musical performance, centred on the conductor, links to the need for a central line of argument in the dissertation. The litany of complaints by orchestral musicians against conductors who it is claimed, often with justification, have very unclear downbeats is metaphorically similar to the dangers of lack of clarity in the lines of argument in a written thesis.

The dissertation that doctoral students must write in universities is the Everest of student academic writing, and the very highest level of university-assessed writing they can do. The most challenging requirement of a PhD is the *original contribution to the field* that it must make. In the UK, the dissertation is examined by two academic experts in the field, one of whom will be a member of the student's university and one will be from a university external to the student. The examiners read the dissertation and prepare an independent report prior to the *viva voce* oral examination where the student has to discuss the examiners' questions. In other countries of the world, the dissertation will be read by two or more examiners without the need for a viva; instead, in some countries in Europe, the student must defend the thesis at a public 'hearing'. In Germany the PhD examination requirements entail publication of the dissertation as a book in order to be finally awarded.

In the case of academic disciplines, and their location in universities, the establishment and maintaining of standards of English language is seen through the expectations of the assessments of writing. The socio-cultural contexts of the academics who maintain the standards include the need for students to master the instrumental aspects of academic language in order to pass their courses. The consummatory aspect of the work by students is reflected in the need for an original contribution. But there is another key marker of standards or conventions of language use upheld by academic disciplines, the use of *citations* and *references*, in a peer-reviewed system.

The idea of proving a proposition, which is part of the definition of *thesis*, requires logic and 'evidence' to support the claims of the proposition. In mathematics, the proof is established in the particular logic based on mathematical symbols, as the story of Fermat's theorem in the first chapter exemplified. For other disciplines, evidence from research is used as part of the 'warrant' for a proposition. If in support of their argument (or to more generally enrich their argument) a researcher refers to other researcher's work, then a citation of the other researcher's name and full information to the other researcher's publication needs to be recorded, so that anyone can check the proof by accessing the research that has been cited. This is also the way that students avoid being thrown off their course, because without citations and references this would be regarded as cheating through *plagiarising* other people's ideas. There are now well established conventions for referencing – the way that citations and references should be formatted. But these conventions are not simply a format. They are inseparable from the lines of argument made in a piece of academic writing.

There are many different systems for referencing. For example, subjects in the humanities, like English literature and history, tend to use the notes/bibliography system. This is where you see a *superscript* number near a word. At the bottom of the page (or sometimes at the end of the book or article) the number will appear again next to a note, which often adds further explanation.[46]

Many social science texts use a different system, the *Harvard* or *author/date system*. Unfortunately the description 'Harvard system' can lead to confusion because Harvard is not one system but more a general description of a range of similar author/date referencing styles. For example, many publishers of educational books claim to use the Harvard system, but their specific guidance differs. This is also true of many academic journals. 'Author/date system' is a more helpful description, which means that citations feature the author's surname followed by the year of publication.

The author/date system I have used most often is what is known as 'APA 6th': this is explained in the American Psychological Association's sixth edition of their *Publication Manual*. The role of APA 6th in establishing certain standards can be seen in its adoption by many social science journals. However, another key aspect of its success is the clarity and comprehensiveness of the guidance of the manual. Guides like the APA 6th establish conventions of writing that writers are required to follow if they want to publish in a journal or book that adopts the style. The guidance is derived from the context of The American Psychological Association, and so it carries social and cultural influences.

[46] The system I have decided to use for this book. The footnote system doesn't interrupt the visual flow of the text as much as the author/date system.

It is no accident that many arts and humanities publications follow an equally important guide that is quite different in its requirements for layout: *The Chicago Manual of Style*. These differences are not just about the technical features of layout (both guides include extensive guidance on referencing; for example); they are also indicative of important differences in the way different disciplines conceive knowledge, build knowledge, and present knowledge through a particular way of structuring language, and the ways that organisations uphold standards for shared communication of ideas. When a writer handles citations and references well, this is not simply a matter of conventions, it is integral to the very lines of argument that are being written. The way that ideas and sources of evidence are understood and used is part of the success or otherwise of written argument. The academic discourse, through its tools and signs, establishes the validity and reliability of knowledge, and to some degree its use, in society.

The establishment of referencing conventions is not only evident in the publication manuals, and hence in the writer's styles, but also through computer software. Computer packages support the writer in supplying citations and references. The writer has to enter the full bibliographic information, but the software can insert citations, and the full reference in the reference list at the end of the document. The software supports a wide range of recognised styles of referencing including footnote systems. One package is also linked in with Microsoft Word functions hence appears in Word menus. This integration goes as far as providing templates for the structure of academic papers, complete with the style of headings including the formatting for their hierarchical arrangement.

The links between the establishment of language conventions and commerce, in the form of software packages, is driven mainly by the need for academics to be more efficient in their production of texts. The packages reflect conventions established by academic disciplines and their associations, or we might say 'guilds' if we link back to the history of the English language. The most important change that digitisation has brought is to enhance the speed with which academic articles can be created. However, the origins of these ideas and products in high-income western countries is one clear sign of the continuation of cultural dominance and control of language. The extent to which the origins of some products, and their control of particular elements of language, is benign or more worrying is not well understood.

Fiction Writing Perspectives

An aspect of guidance from a fiction perspective concerns writing structures and text archetypes. For example, in the UEA creative writing course book, in addition to the siege narratives and the quest narratives, the idea of only two kinds of narrative in the history of human story telling is also mentioned: (1) heroine/hero leaves home, or (2) a stranger comes to town. This is the most extreme reduction of story genres but the idea of a limited number of genres has been explored in various ways.

One popular account in relation to fiction narratives is Christopher Booker's (founder of the Booker Prize) *The Seven Basic Plots: Why We Tell Stories* in which very early on he makes reference to the idea of 'only seven (or six or five) basic stories in the world'. Although this is one of the better argued popular accounts, it is certainly not the first. *The Hero with a Thousand Faces* explored similar ground to Booker's, including its psychoanalytic perspective.[47] Booker's idea of 'a kind of hidden universal language: a nucleus of situations and figures' is intriguing. Many writers' use of such smaller elements seems more plausible than the claims to universality in whole stories and texts. Booker's preference for Freudian-inspired understandings of the human psyche, and other psychological perspectives, perhaps explains his disagreement with the conclusions of the highly regarded researchers of folklore, and award-winning writers, Peter and Iona Opie, that no one all-embracing theory is likely to account for the majority of stories.

There is a rich tradition of fiction writers' guides to writing, and other direct commentaries about their craft, including seminal works such as Orwell's *Politics and the English Language*. Fiction writers' accounts of writing do focus on writing processes but usually with the assumption that the basic skills of writing, such as grammar, have already been acquired. The main context for the advice is usually on becoming a published author and what it is like to be a published author. Accounts about writing narrative fiction are much more frequent than for poetry and non-fiction.

Published more than a decade before Orwell's text, Dorothea Brande's classic advice in *Becoming a* Writer (originally published in 1934) is by turns uplifting and intimidating. She is convinced that writing can be taught, and hence learned, and is metaphysical in her zeal: 'This book, I believe, will be unique; for I think he [the student or amateur writer] is right. I think there is such a magic, and that it is teachable. This book is all about the writer's magic.'[48] But once we get into the heart of Brande's book, if the writer fails at two fundamental requirements: agreed times for writing and agreed amounts of writing each day, then, 'If you fail repeatedly at this exercise, give up writing. Your resistance is actually greater than your desire to write, and you may as well find some other outlet for your energy early as late.'[49] 79.

Brande's suggestion that writers need to become their own best teachers is fundamentally important, and she uses the attractive writing device of

[47] Booker does acknowledge Campbell's books and other similar texts in the tradition of folklore analysis.

[48] Brande, *Becoming a Writer*, 23. [49] Brande, *Becoming a Writer*, 79.

fictionalised, teacher-student interaction, reminiscent of Platonic dialogues. Overall, Brande's most important point is that writers have to develop the ability to read their writing in particular ways, and explicitly say to themselves what needs to be changed, why, and how.

Consistent with the complexities of genre, structure, text archetypes, and the need to break the rules, Stephen King's popular guide *On Writing* is a good example. The book is divided into two halves. The first half is a 'memoir' of King's life, consistent with the subtitle of the book *On Writing: a Memoir of the Craft*, but which King calls a 'CV': 'This is not an autobiography. It is, rather, a kind of *curriculum vitae* – my attempt to show how one writer was formed.' He goes on to argue that writers can't be made, but people with some talent for writing can have those talents 'strengthened and sharpened'.[50] The assumption here is presumably that writers of the stature of King can't be made, but that doesn't mean that writers with more modest success can't be made, as students in universities and children in school have been made year in, year out for hundreds of years.

King's playfulness with genre is also evident in not one but three 'forewords'. The first foreword explains how as a result of his involvement as a musician in a 'rock-and-roll band composed mostly of writers', while on tour, King had a conversation with a band member that led to the book. In response to King's question about what she was never asked about at a question and answer session following a writer's talk, the band member explained to King that 'no one ever asks about the language', and it was this remark that gave King the stimulus and confidence to write a book he had been thinking about for a year or more. However, ironically one thing the book doesn't talk too much about is words and sentences although this is probably because his definition of 'language' is very broad. In the first forward King also raises the issue of popular fiction versus literary fiction:

> nobody ever asks about language. They ask the DeLillos and the Updikes and the Styrons, but they don't ask popular novelists. Yet many of us proles also care about the language, in our own humble way, and care passionately about the art and craft of telling stories on paper.[51]

The issue of how King's fiction is regarded by wider society is clearly an emotive issue for him as a reading of the whole book reveals.[52] The contrast between 'popular' fiction and 'literary' fiction and poetry, is another of the many ways in which conventions of writing have been established, and are maintained through social and cultural practices.

The second foreword in King's book is a provocation:

[50] King, *On Writing*. [51] King, *On Writing*, xi.

[52] Contrary to King's claim that popular writers are not asked about their use of language, he was, for example, interviewed by the *Paris Review* for his views on writing processes and practices.

> This is a short book because most books about writing are filled with bullshit. Fiction writers, present company included, don't understand very much about what they do – not why it works when it's good, not why it doesn't when it's bad. I figured the shorter the book, the less the bullshit.

The irony is, of course, that King went on to write his book at all (in the introductory paragraphs of the memoir half of his book King repeats the point and explains that the book shows how he was 'formed' as a writer, not 'made'). A reluctance to self-analyse, genuine or faux, is not uncommon amongst fiction writers, but in general I have not come across accounts of non-fiction writers who have this same reluctance. The evidence from other writers' reflections that I address in the next chapter suggests that King may not be accurate about fiction writers' capacity to understand what they do.

King's book is unique for its unusual combination of beguiling writing, consistent with his worldwide success as a writer of fiction, but ultimately some lack of rigour about how writing works. For example, his entertaining provocative style seems to lead to contradictions. King says, 'it is impossible to make a competent writer out of a bad writer' and 'it is possible to make a good writer out of a merely competent one'. A developmental perspective on writing suggests that all people can learn to write better including so-called 'bad' writers. King is on safer ground when talking about writers who are recognised historically as great writers, but overall his argument is deflected by perceptions such as, 'a good deal of literary criticism serves only to reinforce a caste system which is as old as the intellectual snobbery which nurtured it.'[53]

In the second half of the book King's advice on writing is structured as a numbered list of sections with several pages per section. His first advice is 'read a lot and write a lot'. The seeming simplicity of this advice is then followed by exploration of how particular ways of reading inform the work of the writer (and here there is similarity with Pinker's approach reviewed earlier in this chapter). Having explored these in more detail, he then turns to the need to have a physical place for writing, and the need for several hours writing every day.

A hallmark of fiction writers' advice is the emphasis on finding ideas for writing linked with the search for the writers' 'voice'. King focuses on the well-known advice to 'write about what you know', not only specialist knowledge that writers may have but also the ways they need to observe and attend to everyday life. The example of the writer John Grisham's former career as a lawyer, and the way he used his legal knowledge in his book (and successful film) *The Firm* is perceptively analysed by King.

The rest of King's book turns to finer details of writing such as narration, description, and dialogue. A key point that King makes, which is relevant to all

[53] King, *On Writing: A Memoir of a Craft*, 161.

forms of writing, is the necessity for at least one main line or theme that reflects and anchors the piece of writing. King says of his own work:

> I have many interests, but only a few that are deep enough to power novels. These deep interests (I won't quite call them obsessions) include how difficult it is – perhaps impossible! – to close Pandora's technobox once it's open (*The Stand, The Tommyknockers, Firestarter*); the question of why, if there is a God, such terrible things happen (*The Stand, Desperation, The Green Mile*); the thin line between reality and fantasy (*The Dark Half, Bag of Bones, The Drawing of the Tree*); and most of all, the terrible attraction violence sometimes has for fundamentally good people (*The Shining, The Dark Half*). I've also written again and again about the fundamental differences between children and adults, and about the healing power of the human imagination.[54]

The trope of the writer's 'voice' is a dominant one in the world of fiction. Al Alvarez's book focuses on this elusive quality.[55] Alvarez based the book on his experience as a writer of poetry, novels, and as a journalist. Consistent with the UEA recognition of a problem with criticism, and the point made by King, Alvarez claims that literary criticism has become 'just another arcane academic discipline with a technical vocabulary and specialised interests all its own'. Alvarez's disparaging comment about academic disciplines is perhaps a product of his own disciplinary and professional background as a journalist. He inadvertently reflects how specialism in particular disciplines develops over time and how new knowledge is accumulated as a result. There is surely space for a range of ways of analysing texts, including how Alvarez first conceptualised criticism, 'as a creative activity in its own right – a writer's way of describing how other writers handle language and what it is that makes them unique'. All these perspectives have been important for my book.

It was one piece of praise that kept Alvarez dreaming about being a writer. Although the 'naïve' first poem that Alvarez sent to a magazine was rejected for publication, the editor praised the penultimate quatrain as 'miraculous'. Further thinking about why the editor liked that bit, and why he did not like the rest of the poem prompted Alvarez to think more deeply, something he described as a first step to developing his ear for other writers' writing, and ultimately his own writer's voice. Other social elements of writing were also important for Alvarez's development of his voice for prose. In particular, his work on a series of seven radio programmes based on interviews with writers who worked under the pressure of political dictatorships, and then interviews with authors from the USA who were friends, helped him write in a style of casual offhand commentary for the programmes that fitted the mix of interviewees' viewpoints. Finding the voice for that casual tone stayed with Alvarez as he further developed his writing.

[54] King, *On Writing*, 246. [55] Alvarez, *The Writer's Voice*.

For Alvarez, and for Pinker, the element that is shared across all different forms of writing is the idea of the writer's 'ear':

> I sometimes feel about my profession much the same as Vladimir Mayakovsky felt about suicide: 'I do not recommend it to others,' he wrote, and then put a gun to his head . . . The art of poetry is altogether different from writing nonfiction, and literary criticism is different from them all. Fifty years of writing for a living have taught me that there is only one thing the four disciplines have in common: in order to write well you must first learn how to listen. And that, in turn, is something writers have in common with their readers. Reading well means opening your ears to the presence behind the words and knowing which notes are true and which are false. It is as much an art as writing well and almost as hard to acquire.[56]

Once again an analogy is made with music, and one that is almost as precise as Lowth's, which I addressed in the last chapter. Music, or text, that is in tune has the authentic sound of the composer's voice (music composer or text composer) according to Alvarez. Text that is out of tune lacks voice. The analogy with music is closer to the music composer than the music performer. For the composer, the notes have to be selected in the first place, and this selection will be 'true' if it helps the music communicate its meaning satisfactorily to the audience. For the performer, when notes are out of tune, or not 'true', this is mainly a technical matter, akin to grammatical mistakes, which are not part of Alvarez's concept of the writer's voice. Understanding the relationship of abstract concepts such as voice to details such as grammar, through the music composer/performer contrast, is an important part of the theory of writing I advance in this book.

Alvarez's concept of writing chimes with the philosophical pragmatic theory that human discourse establishes reality: 'Writing, I mean, is literally a lively art as well as a creative one. Writers don't just "hold, as 'twere, a mirror up to nature" by creating an imitation of life; they create a moment of life itself'.[57] As I show in the next chapter this concept of creating new life was one that drove Hemmingway. Alvarez quotes Freud, making the point that interdisciplinary thinking has been a hallmark of great thinkers, and that the disciplines of the sciences and the arts are not so unrelated (something that Lev Vygotsky also lived out in his scholarship) as Alvarez suggests:

> When, during the celebration of his seventieth birthday, one of his disciples hailed Freud as 'the discoverer of the unconscious', he answered, 'The poets and philosophers before me discovered the unconscious. What I discovered was the scientific method by with the unconscious can be studied.'[58]

I share Alvarez's admiration for the poetry of John Dunne, particularly the beauty of the imagery applied to such raw, real contexts. The first stage of acquiring voice is infatuation with other writers, whom aspiring writers

[56] Alvarez, *The Writer's Voice*, 12. [57] Alvarez, *The Writer's Voice*, 18.
[58] Alvarez, *The Writer's Voice*, 19.

naturally try to emulate. But this infatuation, like most infatuations, doesn't last for all but a small number of favoured authors.

Alvarez is critical of 'high style' epitomised for him in John Lyly's play *Euphues: the Anatomy of Wit*, which was ridiculed by Shakespeare in *Love's Labour's Lost*. The target was the ancient art and craft of rhetoric, or style over substance. The need to guard against high style, as an impediment to finding voice, is portrayed by Alvarez in an anecdote about Kipling, who apparently locked finished writing away in a draw for several weeks then crossed out all the bits that he had been most proud of when he had finished the writing. This is perhaps another caution in relation to some of the US conceptions of style I examined earlier in the chapter.

In the end, although Alvarez's playing with music and literature is appealing, there is more work to be done to understand how writing works. And perhaps this is inevitable in view of the difficulty of the concept of voice. Alvarez's appeal to great writers, and the brilliant anecdotes impress. This line of thinking needs extending to a wider range of writers. It is possible that the features of writing, including the authorship of voice, could be brought even more to the fore through specific attention to writing processes, including attention to research on learning to write and teaching writing.

*

What I have called general guides to language continue to promote and specify standards of language. These standards are inseparable from the underpinning histories, rationales and the social milieu that are part of such guides. In important cases, the history of language is an explicit part of the warrant claimed by these gatekeepers of language. The best guides are responsive to, and in some cases document, language change. A work such as the OED is a powerful example of systematic attention to change, the constant addition of new words, but also the maintenance of a particular view of English rooted in rigorous linguistic scholarship. This is also a prime example of linguistic descriptivism. For writers, paying rigorous attention to linguistically informed conventions does not preclude playfulness with language. On the contrary, it provides a stimulus for imagination and creativity, because it can facilitate reflection on the nature of originality and value.

Knowledge about the craft of writing needs to be acquired, and this knowledge is linguistically informed. Writers build their knowledge through attention to language as it is really used in life, including in real language events, oral and written, of a range of kinds. For the writer of narrative fiction, this approach has the dual advantage of bringing the writer closer to the authenticity of the language of their characters in addition to heightening their awareness of the conventions of language. Rigorous attention to knowledge of the craft of writing includes development of metaunderstanding, with its own metalanguage; for example, ‘reading yourself’, ‘cohesion’, ‘descriptivism’. This is different from the metalanguage associated with grammatical terms such as ‘verb’ or ‘subordinate clause’, which have much more limited uses.

Writing in universities is a very large part of writing worldwide. There are some similarities, but also marked differences, between the development of fiction and poetry writing as part of creative writing courses, versus the development of academic writing. In essence, these differences represent the social and cultural norms for the different forms of writing. One thing that all writing has in common is a single central semantic core that can anchor lines of argument or the vision of a work of fiction. Another commonality is the need for ‘research’ to inform writing, for example, the careful observations, rigorous reading, notes, and other more systematic forms of analysis.

One important function of university writing is work done by academics in order to develop new knowledge as a result of their research. University students also actively engage with this knowledge, and as their learning develops make their own increasingly more original contributions to knowledge in areas that their motivations and interests take them to. The use and deployment of evidence as warrant for the theses and their dissertations are essential, and are very closely connected to more routine conventions, such as citations, references, footnotes, and bibliographies. Using these conventions is still, however, rooted in the social context of written language, for example as recognition of the lives and careers of the authors being cited as well as their contribution to knowledge.

At the metalevel the need to think about writing in large structural ideas is common to both fiction and poetry and non-fiction. For example, the gathering, shaping and finishing that are recommended for fiction and poetry writing are not so dissimilar from some of the broad steps required for writing research publications. The key difference lies in the nature of the creative intent: creativity for its own sake, in fiction and poetry, does have some similarity with the need to make an original contribution in academic work but their raison d'être differs. The writers' task is to heighten their sensitivity to structural possibilities, then consider how to work with them, and break them (often in subtle ways), for the writing purposes that they establish. This attention to structure includes a reasonable developmental perspective where the expectation is that novice writers, such as undergraduates, will initially work more closely with familiar genre features. But the highest standards of writing at any level come from breaking, extending, or building new conventions in ways recognised by readers and society.

A sense of style is important if this means the writers developing their voice. But style can also be an impediment, for example, self-conscious style, ‘high style’ and over-reliance on favoured authors' styles beyond the very early years of experimentation. The metaphor of the ‘ear’ for writing, and the attendant sense of musical and textual intonation, is an essential part of developing voice, as is the concept of 'reading yourself'. The writer's voice comes through constantly trying to express writing through topics that are imbedded in the writer's life and thinking, not because they happen to be fashionable. This is also described as writing about what you know.

The concept of voice has relevance for inexperienced writers and experienced writers alike. For the inexperienced writer, voice is represented in the confidence to communicate with conviction a set of ideas that are personal to the writer. In academic work, the tendency to 'stand on the shoulder of giants' too heavily has to be avoided. The writer's own ideas are paramount, supported by critically appreciative reading of those who are more expert. For experienced professional writers, a distinctive voice is an essential requirement for success in the world of writing. And the voices, and perspectives, of some of those writers who have worldwide success and who have made a contribution that stands the test of time, in fiction, poetry, and non-fiction, are another important source of information about writing processes.

4 Expert Writers

The writers whose work is the focus for this chapter not only have wide recognition, and for most the winning of major prizes such as the Nobel Prize for Literature, but have also been regarded by other writers, including critics, as some of the finest of their generation. Perhaps another way to describe these particular writers is, 'writers' writers'. In any field of human endeavour, we look to the most successful exponents of the art, science, or other domain for their reflections, knowledge, and understanding.

The primary data that underpinned the analysis for this chapter already existed in *The Paris Review Interviews.*[1] *The Paris Review Interviews* are interviews with some of the world's great writers from the 1950s onwards. There are four printed volumes that are a selection of the best of 64 interviews taken from all interviews available prior to each volume. Subsequently, the resource continues to be added to online. As the editor Philip Gourevitch made the selections for the four printed volumes. The revealing insights, in the words of the very writers themselves, are in no small part due to the methodological approach taken by *The Paris Review.* The interviewers were themselves writers who had read their interviewee's works. The interviews, which were undertaken over one or more visits to the writers' homes, sometimes over a period of years, were followed by writers being sent an edited transcript of the interview to review. Hence the benefits of the oral interview, with its revealing 'on the spot' requirement for answers, was balanced against the opportunity for the writers to reflect carefully on the transcript to ensure their answers were as close to their intended beliefs as possible. A unique feature of the interviews is that they focus on the processes of writing, the writer's craft, much more than the outputs of writing.

In addition to the formal interviews the *Paris Review* site also includes a wealth of current and contemporary accounts including its reports in *The Daily.* For example, an interview outside of the usual *Paris Review* interviews was with Karl Ove Knausgård whose writing was generating intense interest at the

[1] Although I had to work with print and online versions, all interviews are now available at www.theparisreview.org/interviews.

time. To take one memorable example of his craft, in the first book of his *My Struggle* cycle of novels, Knausgård (who is the main character as well as the author), as his younger self, explores the philosophical idea that 'the world is linguistically structured', including quoting directly from Nietzsche's idea that 'we have measured the value of the world with categories *that refer to a purely fabricated world*'.[2] The reader discovers that this is leading to the revelation that death is part of a world where reality has become unreality and vice versa. Then the very rare occurrence in the book of a section break of line spaces is used to heighten the point when the reader encounters the 'death' that is in the book's title (the book has no chapters). Knausgård alluded to some of the things that drove his writing,

> I can't speak for other writers, but I write to create something that is better than myself, I think that's the deepest motivation, and it is so because I'm full of self-loathing and shame. Writing doesn't make me a better person, nor a wiser and happier one, but the writing, the text, the novel, is a creation of something outside of the self, an object, kind of neutralized by the objectivity of literature and form. The temper, the voice, the style. All in it is carefully constructed and controlled. This is writing for me – a cold hand on a warm forehead.[3]

My emphasis in this chapter is ultimately on prose writing more than poetry, although the poet Ted Hughes features significantly because of his attention to teaching writing, including to young people. The reason for my emphasis on prose writing is that it is a form that the majority of literate people have to master, whether in story, article, essay, letter, exam, report, or other form. Prose is written in some of the most complex ways, such as Joyce's *Ulysses*, and in some of the purest forms such as traditional tales for children. It is also the case that most writers use a range of forms, including poets who will often publish prose. Paul Auster[4] reflected on some of the difference between non-fiction and imaginative writing:

> The effort is the same [in both non-fiction and novels]. The need to get the sentences right is the same. But a work of the imagination allows you a lot more freedom and manoeuvrability than a work of non-fiction does. On the other hand, that freedom can often be quite scary. What comes next? How do I know the next sentence I write isn't going to lead me off the edge of a cliff? With an autobiographical work, you know the story in advance, and your primary obligation is to tell the truth. But that doesn't make the job any easier. For the epigraph of the first part of *The Invention of Solitude* [non-fiction], I used a sentence from Heraclitus – in Guy Davenport's unorthodox but elegant translation: 'In searching out the truth be ready for the unexpected, for it is difficult to

2 Knausgård, *A Death in the Family*, 244.

3 Barron, 'Completely without Dignity: An Interview with Karl Ove Knausgård', *The Paris Review*, 2016, online.

4 Born 1947, Newark, New Jersey, USA, elected to the American Academy of Arts and Letters, 2006.

find and puzzling when you find it.' In the end, writing is writing. *The Invention of Solitude* might not be a novel, but I think it explores many of the same questions I've tackled in my fiction. In some sense, it's the foundation of all my work.[5]

Later in the chapter we will see that it is not only falling off the edge of the cliff that is the writer's concern, but building the cliff in the first place.

My approach to analysing the interviews began with the initial selection of interviews from the printed volumes of the *Paris Review Interviews*: authors whose published work I had read (in a few cases most of their publications). This was in part to check the extent to which knowing their work might affect appreciation of the writing processes that they followed. Having analysed these early interviews, it became clear there was much of interest without reading the majority of the authors' publications, even were this to have been possible within the timescales for the development of this book.

Following some early reading, the more systematic analysis began. Firstly, I read in full every interview in printed volume one. The analysis, as a result of this reading, focused on the identification of key ideas. Quotes related to the key ideas were typed into MS Word documents. The documents were then imported into *NVivo*, a qualitative data analysis software tool. Using NVivo the quotes were allocated to different categories/codes, as a way to organise and analyse the data, a process called 'coding'. Subsequently the interviews in printed volumes two, three, and four were read, in particular to locate writers' ideas that confirmed, contradicted, enriched, or complicated my ideas about the patterns of writing processes emerging as a result of coding the authors' responses. As the latter parts of the analysis progressed, particularly in relation to volume four, reading every word of the interviews was not always necessary, as some information was not relevant to the emerging findings. The process required progressive focusing of the categories in order to reach sufficient depth of findings.

A final data analysis phase was also undertaken. Now taking the online resource, I used a random number generator to identify further examples of interviews through the technique of stratified random sampling. All interviews from the period 2010 onwards (which were not available in printed form at the time) available on the site were allocated a number, and the author's main contribution was identified, for instance, fiction, biography, translation, poetry, and so on. Then a random selection of authors was made from within each form of main contribution areas. This final selection of post-2010 interviews was used as a method to check that the prior analyses were sufficiently meaningful and robust.

Categories were derived from identification of significant patterns of ideas that recurred in the words of a majority of the writers (this was not a

[5] Auster, *Paris Review Interviews*, Vol. 4, 317.

quantitative analysis of the occurrence of particular words; it was a qualitative analysis of concepts represented in the authors' views). Some of the theoretical framing outlined in Chapter 2 also guided the establishment of categories and their dimensions. The categories were checked and rechecked: sometimes they were amalgamated into a new category, sometimes the quotes might be redistributed and the category subdivided and/or deleted. The final main categories were as follows:

- Creating original ideas for writing;
- Influences on writing;
- Writing and music;
- Writing and teaching;
- Basic processes of writing including the writer's workplace.

Consistent with the inductive approach to data analysis that I took, I selected short phrases from the writers' own words as metaphors, which you will see as part of the subheadings in this chapter. Another important use of metaphor as an analysis technique is seen in my selection of *The Thought Fox* as an introduction and, augmented by attention to the work of Ted Hughes periodically in the chapter, as an 'authorial presence' linking the sections of the chapter.

The process of writing the chapter itself acted as the final form of analysis that resulted in my rechecking the coding. Frequently, I would go back to the interview transcripts to check my findings and their apparent significance, to ensure that the lines of argument appeared rigorous. Inevitably, due to restrictions of space, the examples I use in the chapter are apposite but selective, and only a small fragment of the wealth of the *Paris Review Interviews* that I analysed. The analyses were not *content analysis* that uses frequency counts of particular words, nor is the chapter built on a detailed analysis of literary works. The focus of the chapter is on the much less frequently analysed processes of writing. In fact, as far as I know this is the very first systematic in-depth qualitative analysis and synthesis of the writing processes of great writers derived from robust in-depth interviews.

Beside the Clock's Loneliness: Creating Original Ideas for Writing

Having made my remarks about prose, it is to one of the greatest poets of modern times, and indeed one of his best known poems, that I turn to introduce this first section. Ted Hughes[6] is a particularly important source because he not only wrote poetry and other forms of writing but he also wrote and published an important book to help young people learn to write.

The first stanza of *The Thought Fox* is as follows:

[6] 1930 to 1998. Born Mytholmroyd, Yorkshire, England, Poet Laureate from 1984 to 1998.

I imagine this midnight moment's forest:
Something else is alive
Beside the clock's loneliness
And this blank page where my fingers move,[7]

At one level Hughes' poem is of course about a fox: the fox's movement in the snowy scene captured so beautifully. But it is also the poem's analogy with writing that is brilliant. The writer is awake at midnight, and perhaps at his desk trying to write (as you will see later in this chapter, night-time writing for great writers is not so common). There had been no writing for Hughes at least a year because of writer's block. At first something stirring, barely an idea, not in reach. The movement of the fox perhaps represents the idea's transformation from subconsciousness to consciousness. Then, after waiting for so long, with a shock the idea is there – sharp and hot. Attention in the poem has shifted to the mind because the writing has flowed: in a flurry of creativity, the page was written.

By coincidence having found the poem for this chapter, I saw *Alaska: Earth's Frozen Kingdom*, an episode of a BBC documentary series. I was reminded of the way that Ted Hughes captures the movement of the fox when I saw the antics of the tiny white arctic fox as it stalked polar bears for scraps of meat from their kills, or as it scavenged for the leftovers of food at the wonderfully named most northern human settlement before the North Pole: *Deadhorse*.

Hughes made the important point that poems themselves are the best insight into writers' thinking, and in this regard it appeared on first reading that he shared Hemingway's reticence to explain writing (see later in this chapter). But contradictorily he was very open and insightful about his writing processes, hence in addition to his *Paris Review* interview he published *Poetry in the Making: A Handbook for Writing and Teaching* in 1964. In *Poetry in the Making* Hughes was cautious about definitive meanings of 'The Thought Fox':

> This poem does not have anything you could easily call a meaning. It is about a fox, obviously enough, but a fox that is both a fox and not a fox. What sort of a fox is it that can step right into my head where presumably it still sits . . . smiling to itself when the dogs bark.[8]

Hughes recounted that he could have used 'livelier' words to make the fox be even more real and alive but,

> If I had not caught the real fox there in the words I would have not saved the poem. It would have been thrown in the waste-paper basket as I have thrown so many other hunts that didn't get what I was after. As it is, every time I read the poem the fox comes up again out of the darkness and steps into my head. And I suppose that long after I am

[7] Hughes, 'The Thought Fox'. The complete poem, and Hughes' reading it, is here: http://www.poetryarchive.org/poem/thought-fox.

[8] Hughes, *Poetry in the Making*, 20.

gone, as long as a copy of the poem exists, every time anyone reads it the fox will get up somewhere out of the darkness and come walking towards them.[9]

The portrayal of the fox by Hughes, in the poem and in his own words at interview, is not simply a fiction but instead is real: and as such represents a consummatory act of inner experience, as Dewey philosophised.

Hughes' creativity was closely connected to his perception of his persona as a writer.

You'd suppose any writer worth his salt could be bold and fearless and not give a damn. But in fact very few can. We're at the mercy of the groups that shaped our early days. We're so helplessly social – like cells in an organ.[10]

In further reflections about the life of the writer, and specifically the extent to which writers should be autobiographically present in their own work, he advocated the necessity for personal transformation through writing:

In poetry, living as a public persona in your writing is maybe even more crippling. Once you've contracted to write only the truth about yourself – as in some respected kinds of modern verse, or as in Shakespeare's sonnets – then you can too easily limit yourself to what you imagine are the truths of the ego that claims your conscious biography. Your own equivalent of what Shakespeare got into his plays is simply foregone. But being experimental isn't enough. The plunge has to be for real. The new thing has to be not you or has to seem so till it turns out to be the new you or the other you.[11]

Animals were a profoundly important source of inspiration for Hughes, who remembered that as a child he was thwarted in his attempts to keep foxes by farmers and poultry keepers who killed his fox cubs. Hughes indeed hadn't written for at least a year after his unsatisfactory university experiences: unsatisfactory because he felt that he was in a state of 'total confusion'. He hated the English Literature Tripos (undergraduate degree) at Cambridge, so changed to anthropology. As he was sitting up late in his 'dreary lodgings' in London he got an idea, and in a few minutes 'The Thought Fox' was written. Years later he said that his best poems took as long as it took to write them down, but the less satisfactory ones would be tinkered with, sometimes on and off for a number of years.

In another question during the *Paris Review* interview Hughes was asked about the difference between the function of poetry and the function of prose. Hughes recounted the story of an acquaintance who had *ankylosing spondylitis*. After 40 years of illness, in desperation the acquaintance went to see a medium who told him that he would heal himself if he started to heal others. He took the advice and apparently was cured. Hearing the story was a stimulus for Hughes' hypothesis that

[9] Hughes, *Poetry in the Making*, 20. [10] Hughes, *Poetry in the Making*, 9.
[11] Hughes, *Paris Review Interviews*, Vol. 3, 282.

> Watching and listening to him [the acquaintance], the idea occurred to me that art was perhaps this – the psychological component of the autoimmune system. It works on the artist as a healing. But it works on others too, as a medicine. Hence our great, insatiable thirst for it. However it comes out – whether a design in a carpet, a painting on a wall, the shaping of a doorway – we recognise that medicinal element because of the instant healing effect, and we call it art. It consoles and heals something in use. That's why that aspect of things is so important, and why what we want to preserve in civilisations and societies is their art – because it's a living medicine that we can still use. It still works. We feel it working. Prose, narratives, et cetera, can carry this healing. Poetry does it more intensely. Music, maybe, most intensely of all.[12]

The influence of mysticism, and the hyperbole of the healing metaphor, is an insight to one writer's understanding of creativity, at the level of creative writing's societal and impact on humanity.

The question of creativity in non-fiction was addressed by the biographer Michael Holroyd.[13] Holroyd's passion for non-fiction was clear in his suggestion that the negativity of 'non', in 'non-fiction' is an unhelpful association, preferring instead the idea of creative-writing versus re-creative writing, and the idea of 'non-fiction stories'. Holroyd strongly believes in the importance of narrative story telling for biographical writing. Originality is needed not only in the primary research that underpins an outstanding biography but also in the way the story is told: 'take *Stuart: A Life Backwards*. It was an extraordinary book and a genuinely new way of writing a biography. It was an experiment that came off, not a trick'.[14]

At the most fundamental level, the creation of writing begins with the human intention to create meaning. But this often begins with an uneasy, relatively unfocused desire and need to create, as Louise Erdrich[15] explained:

INTERVIEWER How do your books come into being? Where do they start?

ERDRICH I have little pieces of writing that sit around collecting dust, or whatever they're collecting. They are drawn to other bits of narrative like iron filings. I hate looking for something to write about. I try to have several things going before I end a book. Sometimes I don't have something immediately and I suffer for it.

INTERVIEWER Why?

ERDRICH I feel certain that I'm never going to write again. I'm positive that it's over. The world seems boring. I can't enjoy anything. My family knows I'm moping. I'm not nice to live around, and I'm not a stellar cook. Nothing seems right. The worst times are ending a book tour and

12 Hughes, *Paris Review Interviews*, Vol. 3, 294

13 Michael Holroyd was born in 1935 in Maidenhead, outside London. Holroyd was made a CBE in 1989 and was knighted in 2007 for 'services to English literature'. In 2005 he received the David Cohen Prize for Literature, the first (and still only) time it has been given to a biographer.

14 Holroyd, *Paris Review Interviews*, online, 9.

15 Born 7 June 1954, Little Falls, Minnesota. Honorary Degree of Letters; Pulitzer Prize finalist.

> not having a book to return to. It's sheer emptiness. But I guess that's an essential part of this entire process: You feel your mortality and there's nowhere to go. I walk more, which is good. Then I start rummaging around, thinking, It's all over, so what's there to lose? I go to our bookstore, and others, used bookstores, I talk to the booksellers and look around. I go back to things I didn't finish, but then, if I didn't finish it in the first place, it probably isn't really worth going back to. I go to a historical society and leaf through things. I'll take a drive in the car. Eventually something turns up. That's where I am now. I haven't really engaged with the next book in the same way that I engaged with Shadow Tag. I suppose I could go back to my eternal science-fiction novel, though it is a failure.[16]

Erdrich acknowledged her Native American background as part of her creative stimuli for writing, and she also observed that being a mother meant that a life like Hemingway's, the adventurer-writer life, simply isn't possible.

Paradoxically Ernest Hemingway[17] claimed that the very act of talking about writing could be a problem for a writer:

> 'there is one part of writing that is solid and you do it no harm by talking about it, the other is fragile, and if you talk about it, the structure cracks and you have nothing.' . . . As a result, though a wonderful raconteur, a man of rich humor, and possessed of an amazing fund of knowledge on subjects that interest him, Hemingway finds it difficult to talk about writing – not because he has few ideas on the subject, but rather because he feels so strongly that such ideas should remain unexpressed, that to be asked questions on them 'spooks' him . . . to the point where he is almost inarticulate.[18]

And more to the point, Hemingway said:

> In company with people of your own trade you ordinarily speak of other writers' books. The better the writers, the less they will speak about what they have written themselves. Joyce was a very great writer and he would only explain what he was doing to jerks. Other writers that he respected were supposed to be able to know what he was doing by reading it.[19]

Hemingway's point about reading other writer's work in a particular way relates to my concept of developing the writer's ear. Writers read other writers' writing with a particular analytic mindset that is attuned to the techniques of writing not just the aesthetics of the writing. Hemingway also hinted at the sensitivities that surround the sharing of writing, including the nature of responses to writing that is still not in finished form. And in spite of Hemingway's reticence his interview proved to be revelatory.

[16] Erdrich, *Paris Review Interviews*, online, 10.
[17] Born 21 July 1899, Oak Park, Illinois, USA. Nobel Prize in Literature 1954.
[18] Hemingway, *Paris Review Interviews*, Vol. 1, 37.
[19] Hemingway, *Paris Review Interviews*, Vol. 1, 45.

For Hemingway, writing involved the creation of a whole new thing, a 'birth', that if it succeeded would be immortal.

From things that have happened and from things as they exist and from all things that you know and all those you cannot know, you make something through your invention that is not a representation but a whole new thing truer than anything true and alive, and you make it alive, and if you make it well enough, you give it immortality. That is why you write and for no other reason that you know of. But what about all the reasons that no one knows?[20]

Hemingway recognised the existing sources from which creativity draws, in contrast with the naive idea that originality means creating something that is so new that it has no connection with anything prior to its conception. Saul Bellow's[21] ideas about creativity were also concerned with interpretations of the whole of humanity, and its survival or termination, although his view of the novelist was more modest.

But let us look at one of the dominant ideas of the century, accepted by many modern artists – the idea that humankind has reached a terminal point. We find this terminal assumption in writers like Joyce, Céline, Thomas Mann. In Doctor Faustus politics and art are joined in the destruction of civilisation. Now here is an idea, found in some of the greatest novelists of the twentieth century. How good is this idea? Frightful things have happened, but is the apocalyptic interpretation true? The terminations did not fully terminate. Civilisation is still here. The prophecies have not been borne out. Novelists are wrong to put an interpretation of history at the base of artistic creation – to speak 'the last word'. It is better that the novelist should trust his own sense of life. Less ambitious, more likely to tell the truth.[22]

Thomas Mann's *Doctor Faustus* is indeed an astonishing work, not least the depiction of the musical experiences and life of composer Adrian Leverkühn who is the central character. Mann also provides what I think is one of the most perceptive differentiations of creativity in a work of art (as opposed to other spheres of human activity such as science or mathematics):

There is a great deal of illusion in a work of art; one could go further and say that it is illusory in and of itself, as a 'work'. Its ambition is to make others believe that it was not made but rather simply arose, burst forth from Jupiter's head like Pallas Athena fully adorned in encased armour.[23]

This elusive characteristic of creativity is essential, and begins with the blank page, the blank slate, the blank canvas, or the white snow of Hughes's garden

[20] Hemingway, *Paris Review Interviews*, Vol. 1, 61.

[21] Saul Bellow, born in Lachine, Quebec, Canada. He lived from 10 June 1915 to 5 April 2005. Bellow was awarded the Pulitzer Prize; Nobel Prize for Literature; National Medal of Arts; National Book Award for Fiction, three times; National Book Foundation's lifetime Medal for Distinguished Contribution to American Letters in 1990.

[22] Bellow, *Paris Review Interviews*, Vol. 1, 109.

[23] Mann, *Doctor Faustus*, 192.

and his empty page. The illusion is the deception of the writer, but behind Mann's simple word 'made' is the discipline and hard work necessary for the creativity to be illusory.

Both ends of Bellow's continuum, between apocalypse (or immortality) and trusting one's own 'sense of life', are important for writers who make a lasting impression. For example, the human themes of Hemingway's writing are made seemingly real through the details of writing that draw on his own life experiences, but it is the test of hundreds of years of human history to come that will finally determine the immortality of his work and those of the other writers in the *Paris Review* interviews.

Voices Heard in the Darkness: Influences on Writing

The thoughts that are part of the need and intention to write begin at a primitive biological level in the brain, but these impulses need to be framed as more specific ideas. The broad processes of creativity have to lead to drafts of text. All writing has to have a beginning: a first word, a first sentence, a first paragraph. Peter Carey[24] beautifully articulated this transformation with the simile of the cliff. Even the earth of the cliff itself has to be created:

> It's like standing on the edge of a cliff. This is especially true of the first draft. Every day you're making up the earth you're going to stand on. Normally I know what I want to achieve in a chapter, and I have an idea about where events should take place and I'll have some rough idea of the characters involved. But I might not have fully invented the place. And I certainly won't fully know the characters.[25]

Marilyn Robinson's[26] first book *Housekeeping* (2004) was revered by critics at the level of humanity described by Hemingway, Bellow, and Mann. A *New York Times* review said of her book: 'It's as if, in writing it, she broke through the ordinary human condition with all its dissatisfactions, and achieved a kind of transfiguration'.[27] But in addition to the overarching historical context for human creativity evident in Robinson's work there are a range of other more down to earth influences. Robinson's fiction is informed by careful scholarship, for example, to support the creation of historical figures in her novels, and the reading of 'the most primary and proximate material that I can find. I try to be discreet in my use of historical figures. My John Brown is only a voice heard in the darkness.'[28] Her Christianity is also an important influence on her work but not in any simple moralistic way, more as a framing. She recognises the

[24] Born 1943 Bacchus Marsh, Victoria, Australia. Booker Prize winner twice.

[25] Carey, *Paris Review Interviews*, Vol. 2, 442.

[26] Born 1943, Sandpoint, Idaho, USA. Her novel *Gilead*, won the National Book Critics Circle Award and the Pulitzer Prize.

[27] Robinson, *Paris Review Interviews*, Vol. 4, 438.

[28] Robinson, *Paris Review Interviews*, Vol. 4, 454.

importance of the cultural milieu that writers inhabit: 'We're cultural creatures and meaning doesn't simply generate itself out of thin air; it's sustained in a cultural framework. It's like deciding how much more interesting it would be if you had no skeleton: you would just slide under the door.'[29]

The influence of a cultural milieu on writers is often contemporary or recent events. At the time of American involvement in the Vietnam war, and the subsequent demonstrations, Philip Roth[30] sensed something in the air.

> There's always something behind a book to which it has no seeming connection, something invisible to the reader that has helped to release the writer's initial impulse. I'm thinking about the rage and rebelliousness that were in the air, the vivid examples I saw around me of angry defiance and hysterical oppositions. This gave me a few ideas for my act.[31]

Roth's work engages in many ways with the social, political, and religious events and tropes that are part of societal thinking at the time of his writing.

For Roth, the search for the right idea is also the search for 'something driving down the centre of a book, a magnet to draw everything to it'. The magnet for Roth, and for many writers, is character. For the non-fiction writer, something driving down the centre is also needed, but instead of characters the main lines of argument draw the reader to the text. In a novel, the characters are not only important because they are a necessary feature of the form, but also because they are often used as the essential way the main idea of the book is brought to life.

Roth works tirelessly to find the right characters, but also the right 'predicament' for them. The first attempts to test the characters are 'unpleasant':

> I type out beginnings and they're awful, more of an unconscious parody of my previous book than the breakaway from it that I want . . . I often have to write a hundred pages or more before there's a paragraph that's alive. OK I say to myself, that's your beginning, start there; that's the first paragraph of the book.[32]

Robinson sees her living breathing characters as the inspiration: 'The one consistent thing among my novels is that there's a character who stays in my mind. It's a character with complexity that I want to know better.' Robinson forms such a strong bond with her characters that when a novel is finished she misses the characters so much she feels 'sort of bereaved'. So powerful was this feeling after finishing *Gilead* that Robinson decided to work further with some of the characters she felt had not been fully realised, and this resulted in her book *Home*.

[29] Robinson, *Paris Review Interviews*, Vol. 4, 448.
[30] Born 1933, Newark, New Jersey, USA. National Book Foundation Medal for Distinguished Contribution to American Letters, 2002.
[31] Roth, *Paris Review Interviews*, Vol. 4, 223.
[32] Roth, *Paris Review Interviews*, Vol. 4, 206.

The personal experiences of any writer are some of the most important influences on their work. But, as Roth suggests, it is not the specifics of the author's experiences that directly influence the text but more particular moments and experiences in life that become the basis for the author's improvisation that provides authenticity for their characters:

> Novelists are frequently as interested in what hasn't happened to them as in what has. What may be taken by the innocent for naked autobiography is, as I've been suggesting, more than likely mock autobiography or hypothetical autobiography or autobiography grandiosely enlarged . . . Novelists are even interested in what happens to other people and, like liars and con men everywhere, will pretend that something dramatic or awful or hair-raising or splendid that happened to someone else actually happened to them. The physical particulars and moral circumstances of Zuckerman's mother's death have practically nothing to do with the death of my own mother. The death of the mother of one of my dearest friends – whose account of her suffering stuck in my mind long after he'd told me about it – furnished the most telling details for the mother's death in The Anatomy Lesson.[33]

Sometimes even the brilliant conception, through characters, through the cultural milieu, or through the building of the cliff, may not be enough on its own to begin a truly ground-breaking piece of writing. Gabriel García Márquez[34] had an idea about a book that he'd always wanted to write but he felt there was something missing:

> After *The Evil Hour* I did not write anything for five years. I had an idea of what I always wanted to do, but there was something missing and I was not sure what it was until one day I discovered the right tone – the tone that I eventually used in *One Hundred Years of Solitude*. It was based on the way my grandmother used to tell her stories. She told things that sounded supernatural and fantastic, but she told them with complete naturalness. When I finally discovered the tone I had to use, I sat down for eighteen months and worked every day.[35]

Márquez's description of tone is related to Alvarez's thoughts on voice that I addressed in the previous chapter. But Márquez's comments hint at the possibility of a different voice for a different novel, hence voice that changes.

The stimulus of what writers read, and the way it influences their writing, is relevant to all writers but varies widely. Ted Hughes 'met' W.B. Yeats, 'via the third part of his poem "The Wandering of Oisin", . . . Yeats sucked me in through the Irish folklore and myth and the occult business.'[36] And by the time Hughes got to the University of Cambridge he had what he called his sacred canon: 'Chaucer, Shakespeare, Marlowe, Blake, Wordsworth, Keats,

[33] Roth, *Paris Review Interviews*, Vol. 4, 213.
[34] 1927 to 2014. Born Aracataca, Columbia. Nobel Prize for Literature, 1982.
[35] Márquez, *Paris Review Interviews*, Vol. 2, 188.
[36] Hughes, *Paris Review Interviews*, Vol. 3, 274.

Coleridge, Hopkins, Yeats, Eliot. I knew no American poetry at all except Eliot . . . The only modern foreign poet I knew was Rilke in Spender's and Leishman's translation.'[37]

In addition to classic authors' influence in general, it is often seemingly small details of particular texts that are major influences. Márquez was lent Kafka's book of short stories *The Metamorphosis*:

> The first line reads, 'When Gregor Samsa woke up one morning from unsettling dreams, he found himself changed in his bed into a monstrous vermin . . .' When I read the line I thought to myself that I didn't know anyone was allowed to write things like that. If I had known, I would have started writing a long time ago. So I immediately started writing short stories.[38]

It was almost as if Kafka gave Márquez permission to find his writer's voice. But in spite of Márquez's famed style of magical realism he drew directly from his own experiences of life.

> but if I had to give a young writer some advice I would say to write about something that has happened to him; it's always easy to tell whether a writer is writing about something that has happened to him or something he has read or been told. Pablo Neruda has a line in a poem that says God help me from inventing when I sing. It always amuses me that the biggest praise from my work comes for the imagination, while the truth is that there's not a single line in all my work that does not have a basis in reality. The problem is that Caribbean reality resembles the wildest imagination.[39]

Translators, whose work is much less often recognised in the way other authors' work is, have a much more direct relationship with other texts as stimulus for writing. Richard Pevear and Larissa Volokhonsky[40] are unique not only for their outstanding translations of Russian literature but also because they have written together. Their observations on the stimulus of previous translations and the need for new work focuses mainly on trying to give the author's authentic voice. While talking about their translation of *The Brothers Karamazov*, they used the description 'metropolitan cosmopolitan' (akin to hoity-toity) to try and be faithful to Dostoevsky's sarcastic portrayal of the character Mr Miusov, and avoid the blandness they detected in others' translations.

[37] Hughes, *Paris Review Interviews*, Vol. 3.

[38] Márquez, *Paris Review Interviews*, Vol. 2, 184.

[39] Márquez, *Paris Review Interviews*, Vol. 2, 186.

[40] Richard Pevear and Larissa Volokhonsky. Richard Pevear was born in Waltham, Massachusetts, USA, on 21 April 1943. Larissa Volokhonsky was born in Leningrad. Pevear and Volokhonsky have won the pen Translation Prize twice. Pevear, who has also translated French and Italian works, is Distinguished Professor Emeritus of Comparative Literature at the American University of Paris.

INTERVIEWER What had the other translators said?

VOLOKHONSKY 'Who had been in capitals and abroad.' They would give the information but not the voice. This is the kind of thing I began to notice throughout the novel. Sometimes three times, five times on a page.

PEVEAR And I discovered during our work together on Dostoevsky that he was not a brooding, obsessed man, but a very playful, free spirit. You see it in his style. The style of Dostoevsky is extremely varied. He would practice writing pages in different voices. He shows characters through the voice, through the way they use or misuse language. Which meant a lot of people used to say that he didn't write very well! For example, there is a little note at the beginning of Karamazov, 'From the Author', about how he came to write the book. The 'author' is not Dostoevsky – he makes that perfectly clear – although everybody seems to think that Dostoevsky is the narrator. But the narrator isn't a writer at all. He just happens to live in the town where the novel is set. He got interested in the story of the Karamazov brothers and the murder of their father and wanted to record it. The whole point of this preface is to introduce all possible voicings of this narrator, who writes absurd things like, 'Being at a loss to resolve these questions, I am resolved to leave them without any resolution.' And of course all the translators vary the words, because Flaubert said you should never use the same word twice on the same page. Finally he says, 'Well, that is the end of my introduction. I quite agree that it is superfluous, but since it is already written, let it stand.' Dostoevsky gets you into the entire question of whether this man is trustworthy. Does he know what he's talking about? The uncertainty surrounding this narrator is very important, and all of that is introduced just by the way it's written. So the light suddenly went on.

VOLOKHONSKY I said to Richard, You are reading a different book.

PEVEAR It occurred to us that there was a whole other register to Dostoevsky, and the translators hadn't translated it. There was something to be done there.[41]

Although classics from literary canons are common influences for most writers, there are other interesting ways that texts of many kinds influence writing. Jack Kerouac's[42] best known work *On the Road* is lauded for framing the style of the Beat Generation of young people in the late 1950s and 1960s. It is also known for its style of *spontaneous prose*, a method that Kerouac listed not entirely coherently in his *30 Essentials for Spontaneous Prose*. The influence for *On the Road* was a personal letter that inspired the book and the spontaneous style, a letter that has a remarkable story of its own. Kerouac used to exchange letters with his friend Neal Cassady, and it was the style of Cassady's letters that attracted Kerouac:

[41] Richard Pevear and Larissa Volokhonsky, *Paris Review Interviews* online, 4.

[42] 1922 to 1969. Born Lowell, Massachusetts, USA. Recognised for his contribution to an original style of writing.

all first person, fast, mad, confessional, completely serious, all detailed – with real names in his case, however, being letters ... The letter, the main letter was forty thousand words long, mind you, a whole short novel. It was the greatest piece of writing I ever saw, better'n anybody in America, or at least enough to make Melville, Twain, Dreiser, Wolfe, I dunno who, spin in their graves ... We also did so much fast talking between the two of us, on tape recorders, way back in 1952, and listened to them so much, we both got the secret of LINGO in telling a tale and figured that was the only way to express the speed and tension and ecstatic tomfoolery of the age.[43]

In 1953 Kerouac lent the letter to another famous beat generation author Allen Ginsburg. Ginsburg lent it to Gerd Stern, who lived on a houseboat in Sausalito near California. Tragically Stern lost the letter, presumed overboard.

Writers find ways to link the influence of their favoured authors and texts with their own creative ideas. The relationship between the influence of canons of great literature and more technical features such as plot and character can be seen as similar in scale to the relationship between the immortality of a work and trusting one's own 'sense of life'. Great writing unites profound subjects that will stand the test of time, with the minutiae of life, communicated through the ubiquitous human language of words, sentences, and larger text structures.

A Tenor Man Drawing a Breath: Writing and Music

Music is frequently a point of reference, a metaphor, a means of explanation for writers' descriptions of writing processes. The influence of music took two main forms for Hughes. Firstly, it was a presence in his life. For example, during his years of 'chaos and confusion' the music of Beethoven was Hughes' 'therapy'. In addition to the emotional appeal of Beethoven's music the attraction may also have been structure and form, the concision of the compositions seen in the building of great works from fragments. Secondly, the influence of music on Hughes was the concrete elements of pitch, pacing, inflections, and shapes:

Take any passage of 'The Waste Land', or maybe a better example is Eliot's poem 'Marina'. Every word in those poems is as formally fixed, as locked into flexible laws, as words can be. The music of those words, the musical inevitability of the pitch, the pacing, the combination of inflections – all that is in some way absolute, unalterable, the ultimate perfect containment of unusually powerful poetic forces. You could say the same of many other examples: Smart's 'Jubilate Agno', any passages in Shakespeare's blank verse, Shakespeare's prose. To my mind, the best kind of verse usually called free always aspires towards that kind of formal inevitability – a fixed, unalterable, musical, and yet hidden dramatic shape.[44]

[43] Kerouac, *Paris Review Interviews*, Vol. 4, 84.
[44] Hughes, *Paris Review Interviews*, Vol. 3, 303.

The idea of 'flexible laws' is particularly helpful in relation to the need to understand conventions of writing but also be able to play with and disrupt conventions. The way that Hughes used to listen to Beethoven also prompts reflection on the more straightforward issue of whether to have music playing, when the writer is writing, or not. In Stephen King's[45] earlier years of writing he used pop music as a means to stimulate the pace of the plots in his writing.

> But I was younger then, and frankly my brains used to work better than they do now. Now I'll only listen to music at the end of a day's work, when I roll back to the beginning of what I did that day and go over it on the screen. A lot of times the music will drive my wife crazy because it will be the same thing over and over and over again . . . I'm not really listening to the music – it's just something there in the background.[46]

For Jack Kerouac the music influence was not so much classical music but more jazz. In general terms it was the structural aspects of music compared with the structural aspects of poetry that interested him. Kerouac's understanding of jazz solos framed by the musical structures of *bars* and *beats* prompted him to use this idea to structure his poetry. In a startling example he said:

> But as for my regular English verse, I knocked it off fast like the prose, using, get this, the size of the notebook page for the form and length of the poem, just as a musician has to get out, a jazz musician, his statement within a certain number of bars, within one chorus, which spills over into the next, but he has to stop where the chorus page stops.[47]

Kerouac was also interested in the constrained structure of forms like the Japanese Haiku poem.

'Phrases', in a technical sense, are common to both written text and to music. In addition to the structure of musical bars and beats, the tunes played on any wind instrument, or those sung by the human voice, are constrained by the human capacity to breathe. And even other instruments, such as string instruments, require control of breathing in relation to musical phrases. The best players fit their breathing to the 'phrases' of music, a technique known by musicians as 'phrasing'. Phrases in music are melodic fragments that have a completeness in their own way but are a vital building block of a melody. So they will be part of a melody, but a distinctive part that requires the musician to provide some articulation at the point of the phrase boundary. It is the capacity to understand and represent phrases in music that is often equated with being a 'musical' player rather than one who is technically proficient but without real musicality. A phrase in a sentence is also a fragment, usually of a clause. And when read aloud, the reader also needs to articulate textual phrases carefully, something that is one of

45 Born 1947, Portland, Maine, USA. Medal for Distinguished Contribution to American Letters 2003.

46 Hughes, *Paris Review Interviews*, Vol. 3, 479.

47 Kerouac, *Paris Review Interviews*, Vol. 4, 87.

the historical legacies of punctuation in writing, encapsulated in ideas about punctuation indicating lengths of pauses in written text (as we saw in Louth's text in Chapter 3).

Kerouac realised that the ways in which jazz melodies are played by a 'tenor man' related to the way he wanted to express himself in writing:

> Yes, jazz and bob, in the sense of, say, a tenor man drawing a breath and blowing a phrase on his saxophone till he runs out of breath, and when he does, his sentence, his statement's been made ... That's how I therefore separate my sentences, as breath separations of the mind ... Then there's the raciness and freedom and humor of jazz instead of all that dreary analysis and things like. James entered the room, and lit a cigarette. He thought Jane might have thought this too vague a gesture ... You know the stuff.[48]

Kerouac's 'separations of the mind' also has resonances with the distinction between oral and written language. Speech is more informal than writing and is 'punctuated' by pauses to breathe 'ums' and 'ahs' etc. Speech takes place in a social context where the other person in the conversation may interject, answer, seek clarification, and so on. Whereas writing, at its time of production, is nearly always a private act. The words are carefully crafted and edited in order to have an effect on a reader who is not in close proximity. Body language and intonation have no part in writing. Kerouac's spontaneous writing was built to some degree on an approximation of speech, as his experimentation with tape recorders showed. But speech written down is just that, an approximation. In fact no novel would be published if it faithfully reproduced accurate transcriptions of real speech; it would simply be too tedious to read.

Jazz music was also an important influence on Haruki Murakami:[49]

> I've been listening to jazz since I was thirteen or fourteen years old. Music is a very strong influence: the chords, the melodies, the rhythm, the feeling of the blues are helpful when I write. I wanted to be a musician, but I couldn't play the instruments very well, so I became a writer. Writing a book is just like playing music; first I play the theme, then I improvise, then there is a conclusion, of a kind. . . . Jazz is a journey for me, a mental journey. No different than writing. . . . I like classical music as well, particularly baroque music. And in my new book, Kafka on the Shore, the protagonist, the boy, listens to Radiohead and Prince. I was so surprised: some member of Radiohead likes my books! . . . I read the Japanese liner notes for Kid A the other day, and he said that he likes my books, and I was so proud.[50]

The influence of music on writing is perhaps not surprising if you consider that sounds and music were the substrate from which human language evolved, and so one of the very first forms of artistic expression that humans developed. The

[48] Kerouac, *Paris Review Interviews*, Vol. 4, 103.

[49] Born 1949, Kyoto, Japan. Franz Kafka Prize 2006.

[50] Murakami, *Paris Review Interviews*, Vol. 4, 366.

ability to make musical sounds with the voice, and to use objects percussively, all came before the ability to write. These links from music to our primitive ancestry were important to William Faulkner.[51]

> A writer is trying to create believable people in credible moving situations in the most moving way he can. Obviously he must use the tools of his environment that he knows. I would say that music is the easiest means in which to express oneself, since it came first in man's experience and history. But since words are my talent, I must try to express clumsily in words what the pure music would have done better. That is, music would express better and simpler, but I prefer to use words, as I prefer to read rather than listen. I prefer silence to sound, and the image produced by words occurs in silence. That is, the thunder and the music of the prose take place in silence.[52]

Links between music and poetry are more concrete than the links between music and prose. Rhythm is a fundamental component of poetry and music,[53] and songs are creations that often use poems to inform original musical composition that intimately combine the words of texts with the melodies and harmonies of musical notes. Music perhaps does have a particular physiological power to engage the listener in an immediate visceral way that text can rarely achieve. And music is communication of a 'simpler' kind because it cannot portray the complexities of meaning that writing can, hence the importance of joining writing and music in song, opera, and musical theatre.

You Throw the Rock and You Get the Splash: Writers, Writing, and Teaching

One of the many transformations in *The Thought Fox* is the personification of the clock's movement from lonely to somehow contentedly ticking away as a friendly companion: a move from loneliness to social partnership with the writer (and the transformation of the writer's psyche). The significance of writers' solitude, and their conceptualisations of writing processes, can be further understood by reflecting on one of the contexts that is undoubtedly social: the context of teaching writing to others.

In the *Paris Review Interviews* writers are divided on the extent to which writing, and particularly the creative aspects of writing, can be taught (this difference of opinion also exists for creativity researchers: see Chapter Five). Robert Stone,[54] an actor and writer, was dubious about whether you could learn from creative writing classes, and yet he did some writing teaching himself. One of his techniques was to take aspiring writers to 'bars and race tracks to

[51] 1897 to 1962. Born Oxford, Mississippi, USA. Nobel Prize in Literature 1949.
[52] Faulkner, *Paris Review Interviews*, Vol. 2, 48.
[53] For more on the technical links between music, particularly jazz, and free verse see, Andrews, *A Prosody of Free Verse*.
[54] 1937 to 2015. Born Brooklyn, New York, USA. National Book Award 1975.

listen to dialogue',[55] but he recognised the limitations of this technique, and that writing classes could have some value. In essence his philosophy was, 'You know, you throw the rock and you get the splash.' Or in other words you set the environment for creativity to flourish, then encourage the writing and see what happens.

Richard Price[56] held similar views to Stone in that he felt that you couldn't teach talent but you could create conditions to help aspiring writers find their story: 'Oftentimes, it's a matter of lining up the archer with the target . . . What do you know that I don't know?'[57] Price's philosophy is also interesting for his view that knowledge is an important part of being a fiction writer, something more usually linked to non-fiction writing. He told a wonderful story about a student in one of his classes. The student was writing about black people in the South Bronx, and their lives on drugs. But Price felt it was 'over-the-top to the point of being silly'.[58] He asked the student, what do you know that I don't know:

> He turned out to be one of those kids in the early eighties who was bombing trains with graffiti – one of these guys who was part of the whole train-signing subculture, you know, Turk 182. He wrote a story, over a hundred pages long, about what it was like to be one of these guys – fifteen pages on how to steal aerosol cans from hardware stores. He could describe the smell of spray paint mixing with that rush of tunnel air when someone jerked open the connecting door on a moving train that you were 'decorating'. He wrote about the Atlantic Avenue station in Brooklyn where all the graffiti signers would hang out, their informal clubhouse, how they kept scrapbooks of each other's tags . . . That is the job of the writing teacher: what do you think you should be writing about?[59]

Price also had another technique for encouraging writing. When he was working at Yale University, he hated setting teaching assignments or tasks, but he came up with the idea of asking the students to find a photograph of their family taken at least one year before they were born, and then to write a story about what happens immediately after the family members break the pose held for the photograph. Price's sting in his tale was the recollection that 'Tom McGuane once said, I've done a lot of horrible things in my life but I have never taught creative writing.'! Kurt Vonnegut[60] also had reservations, and dismissively likened the teaching of creative writing to the way a golf professional might point out things like flaws in the golf swing. At the same time the ambivalence of his view was shown in the fact that he had taught for

[55] Stone, *Paris Review Interviews*, Vol. 1, 331.
[56] Born 1949, The Bronx, New York City, USA.
[57] Price, *Paris Review Interviews*, Vol. 1, 403.
[58] Price, *Paris Review Interviews*, Vol. 1, 402.
[59] Price, *Paris Review Interviews*, Vol. 1, 403.
[60] 1922 to 2007. Born Indianapolis, Indiana, USA.

two years at the University of Iowa, and he had obvious pride about some of his ex-students: Gail Godwin, John Irving, Jonathan Penner, Bruce Dobbler, John Casey, and Jane Casey.

Distinctions between things that could be taught and those that could not be taught also concerned William Styron[61], to a somewhat extreme position:

> A writing course can only give you a start, and help a little. It can't teach writing. The professor should weed out the good from the bad, cull them like a farmer, and not encourage the ones who haven't got something . . . The average teacher . . . can teach you something about matters of technique. You know – don't tell a story from two points of view and that sort of thing. But I don't think even the most conscientious and astute teachers can teach anything about style. Style comes only after long, hard practice and writing.[62]

But perhaps, like Queen Gertrude in Shakespeare's *Hamlet*, Styron doth protest too much?

The most true account of this issue, and a really extensive set of perceptive reflections, comes from John Gardener.[63] In the 1970s John Gardener's work was regarded in the eyes of many critics and reviewers as both highly original and paradoxically with some elements of conservatism, in comparison with some of the more experimental writers of his generation. His scholarly approach, and perhaps some of the reason for his perceptive observations about teaching, was influenced by not only his reading of the classics such as Virgil and Dante but also the critical controversies including debates about mistakes in translations of these classical works.[64] Gardener's honesty is revealed in his shock discovery that (in contrast to the more negative perspectives on whether writing could be taught by Stone, Styron, and Price) he found it 'fairly easy to transform an eager, intelligent student to a publishing creative writer'. In fact so shocking was this to him that he quit creative writing teaching:

> Silly as it sounds, that discovery was a shock to my ego and changed my whole approach to writing fiction. I was twenty-four, twenty-five at the time. Since I found out that anyone has stories he can tell and, once you've shown him a little technique, can tell them relatively well, I was determined to set myself apart from the herd – I was reading that devil Nietzsche then – by writing as other people couldn't. Also, I quit teaching creative writing, maybe partly from annoyance that my students were as good as I was, but mainly in hopes of learning the things I had to know to become a good writer. I began teaching history of criticism courses, which turned out to be one of the most valuable experiences of my life.[65]

[61] 1925 to 2006. Born Newport News, Virginia, USA. Prix mondial Cino Del Duca 1985.
[62] Styron, *Paris Review Interviews*, Vol. 4, 4.
[63] 1933 to 1982. Born Batavia, New York, USA.
[64] Gardner, *Paris Review Interviews*, Vol. 2, 144.
[65] Gardner, *Paris Review Interviews*, Vol. 2, 166.

It was not that Gardener didn't value teaching creative writing; he felt that 'When you teach creative writing, you discover a great deal.'[66] Gardner's view was that in contrast to classical and medieval literature, which by virtue that it has survived to the present day is nearly always outstanding, the work of students can be a little thin, so the teacher has to find ways to help the student deal with this. As part of the creative writing teaching process: 'when you teach creative writing, you see a thousand ways that a piece can go wrong. So [creative writing] is helpful to me.' Contrary to the negative perspectives, Gardener's view was not only that creative writing could be taught but 'when you get a good creative writing class it's magisterial'. His enthusiasm for teaching was clear in his view that by working with intelligent students and teachers as part of literary criticism his own writing developed

> a clear idea of my audience, or anyway of a hypothetical audience. I don't think a writer can write well without some such notions . . . What I notice now is that all around me there are first-rate writers, and in nearly every case it seems to me that *what makes the first rate is their similar involvement in teaching and scholarship*. There are exceptions – maybe William Gaddis, I'm not sure. A brilliant writer, though I disapprove of him. Perhaps the most important exception is John Updike, who, unlike John Hawkes, Bill Gass, Stanley Elkin, and Saul Bellow and so on, is not a teacher. But the exception means nothing, because, teacher or not, he's the most academic of all.[67]

Hughes was also upbeat in his reflections about writing and teaching. His earliest influence was his discovery of the poems of Rudyard Kipling, when he was age fourteen or fifteen, which inspired him to write and to show his work to his school English teacher. It appears his English teacher was not uncritically encouraging, but the crucial moment to Hughes' development as a writer was when she told Hughes that a particular phrase was 'real poetry'. Some years later Hughes did some teaching for the University of Massachusetts that led to work with the Arvon Writing Foundation in England.[68] His description of the experience reveals again the powerful links between writing, education, and people's lives and life chances:

> But the founders of Arvon, two poets, went ahead and invited me to give a reading of my verses to the first course. The students were a group of fourteen-year-olds from a local school. Within that one week they had produced work that astonished me. Within five days, in fact. They were in an incredible state of creative excitement.[69]

Involvement in well-established writing courses was also part of the development of other writers. I referred to the importance of the liberal arts traditions at

[66] Gardener, *Paris Review Interviews*, Vol. 2, 167.

[67] Gardener, *Paris Review Interviews*, Vol. 2, 170. Italics added.

[68] In 2017 I began an experimental trial, with 100 schools in England, to evaluate an Arvon approach to supporting the teaching of writing. The approach builds on previous research carried out by academics Teresa Cremin and Debra Myhill in collaboration with Arvon.

[69] Hughes, *Paris Review Interviews*, Vol. 3, 295.

Dartmouth College in relation to the development of the BASIC computer language. The relationship between writing and the teaching of writing is evident in Louise Erdrich's biography, which included an MFA in creative writing from Johns Hopkins University. She studied English at Dartmouth where she met her husband Michael Dorris who founded the college's new Native American Studies program.[70] Even the venue for the interview reflected the importance of teaching:

> Erdrich lives in Minneapolis, but we met in the Fargo Econo Lodge parking lot. From there, with Erdrich's eight-year-old daughter, Kiizh, we drove five hours up to the Turtle Mountain Chippewa reservation, on the Manitoba border. Every August, when tick season has subsided, Erdrich and her sister Heid spend a week in a former monastery here to attend the Little Shell Powwow and to conduct a writing workshop at the Turtle Mountain Community College. One afternoon, participants took turns reciting poetry under a basswood tree beside the single-room house where Erdrich's mother grew up. Another day, they ate homemade enchiladas and sang 'Desperado' and 'Me and Bobby McGee', accompanied by a fellow workshopper on the guitar. In class, the writing is personal, the criticism charitable. It helps that Erdrich does the exercises, too – reading out the results in her mellifluous, often mischievous voice. In tidy fulfilment of an assignment entitled 'very short fiction', she wrote, 'You went out for the afternoon and came back with your dress on inside out.'[71]

But it is perhaps Joyce Oates[72] whose enthusiasm for the place of teaching in writing is the most infectious. Oates has been so prolific in her writing that she had three different publishers, including one publisher she used as the place to locate her more experimental work so that it didn't get wasted by rejection from her more conservative other two publishers. Oates is currently Professor in the Humanities with the Program in Creative Writing at Princeton University. In reflections on a previous university role at the University of Windsor she explained the level of her teaching commitment:

> One [class] is creative writing, one is the graduate seminar (in the Modern Period), the third is an oversize (one hundred and fifteen students) undergraduate course that is lively and stimulating but really too swollen to be satisfying to me. There is, generally, a closeness between students and faculty at Windsor that is very rewarding, however.[73]

The value of teaching for Oates was her view that until you teach a text to intelligent and responsive students the text has not been fully experienced. And for writers it is not just the influences of the particular authors who are part of their reading in general that is important, but also the particular analytical qualities that writers need to develop to be able to understand how writing is

[70] Tragically Michael Dorris committed suicide in 1997.

[71] Erdrich, *Paris Review Interviews* online, 1.

[72] Born 1938, Lockport, New York, USA. Awarded National Humanities Medal 2010.

[73] Oates, *Paris Review Interviews*, Vol. 3, 175.

done, without the need of the 'explanation for jerks' (as according to Hemingway Joyce pointed out).

I hope that the highly significant connections between writing and teaching mean we can safely contest a remark from the renowned playwright, George Bernard Shaw (and Oscar Wilde's aphorism from Chapter 3). Shaw wrote, 'He who can does. He who cannot teaches.' The context for Shaw's unfortunate remark is curious. After the end of his play script for his *Man and Superman* (1903) he wrote the postscript 'Maxims for Revolutionists'. It was this that contained the remark about doing vs. teaching:

Maxims for Revolutionists	Education
When a man teaches something he does not know to somebody else who has no aptitude for it, and gives him a certificate of proficiency, the latter has completed the education of a gentleman.	*31*
A fool's brain digests philosophy into folly, science into superstition, and art into pedantry. Hence University education.	*32*
The best brought-up children are those who have seen their parents as they are. Hypocrisy is not the parent's first duty.	*33*
The vilest abortionist is he who attempts to mould a child's character.	*34*
At the University every great treatise is postponed until its author attains impartial judgment and perfect knowledge. If a horse could wait as long for its shoes and would pay for them in advance, our blacksmiths would all be college dons.	*35*
He who can, does. He who cannot, teaches.	*36*
A learned man is an idler who kills time with study. Beware of his false knowledge: it is more dangerous than ignorance.	*37*
Activity is the only road to knowledge.	*38*
Every fool believes what his teachers tell him, and calls his credulity science or morality as confidently as his father called it divine revelation.	*39*
No man fully capable of his own language ever masters another.	*40*
No man can be a pure specialist without being in the strict sense an idiot.	*41*
Do not give your children moral and religious instruction unless you are quite sure they will not take it too seriously. Better be the mother of Henri Quatre and Nell Gwynne than of Robespierre and Queen Mary Tudor.	*42*

Some of Shaw's maxims are more significant than 'He who can, does. He who cannot, teaches': for example, the idea that activity is strongly linked with knowledge (although activity is not the 'only road' to learning). Literal analysis of Shaw's maxims is, of course, risky as these maxims are necessarily 'revolutionary' given their context in his play. However, as the evidence from the writers I analysed for this chapter showed, rather than being separate occupations, 'doing' and 'teaching' are often strongly linked. Most writers and other artists usually both 'do' their art, and 'teach' their art.

Keeping the Machine Running: The Basic Processes of Writing

When writing was going well Hughes said that he felt a sense of 'effortless concentration'. In order to create the right atmosphere for this, in his early years he spent a year writing with the windows of his flat covered with brown paper, and ear plugs in his ears to avoid distractions. A special kind of concentration was also important for Robinson:

> The difficulty of [writing] cannot be overstated. But at its best, it involves a state of concentration that is a satisfying experience, no matter how difficult or frustrating. The sense of being focused like that is a marvellous feeling. It's one of the reasons I'm so willing to seclude myself and am a little bit grouchy when I have to deal with the reasonable expectations of the world.[74]

And Kerouac in his inimitable style saw the concentration as a kind of silent meditation, while going at 100 miles per hour:

> Remember that scene in La Dolce Vita where the old priest is mad because a mob of maniacs has shown up to see the tree where the kids see the Virgin Mary? He says, 'Visions are not available in all this frenetic foolishness and yelling and pushing; visions are only obtainable in silence and meditation.' Thar. Yup.[75]

Márquez was also convinced that there was a special state of mind which allowed writing to flow. But he needed to work in 'surroundings that are familiar and have already been warmed up with my work. I cannot write in hotels or borrowed rooms or on borrowed typewriters.' Styron was brutally honest:

> Do you enjoy writing?
>
> I certainly don't. I get a fine, warm feeling when I'm doing well, but that pleasure is pretty much negated by the pain of getting started each day. Let's face it, writing is hell.[76]

The sense of keeping writing moving at a regular pace is a concern for most writers. The most extreme opposite of movement is a standstill, or writers' block, yet hardly any of the writers in the *Paris Review* volumes refer to writer's block, presumably because they were all extremely accomplished and experienced writers when interviewed. However, Márquez had a form of block, five years, as he searched for the right voice for *One Hundred Years of Solitude*. Roth talked about having to write hundreds of pages to find the right

[74] Robinson, *Paris Review Interviews*, Vol. 4, 456.
[75] Kerouac, *Paris Review Interviews*, Vol. 4, 87.
[76] Styron, *Paris Review Interviews*, Vol. 4, 4.

paragraph that was the spur to a whole novel. Hughes talked about a similar process:

The nearest I've ever felt to a block was a sort of unfitness in the athletic sense – the need for an all-out, sustained effort of writing simply to get myself in chapter before starting on what I imagined would be the real thing. One whole book arrived like that, not a very long book, but one which I felt I needed to galvanise my inertia, break through the huge sloth I was up against . . . That's displaced activity. Much of what we do at any level is a bit like that, I fancy . . . The big problem for those who write verse is keeping the machine running without simply exercising evasion of the real confrontation. If Ulanova, the ballerina, missed one day of practice, she couldn't get back to peak fitness without a week of hard work. Dickens said the same about his writing – if he missed a day he needed a week of hard slog to get back into the flow.[77]

Similarly, musicians have to maintain daily practice if they are to perform at optimum levels. For most writers their writing is done in the morning, often first thing in the morning, and the number of words per day between 500 and 2,000.

KING: I used to write two thousand words a day and sometimes even more. But now it's just a paltry thousand words a day.[78]

MÁRQUEZ: I find it harder to write now than before, both novels and journalism . . . Now the output is comparatively small. On a good working day, working from nine o'clock in the morning to two or three in the afternoon, the most I can write is a short paragraph of four or five lines, which I usually tear up the next day.[79]

ROTH: I work all day, morning and afternoon, just about every day. If I sit like that for two or three years, at the end I have a book.[80]

HEMINGWAY: When I am working on a book or a story I write every morning as soon after first light as possible. There is no one to disturb you and it is cool or cold and you come to your work and warm as you write. You read what you have written and, as you always stop when you know what is going to happen next, you go on from there. You write until you come to a place where you still have your juice and know what will happen next and you stop and try to live through until the next day when you hit it again. You have started at six in the morning, say, and may go on until noon or be through before that. When you stop you are as empty, and at the same time never empty but filling, as when you have made love to someone you love. Nothing can hurt you, nothing can happen, nothing means anything until the next day when you do it again. It is the wait until the next day that is hard to get through.[81]

STYRON: When I'm writing steadily – that is, when I'm involved in a project that I'm really interested in, one of those rare pieces that has a foreseeable end – I average two-and-a-half or three pages a day,

77 Hughes, *Paris Review Interviews*, Vol. 3, 284.
78 King, *Paris Review Interviews*, Vol. 2, 480.
79 Marquez, *Paris Review Interviews*, Vol. 2, 183.
80 Roth, *Paris Review Interviews*, Vol. 4, 207.
81 Hemingway, *Paris Review Interviews*, Vol. 4, 38.

> longhand on yellow sheets. I spend about five hours at it, of which very little is spent actually writing. I try to get a feeling of what's going on in the story before I put it down on paper, but actually most of this breaking-in period is one long, fantastic daydream, in which I think about anything but the work at hand. I can't turn out slews of stuff each day. I wish I could. I seem to have some neurotic need to perfect each paragraph – each sentence, even – as I go along.[82]

Kerouac preferred 'midnight to dawn', literally burning the midnight oil. Robinson is much more led by the creative impulse than the need for the discipline of a daily ritual:

> I really am incapable of discipline. I write when something makes a strong claim on me. When I don't feel like writing, I absolutely don't feel like writing. I tried that work ethic thing a couple of times – I can't say I exhausted its possibilities – but if there's not something on my mind that I really want to write about, I tend to write something that I hate.[83]

As for the physical environment for writing, the vast majority of writers need a designated familiar place with the right tools for the job. 'The Desk in the room, near the bed, with a good light . . . a drink when you get tired' (Kerouac); the same for King but also a comfortable chair, a refuge with no distractions; and for Robinson, but also with the option of the couch; a meticulously organised office for Roth. Truman Capote[84] and Hemingway had some more unusual conditions for their work:

CAPOTE: I am a completely horizontal author. I can't think unless I'm lying down, either in bed or stretched on a couch and with a cigarette and coffee handy. I've got to be puffing and sipping.[85]

HEMINGWAY: A working habit he has had from the beginning, Hemingway stands when he writes. He stands in a pair of his oversized loafers on the worn skin of a lesser kudu – the typewriter and the reading board chest-high opposite him.[86]

The editorial work of making revisions was seen by many of the writers as essential. These revisions could be done in the mind prior to setting down on paper, like Robinson, who simply tosses the paper and tries again if something is really wrong, or for the majority of writers a painstaking repetitive process, something trenchantly described by Hemingway:

[82] Styron, *Paris Review Interviews*, Vol. 4, 4.
[83] Robinson, *Paris Review Interviews*, Vol. 4, 4.
[84] 1924 to 1984. Born New Orleans, Louisiana, USA.
[85] Capote, *Paris Review Interviews*, Vol. 1, 28.
[86] Hemingway, *Paris Review Interviews*, Vol. 1, 35.

How much rewriting do you do?

It depends. I rewrote the ending of Farewell to Arms, the last page of it, thirty-nine times before I was satisfied.

Was there some technical problem there? What was it that had stumped you?

Getting the words right.[87] (p. 39)

As most of the interviews were undertaken with experienced writers whose work took place mainly before the wide adoption of computers, very few said that they were using computers for composing or for revisions. King, however, had some interesting views on the ways in which using a computer was different:

One of the ways the computer has changed the way I work is that I have a much greater tendency to edit 'in the camera' to make changes on screen. With Cell that's what I did. I read it over, I had editorial corrections, I was able to make my own corrections, and to me that's like ice skating. It's an OK way to do the work, but it isn't optimal. With Lisey I had the copy beside the computer and I created blank documents and retyped the whole thing. To me that's like swimming, and that's preferable. It's like you're writing the book over again. It's literally a rewriting.[88]

Views on pens and paper versus keyboards seemed to be divided. Having begun the chapter with Hughes, it is appropriate to end with his romantic view of the pen or the pencil, a view that would perhaps have received a sympathetic hearing from a significant number of the writers who were interviewed:

I realized instantly that when I composed directly onto the typewriter my sentences became three times as long, much longer. My subordinate clauses flowered and multiplied and ramified away down the length of the page, all much more eloquently than anything I would have written by hand . . . When you sit with your pen, every year of your life is right there, wired into the communication between your brain and your writing hand . . . Maybe what I'm saying applies only to those who have gone through the long conditioning of writing only with a pen or pencil up through their mid-twenties. For those who start early on a typewriter or, these days, on a computer screen, things must be different . . . Maybe the crucial element in handwriting is that the hand is simultaneously drawing. I know I'm very conscious of hidden imagery in handwriting – a subtext of a rudimentary picture language. Perhaps that tends to enforce more cooperation from the other side of the brain. And perhaps that extra load of right-brain suggestions prompts a different succession of words and ideas.[89]

As I show in Chapter 7, there is some neuro-scientific evidence linking the importance of the tools of writing with the signs that authors create.

*

The thinking for a new piece of writing is at first highly abstract. Sometimes barely conscious thoughts at all, more a sense that there might be something emerging. For many writers, and essential for the most eminent writers, the

[87] Hemingway, *Paris Review Interviews*, Vol., 39.
[88] King, *Paris Review Interviews*, Vol. 2, 481.
[89] Hughes, *Paris Review Interviews*, Vol. 3, 277.

intent to conceive something original is paramount. The intended readership is another vital element that will have profound consequences for the nature of the writing. For a very small minority of writers, their contribution is to human civilisation, through the birth and immortality of a work. For all writers, the need for sufficient time to think about the nature of the contribution, not just the possible topics for writing, is an important element. Although the impulse to engage daily with the process of writing, to get on with the task, needs to be heeded (and is sometimes a technique for generating an idea), the time spent thinking about the overall concept, is also important. A sense of realism about what a piece of writing might achieve is part of this thinking.

Generating ideas for writing is a creative process, and it is a creative process that needs some explicit understanding. If writers believe that creativity means the production of something that has in every sense never been seen or heard before, then they will struggle to write. But if they understand that all writers, indeed all artists, deliberately build on existing traditions of work in their field in order to produce something original, they are more likely to write well. The intent is to 'make others believe that it was not made but rather simply arose',[90] a kind of alchemy perhaps.

For the novelist, character is one of the most important elements needed to generate ideas and sustain writing. The bonds that writers form with their characters seem so strong it is often as if the characters become real people. In a way, this is perhaps akin to the techniques of the method actor. Building fictional characters on the observed characteristics of real people is common. And although characters are important, they also need to exist in a created social and cultural milieu, which is related to the writer's real experiences of life. The characters also need to encounter problems, predicaments, challenges; in other words they need to encounter life.

Characters are not just important for their personalities; they are a vital element that brings structural coherence to a story. Structural coherence is vital to any text. For non-fiction, it is reflected in the cumulative building of lines of argument that are driven through to the concluding words. Characters can also be part of non-fiction. The examples, vignettes, and case studies of non-fiction writing often depict people and their lives. The words of these 'characters' may, for example, have come originally from audio recordings but these words still have to be moulded and crafted by the writer. And questions about authorial presence in the text are relevant to fiction and non-fiction narratives alike.

Other texts are also a fundamental part of generating ideas for writing. In the context of education, Margaret Meek titled one of her books *How Texts Teach What Readers Learn*. We might rephrase that to 'how texts teach what writers

[90] Mann, *Doctor Faustus*, 192.

write'. For eminent writers this is even more important than the advice to 'read like a writer'; it is about trying to *inhabit* the world of another writer. Reading like a writer is indeed helpful because it is the ability to suspend the emotional engagement that the writer hopes to draw you into (the alchemy), or suspend the thrilling ride of an intellectual argument, so that you can see structures, language use, organising principles, philosophical underpinnings. Inhabiting the world of the writer should lead to the courage to take risks and to create your own voice because you have developed the 'Ears. Ears. To hear the language', a sense which for Maya Angelou[91] came in part from the 'musical beauty of the language of the Bible' and her ability to speak many languages. Texts that have stood the test of time, the classics, but the classics that are personally meaningful to each individual writer, are an essential influence for many writers. However, the search for texts and authors, that will come to be a strong influence on the writer, is also a search of the widest possible range, that supports the drive for originality. The magpie mentality to locate and save interesting texts, including extracts, may be part of this, and like Kerouac's letter, for some the search leads to that single text that 'blows you away'.

The task of finding and selecting the meanings to communicate, initially at the level of the whole contribution that the writing might make, then to increasingly smaller details, is fundamental to the process of writing. Establishing the overall ideas for writing is a complex process of thought. All other elements of the techniques of writing have to be sidelined while the ideas are formed, refined, and pursued relentlessly. But ultimately the ideas have to be tested through the physical writing of words and sentences. There is an intimate and recursive relationship between the ideas to be expressed, their expression in words, the further comparison between the words and the idea, and the subsequent editing of words.

The difficulties in expressing orally the subtleties of the craft of writing are alleviated for many writers through musical metaphors. For example, Angelou's ears for language were attuned through her musical ear. In addition to metaphorical explanations, there are also many direct links between writing music and writing text. Improvisation, as a musical process, was seen as similar to the process of writing. In music, improvisation is constrained by the limits of musical structure and the physical demands of singing or playing an instrument. Similarly, in writing the textual structure and the limits of the author's physical capacity to produce the words act as boundaries. Understanding and working with these boundaries is a necessary part of a satisfactory composition. The musical concept of rhythm is most prominent in the spoken language of characters (although the narrator's voice must also have the right rhythm); for non-fiction, rhythm comes through the building blocks of the argument: when

[91] Angelou, *Paris Review Interviews*, Vol. 4, 255. Born 1928, St Louis, Missouri, USA.

to subtly repeat points, how one point follows the next without the need for clumsy coordinating phrases. The melodies of music are the themes of writing; the chords are the layers of meanings; and the language must have the right rhythms. Many writers are technically proficient but can they 'blow like the tenor man'?

Although writing is for many hours, days, weeks, months, and years a solitary pursuit, it is also punctuated by the social context of the writer's personal and professional life. The first reader, when the writer has decided some text is ready, is so often someone personally close. Once publication approaches, the number of people with whom the writer interacts grows (and forms like writing for films and television are generally more collaborative). There are also significant risks with not sharing writing with others because of the almost impossible task writers face in distancing themselves sufficiently from their writing to take an objective and critical view.

Another major social factor for writers, and a significant influence on their writing, is the work they do to help other writers: formal teaching is a very important part of this. The idea that you learn more about your own writing by teaching others is borne out in the interviews. This suggests that in order to write well writers need to share their craft with others. Although not all writers can engage in formal teaching of writing, there are many opportunities for volunteering, for example, to support young people's writing. If writers teach others in these ways, they may also reflect on the extent to which the creativity of writing can be taught. It is not the final answer to the conundrum of whether creativity can be taught that matters as much as the process of actively thinking about the place of creativity in writing.

5 Creativity and Writing

Writing is one of the most potent forms of creative expression, as the work of some of the greatest writers has shown. One dimension of judgements about creativity is the test of time, measured in hundreds of years for the highest levels of creativity. The creative expression that is a part of written composition is also present in a range of other forms. Visual art, dance, architecture, drama, and music all involve creative composition of drawings, paintings, sculptures, dances, buildings, and music. A fundamental element of composition is the need for the composer to generate original ideas from a blank space: whether page (manuscript or screen), canvas, or metaphorical slate. As I mentioned in the previous chapter Thomas Mann articulates the special creativity of artists beautifully in his novel *Doctor Faustus*, inspired by the Faust legend, a legend that has itself been subject to a range of literary and musical interpretations.

Another example of a very high level of creativity, in text and music combined, is Franz Joseph Haydn's oratorio *The Creation*. In addition to the importance of *The Creation* as a representation of creativity, it is an interesting example for a number of reasons. Its subject is creativity, or more accurately, creation itself. *The Creation* also draws on what is perhaps the most influential text ever written: the Bible, a work which raises profound philosophical questions about the role played by creativity in its own composition. What's more, the Book of Genesis describes what many people would see as the ultimate creative act: God's creation of the universe and all living things.

> In the beginning God created the heaven and the earth. And the earth was without form, and void; and darkness was upon the face of the deep. And the Spirit of God moved upon the face of the waters. And God said, Let there be light: and there was light. And God saw the light, that it was good: and God divided the light from the darkness.

For the time of its composition (1798), the beginning of *The Creation* represented a particularly original opening for a piece of western classical music. The first page of the full score reveals Haydn's depiction of 'the representation of chaos'. In the first movement, Haydn's music captures the world 'without form or void', in an extract which revolutionised the harmonic landscape of music. Building on the representation of chaos, the voices and orchestral accompaniment moves inexorably to the words, 'and, there, was . . . LIGHT!' The signification of the word 'light' is matched by musical harmony, dynamics, and orchestration of such brilliance and power that even those who know the piece well continue to be moved and even startled during its performance. It is the addition of words to music, such as in opera and songs more widely, that provokes the dramatic transformation of meaning-making possibilities in the creative work.

This chapter begins with a topic that is both seminal to the creativity research field but also of enduring importance: how creativity might be defined. As part of Vygotsky's contribution to socio-cultural theory, he wrote an important paper on creativity and imagination with which I begin a theoretical exploration of creativity. The modern era of creativity research, from the 1950s onwards, is reviewed, including some of the latest advances in cognitive neuroscience. The final part of the chapter reports for the first time the findings of a longitudinal study of creativity and writing in young people.

Defining Creativity

Vygotsky's *Imagination and Creativity in Childhood* begins with a powerful assertion:

> Any human act that gives rise to something new is referred to as a creative act, regardless of whether what is created is a physical object or some mental or emotional construct that lives within the person who created it and is known only to him.[1]

This all-embracing definition of 'any human act' emphasises originality as the creation of 'something new'. However if the creativity 'lives within the person who created it and is known only to him' the person cannot be sure something 'new' has been created. Newness is dependent, to varying degrees, on comparison. Vygotsky emphasised that the creation of something new is a result of a particular kind of thinking that uses previous experience recorded in memory in a 'creative or combinatorial' way. The example of Vygotsky imagining the future life of humanity under socialism is offered. As humanity under socialism has never existed, he has to combine his experience of other forms of political ideology in order to imagine the new condition. He termed this combination of the known with the unknown, 'imagination or fantasy'. Vygotsky was influenced by Theodule Ribot's idea that the process of invention is centrally about imagination (Ribot did not use the term 'creativity').

According to Vygotsky, everyday creativity is the rule not the exception reserved for a few selected individuals recognised through history. The

[1] Vygotsky, 'Imagination and Creativity in Childhood', 7.

example he gives exemplifies imagination rather than creativity, something which is closely linked to creativity but for reasons I will advance is not synonymous with creativity.

A child who sits astride a stick and pretends to be riding a horse; a little girl who plays with a doll and imagines she is its mother; a boy who in his games becomes a pirate, a soldier, or a sailor, all these children at play represent examples of the most authentic, truest creativity.[2]

One of the reasons that this kind of play in childhood is difficult to describe as 'new' is because it is a widely shared, and arguably normal trait of childhood.

In the same academic paper, Vygotsky had some prescient thoughts about writing, teaching, and creativity. He was critical of the teacher assigning a topic for writing, which children had to write about in the style of adults because,

It was a rare case that this work was linked with a goal that was understandable, interesting, and within the capacity of the children. The teachers who thus incorrectly guided their pupils' literary creativity, often killed the spontaneous beauty, individuality, and vitality of children's language and impeded their mastery of written language as a special way of expressing one's thoughts and feelings. Instead, the children developed, to use Blonskii's expression, the type of school jargon that is produced by the purely mechanical inculcation of children with the artificial bookish language of adults.[3]

A 'case study' is then described by Vygotsky, remarkable because it was Leo Tolstoy who wrote the case study based on an experience he had working with 'peasant children' to encourage their creative writing.[4] Tolstoy's initial approach to teaching writing was to set writing topics for the children, rather like the teachers described by Vygotsky. Dissatisfied with the children's progress, Tolstoy changed his approach, and was so amazed by the change in the children that he said of the work of one of the children in particular,

It seemed very strange to me that a half-literate peasant boy would suddenly show such conscious artistry, a level of development so high that Goethe couldn't reach it. It seemed so strange and humiliating that I, the author of [*Childhood*], which has enjoyed some success and has been acknowledged by the educated public to show artistic talent, not only could not do anything to help or instruct eleven-year-old Semka or Fedka, but that it was merely a fortunate burst of inspiration that allowed me to follow and understand them. It seemed so strange to me, that I didn't believe what happened yesterday.[5]

[2] Vygotsky, 'Imagination and Creativity in Childhood', 11.

[3] Vygotsky, 'Imagination and Creativity in Childhood', 45.

[4] Described in an article called, '"Who should learn to write from whom: peasant children from us, or us from them?" [Komu u kogo uchit'sia pisat'—krest'ianskikh rebiatam u nas ili nam u krest'ianskikh rebiat].'

[5] Vygotsky, 'Imagination and Creativity in Childhood', 48.

In order to achieve these results, Tolstoy had changed his approach to teaching by starting the creativity for a new story though collaboration with the children. He encouraged the children to suggest ideas which Tolstoy wrote down for them (this technique is now common in early years classrooms and is known as 'scribing for the child' or 'teacher as scribe'). One child in particular became so motivated that he developed his ear for particular language constructions to the extent that he became angry if Tolstoy did not write the words exactly as the child had intended. Vygotsky observed that the order of words 'is to literature what melody is to music, or pattern is to a picture'.[6] On the basis of his experience Tolstoy created a theory of creative writing teaching:

> All he needed from me was the material in order to fill it out harmoniously and completely. As soon as I gave him complete freedom, stopped trying to instruct him, he wrote a poetic work whose like had never been seen in Russian literature. And thus, I am convinced, we must not try to teach children in general and particularly peasant children how to write and compose, how to set about writing. If what I did to attain this goal can be called techniques, then these techniques were as follows. First: offer the greatest and widest choice of topics, without selecting those you think are particularly suited to children, but proposing the most serious topics that interest you yourself. Second: give the children works by children to read as models, and only such works. Third (of particular importance): never criticize the child when looking over his composition, either for neatness, penmanship, spelling, and especially not for the structure of sentences or logic. Fourth: because the difficulty of creative writing lies not in the length or content, but in the artistic value of the topic, then the sequence in which the topics are presented must be determined not by length, nor content, nor language, but by the nature of the mechanism underlying the creative work.[7]

As I show in Chapter 6, Tolstoy's pedagogical theory has many resonances with what we now know from research is effective in the teaching of writing. For example, the importance of choice and decision-making, using models of writing, and attending carefully to the nature of feedback to children about their writing.

Creativity research in the modern era can, in relation to psychological work, can be traced back to the presidential address to the American Psychological Association (APA) in 1950.

> The subject of creativity has been neglected by psychologists. The immediate problem has two aspects. (1) How can we discover creative promise in our children and our youth? (2) How can we promote the development of creative personalities? Creative talent cannot be accounted for adequately in terms of IQ. A new way of thinking about creativity and creative productivity is seen in the factorial conceptions of personality. By application of factor analysis a fruitful exploratory approach can be made. Carefully constructed hypotheses concerning primary abilities will lead to the use of novel types

[6] Vygotsky, 'Imagination and Creativity in Childhood', 49.
[7] Vygotsky, 'Imagination and Creativity in Childhood', 49.

of tests. New factors will be discovered that will provide us with means to select individuals with creative personalities. The properties of primary abilities should be studied to improve educational methods and further their utilization.[8]

One of the powerful influences on the drive towards creativity in this period was American government fear about military supremacy.[9] Such fear resulted in funding from government for projects that might result in enhanced creativity in pupils, and citizens more widely, who might provide creative solutions to military problems. The feelings of discomfort that some feel about the overall purpose for the creativity research funding in this period of US history links with a line of debate in the creativity field that questions whether something that is evil can be regarded as creative. This is a debate that importantly, for my purposes, also raises the question of the *value* of any creative act and its outcomes. As is clear from the APA presidential address, creativity was to become a significant area of study.

In 1953, Morris Stein published a paper that articulated a number of key parameters that are entirely relevant today. Stein's interest in creativity was broad including personality and processes, and how these might relate to culture and society. Stein's definition of creativity was 'The creative work is a novel work that is accepted as tenable or useful or satisfying by a group in some point in time.'[10] His idea of novelty recognised the use of existing knowledge, but also that to be creative the work has to have elements that are new. Stein also dealt directly with children's creativity, recognising, for example, that the child who fixes something on their bike for the first time exhibits some of the characteristics of creativity but is distinguished by being regarded through an internal frame of reference for the creativity rather than an external frame. Recognition that creativity exists in different areas of human endeavour, such as physics or art, and that creativity is different in these areas caused by the interaction between the individual person and their external environment for creativity was also drawn attention to by Stein.

As far as *value* as a definitional construct of creativity Stein identified and equated the following concepts: tenable, in relation to ideas; useful, in relation to things; and satisfying in relation to aesthetic experiences. And of vital importance, in contradiction to Vygotsky's idea of a construct that lives within the person who created it and is known only to him:

My essential purpose here is to develop the thesis that the results of the creative process must be communicated to others. Communication with the self alone is insufficient. The creative person must achieve, as Sullivan says in another context, 'consensual validation'.[11]

[8] Guilford, 'Creativity', 444–454.
[9] Feldman and Benjamin, 'Creativity and Education', 319–336.
[10] Stein, 'Creativity and Culture', 311. [11] Stein, 'Creativity and Culture', 316.

In a further remarkably prescient observation, taking into account Stein's background as a psychologist rather than an educator, he noted the capacity of culture to either limit creativity or to provide spaces for creativity, and commented specifically about children and their education:

> A culture also fosters creativity to the extent that its parent-child relationships and child-rearing techniques do or do not result in the setting up of rigid boundaries in the inner personal regions. Techniques that result in excessive repression or guilt restrict internal freedom and interfere with the process of hypothesis formation. Attention must also be directed toward the broader aspects of education. For example, does the culture tolerate deviation from the traditional, the status quo, or does it insist upon conformity, whether in politics, science, or at school? Does the culture permit the individual to seek new experiences on his own, or do the bearers of culture (parents, teachers, and so on) 'spoon-feed' the young so that they constantly find ready-made solutions available to them as they come upon a situation that is lacking in closure? Furthermore, to what extent do the adults accept or reward and thus reinforce the creative experience that the individual has had? For example, in the case I spoke of earlier – the child who fixed his tricycle bell – his experience could have been handled either by a depreciation of his experience and verbalized as, 'Oh, anyone could have done that!' or the magnitude of his experience for himself could have been recognized and he could have been encouraged to seek similar experiences in the future. Experiences of this kind should be studied both in the home and in formal educational systems.[12]

Psychological research through the 1970s and 80s was largely concerned with more detailed attempts to define and ultimately measure creativity. The 'Torrance tests of creativity' were one of the most well-known examples of such measurement. This work was in the tradition of psychometric assessment that resulted in the frequently cited ideas of 'technological inventiveness' and 'ideational fluency'.[13] However, like so many standardised tests the Torrance tests of creativity came under increasing criticism due to the telling argument that creativity was much more complex than even these well-thought-through tests were showing.

Some thirty years after the address to the APA and Stein's paper, a notable definition arising from this kind of psychological perspective was Vernon's: 'Creativity means a person's capacity to produce new or original ideas, insights, restructurings, inventions, or artistic objects, which are accepted by experts as being of scientific, aesthetic, social, or technological value.'[14] Key ideas that are part of Vernon's definition included the idea of creativity as part of an individual person's capacity but also the notion of acceptance by others as part of how creativity is defined, and the notion of the creativity being valued by such 'experts'.

[12] Stein, 'Creativity and Culture', 319.
[13] Feldman and Benjamin, 'Creativity and Education', 319–336.
[14] Vernon, 'The Nature-Nurture Problem in Creativity', 93–110.

In the 1990s another important creativity theorist Csikszentmihályi focused on personality, motivation, and the discovery of new problems.[15] His research with several hundred artists sought to understand why some produced work that would be judged to be creative, while others did not. As far as personality was concerned, it was found that more creative student artists tended to be self-sufficient and not particularly interested in social norms or acceptance and tended to exhibit greater sensitivity and openness to experiences and impulses. However, the trait that most consistently distinguished these artists from others was 'a cold and aloof disposition'.[16]

Like other researchers Csikszentmihályi and his team failed to find any relationship between traditional measures of intelligence and criteria for creative accomplishment. Csikszentmihályi realised that for many creative individuals the *formulation* of a problem is more important than its solution. Thus he set out to investigate the *discovery orientation* of artists. When presented with visually interesting objects and drawing materials, a group of students were encouraged to do what they wanted, and finish when they had produced a drawing that they liked. The variables used to measure the students' discovery orientation included the number of objects that they touched: the higher the number the more likely the problem was being approached from a discovery orientation. Another variable was the number of changes the person introduced into the drawing process. The established artists and teachers who rated the drawings, rated those produced by students who had used discovery orientation more highly in terms of originality than those produced by students who had used a more predictable problem-solving approach. In terms of artistic career success some seven years later, the correlation was still significant.

Csikszentmihályi's well-known 'systems perspective'[17] viewed creativity as the result of interaction between three subsystems: the person, the field, and the domain. The domain is a system that has a set of rules. This might be a subject like mathematics, or a religion, a game, or a sport. For example western classical music is a 'domain' that requires the composition of sound and silence to create pieces of music for the benefit of performers and audiences. The 'field' is part of the social system which has the power to influence the structure of the domain. The most important function of the field is to maintain the domain as it is, but the field will also act as a gatekeeper to allow changes to the domain to take place. The role of the person is to create ideas that lead to variations in the domain as judged by the field. Variations of this kind represent exceptional creativity. Haydn's

[15] Csikszentmihályi, 'The Domain of Creativity'.
[16] Csikszentmihályi, 'The Domain of Creativity', 192.
[17] Csikszentmihályi, 'The Domain of Creativity', 205.

compositions, including *The Creation*, but in particular his contribution to the invention of the string quartet form, have been judged by the field, for more than two hundred years, to have transformed the domain of western classical music.

The importance of processes of judgement, and the importance of heuristic rather than algorithmic processes, was taken forward by other researchers: for example, by using the judgements of practising poets to assess creativity in the context of poetry writing tasks.[18] Teresa Amabile has made a significant contribution to the creativity research field. Because of her dissatisfaction with standardised creativity tests, she used tests/activities that required the creation of some kind of real-world product, for example, making paper collages or writing poems such as cinquains or haikus. These were then judged by experts, such as studio artists or practising poets, who rated the collages for creativity and other dimensions. Like Stein Amabile called this process *consensual assessment.*[19] The conceptual definition of creativity that she used was 'A product or response will be judged as creative to the extent that (a) it is both a novel and appropriate, useful, correct, or valuable response to the task at hand, and (b) the task is heuristic rather than algorithmic'.[20] Amabile made the point that, although creativity is often very difficult for people ('judges') to define, they can recognise creativity when they see it. They also have considerable agreement about their judgements, particularly with products, but less so with creativity in persons or creative processes. She also argued, correctly in my view, that creativity is a continuous rather than discontinuous quality which begins at one end of the creative continuum with children's every-day creativity, and ends with Haydn and Hemingway at the other end. The difference is not the presence of creativity per se but the ability, cognitive style, motivational levels, and circumstances of the different people concerned.

From the 2000s onwards, cognitive work on creativity was informed by neuroscientific findings. Important evidence of the way in which coordinated areas of the brain handle creativity comes from Rex Jung and colleagues. One of their research papers begins with an intriguing view of the story of definitions of creativity with the argument that an encompassing definition results in 'unedifying academic arguments'. As a comparison they claimed that 'gene' had no commonly accepted definition, but in spite of this, research was still done. However, having opened this debate, and consistent with my position in this chapter, they settle on,

[18] Amabile, 'Motivation and Creativity: Effects of Motivational Orientation on Creative Writers', 393–99; Csikszentmihályi, 'The Domain of Creativity', 190–214.

[19] Amabile, 'Social Psychology of Creativity', 997–1013.

[20] Amabile, 'Social Psychology of Creativity', 66.

a broadly accepted definition of creativity, which refers to *the production of something both novel and useful* . . . This definition is plausible, is broadly applicable, and would appear to hold true across much of evolutionary time. As such, it also refers to the workings of the brain.[21]

The aim of Jung et al.'s work was to approximate how creative cognition might be related to the neurology of the human brain, as established through brain imaging research using a range of techniques. They debunk the idea that cognitive functions such as creativity happen in discrete zones of the brain, arguing instead that the ideas of networks of hubs is a more appropriate metaphor. Indeed the human brain is optimised to bind together information from multiple sources. The important ideas of stimulus-dependent thought versus stimulus-independent thought, and attention switching between salient environmental stimuli are features of such networks. Task-unrelated thoughts, or perhaps something akin to day-dreaming, do appear to be an important part of thinking that supports creativity. The authors propose the idea of a default mode network (DMN) that, through blind variation and selective retention (BVSR) (measured by tests of divergent and convergent thinking respectively), serves to take the person's informed guesses towards increasingly probable solutions. If the DMN supports an uninhibited search for things novel and of value, then a cognitive control network (CCN) is used in the refinement and selective retention of some ideas above others.

As far as further links between language and music are concerned, one rather interesting neuroscientific study looked at the improvisation processes of jazz musicians. Charles Limb and Allen Braun made the point that improvisation as a feature of human behaviour occurs not just in music but is also is closely related both to creativity 'and perhaps most importantly, the use of natural language, all of which are unscripted behaviors that capitalize on the generative capacity of the brain'.[22] The most important implication of this research for the practice of writing was to underline the vital importance of opportunities for thinking in a way that is unstructured in order to allow the brain the time and space it needs to produce original thoughts.

There is, though, one issue with the methodology of this research. It relies on the hypothesis that the improvisation of the jazz musician, or as Kerouac said, 'blowing like the tenor man', is the most typical form of creative processes. It was argued by the authors that the live spontaneity of improvisation was the key. But creativity is not just moments of spontaneity, it is also long periods of intensive hard work. The writer who creates the ground-breaking new book has spent months and years crafting it. Even the relative spontaneity of the main

[21] Jung, Brittany, Carrasco, and Flores, 'The Structure of Creative Cognition in the Human Brain', 1.

[22] Limb, C. J., and Braun, A. R. 'Neural Substrates of Spontaneous Musical Performance', 1.

idea behind the book is not static. In fact, during the processes of creating the book, the main idea may become modified as a result of the processes of writing. Similarly the classical music composer takes extended periods of time to write the music. This time may involve testing sections of the emerging music, perhaps on a keyboard, in order to support the revisions. Longitudinal research is needed to try and capture more of the extended processes that characterise much creativity. Research on musical composition processes, focused on musically creative people (as identified by the people themselves), found evidence that networks of specific regions in the brain linked, a) domain-general capacities (e.g. defocusing to allow free flow of ideas); b) domain-specific knowledge and skills (developed through years of practice), and c) emotion-affiliated thoughts, 'facilitate and motivate the drive to create music'.[23]

Whether it is possible to adequately define creativity, and what such definitions might be remains a contested issue. However, there are two key features and a key process that are widely acknowledged, including in creativity theory and in research from different traditions, wider sources such as dictionaries, and in people's commonly held perceptions: *originality* and *value*, as judged by people with appropriate knowledge.

The proposition of originality and value as fundamental to creativity is sometimes challenged on the basis that not everyone can produce something that is original. However, the definitional concept of originality for creativity recognises that all creative processes, products, and acts derive from a history in their respective context, fields, and traditions so to some degree are imitative.[24] The definition also recognises that even a young child in the production of, for example, a piece of writing can produce something that is original when assessed by people with appropriate expertise to make such judgements.

The idea of value is less well researched. It immediately raises the question of value to whom? At the level of a young child's creativity, the value is likely to be mainly to the individual child, possibly to peers, and in the eyes of a perceptive adult. But for a teacher, a child's creativity can also be judged to be of value more generally through comparison of the child's writing with typical child development as a result of the teacher's knowledge. Occasionally, children demonstrate a more profound and rare form of creativity with wider appeal, such as the creativity of the child described by Tolstoy earlier in this chapter.

Determination of originality and value requires a process of consensual judgement by appropriately qualified people. So it is entirely possible that a

23 Bashwiner, Wertz, Flores, and Jung, 'Musical Creativity "Revealed" in Brain Structure', 1–8.
24 Banaji and Burn, *The Rhetorics of Creativity*.

child could demonstrate creativity as judged by peers and/or by teachers, teaching assistants, and parents/carers. The definition does not imply any particular level of creativity because that is dependent on the kind of originality being judged. It may be that judgements are being made in relation to the kind of creativity that might stand the test of time, perhaps, for example, as part of consideration for a Nobel prize. Equally it may be that the judgements are being made by a teacher and a researcher about a piece of writing that a child has carried out.

Teaching and Fostering Creativity

A fundamental consideration in teaching the originality and value that are part of creativity is the kinds of conditions that are likely to promote or inhibit learners' creativity development. One condition is the extent to which learners are motivated to create. Motivation is something that can be facilitated by teachers and by education systems. Research has shown that intrinsic motivation enhances creativity, whereas extrinsic motivation, stimulated by an external goal, can be a 'killer' of creativity. To take an example from education, 'high stakes' school testing systems (that use pupil test scores to hold teachers accountable and which are published in league tables, for example in England) have a negative effect on intrinsic motivation because the system is heavily focused on the extrinsic factors related to the high stakes tests. However, this negative effect can be mitigated by 'immunisation procedures'.[25] These procedures involve teachers helping children to understand the value of intrinsic motivation, in spite of a range of extrinsic motivators that may be present in classrooms. However, the research showed that the immunisation approach only maintained baseline motivation and creativity, not the unusually high levels of intrinsic motivation and creativity that are possible in the ideal classroom environment.

The translation of research findings, such as those about motivation and creativity, into teachers' and schools' practices is not always made clear. However, Hennessey advocates the 'open classroom' of the 1970s in America, inspired by the British infant classroom model of the 1960s, as the ideal practical realisation of what she and her colleagues have discovered about the optimal classroom conditions for creativity. Some of the features of the infant classroom model were a strong focus on arts subjects; daily opportunities provided for children's free play; a high degree of autonomy for children in their classroom activities; child-centred teaching; hands-on learning; and conceptual links made between different subjects of the curriculum through topic-based planning.

[25] Hennessey, 'Intrinsic Motivation and Creativity in the Classroom', 343.

A recent contribution from educational scholarship has been to question what is meant by 'experts' in relation to consensual judgement of creativity, a contribution that links with ideas such as creativity vs. Creativity, or everyday creativity vs. 'sublime' creativity.[26] As part of this work, Russell Jones and I have argued that such judgements can be made by children and young people themselves, by their teachers, and by others with the capacity to make informed judgements in relation to children's development.[27]

There are hundreds of programmes that claim to enhance or 'teach' creativity. These range from detailed approaches carried out over quite lengthy periods of time to specific techniques, such as SCAMPER, which encourages novelty by Substituting, Combining, Adapting, Magnifying, Putting to a different use, Eliminating, and Rearranging/Reversing.[28] Another example is the use of brainstorming which has been extended to include more structured ways of generating ideas, such as mind-maps and other visual techniques which use hierarchies of categories. Many of the packages begin their lives in the business sector, such as Edward de Bono's lateral thinking approach. A number of factors had been identified which focused on the need to:

- Reward curiosity and exploration;
- Build motivation, particularly internal motivation;
- Encourage risk-taking;
- Have high expectations/beliefs about the creative potential of students: this applies to both teachers' views of their pupils, and pupils' own self-image;
- Give opportunities for choice and discovery;
- Develop students' self-management skills; and
- Support domain-specific knowledge: pupils need to understand as much as possible about the domain (e.g. the subject area) that they are doing the creative work in.[29]

It appears that creativity can be developed, for example, by the ways that teachers and other adults work with pupils and students. However, In spite of great interest in the area, and much financial success for the designers of some approaches, it was argued from a psychological perspective that 'A clear, unequivocal, and incontestable answer to the question of how creativity can be enhanced has not been found.'[30] More recent research has used the definitional concepts of originality and value, as judged though consensual assessment, to examine creativity in writing. The final half of this chapter is an example of a three-year research and development project that colleagues and I worked on for which creativity and writing were central.

[26] Craft, *Creativity across the Primary Curriculum*.
[27] Jones and Wyse, *Creativity in the Primary Curriculum*.
[28] Cropley, *Creativity in Education and Learning*. [29] Nicholson, 'Enhancing Creativity', 407.
[30] Nicholson, 'Enhancing Creativity', 409.

Creativity, Writing, and *The Ministry of Stories*

In the afternoon sun two boys meandered their way down Valencia street. Too-familiar shop fronts only occasionally merited a glance. Even the skeletal bike, locked to a parking meter with no wheels, brakes, chain, wasn't enough to detain them.

'What you wanna do?'

'Dunno'

'Go to yours?'

'Maybe.'

More shops, familiar names selling unfamiliar products, *Ginko, Aggregate Supplies*.

A plastic bottle was sport for a minute until it flipped into the entrance way to a shop door. The boys paused:

826 Valencia: SAN FRANCISCO'S ONLY INDEPENDENT PIRATE SUPPLY STORE (for the working buccaneer).

'Leon told me about this place.'

'Let's have a look.'

Now inside there was plenty to detain them: peg legs; arm hooks; eye patches; replacement eyes; planks sold by the foot; the treasure vat.

A man with peg leg and eye patch approached them. The parrot on his shoulder squawked, 'pieces to write, pieces to write'. Long John Silver's hooked arm motioned smoothly from left to right across the scene of young people and adults talking, laughing, concentrating, thinking, and writing.

'You brave enough me hearties?'

They shrugged their shoulders and smiled; they were hooked.

That's how I imagine some children and young people come across *826Valencia*, novelist Dave Egger's and educator Ninive Calegari's first writing centre, in San Francisco. Just like the other writers I've talked about in this book, Dave Eggers had strong interests in education. His mother was a teacher, his sister became a teacher, as did many of Egger's friends from college. As he worked on his Pulitzer Prize–winning book *A Heartbreaking Work of Staggering Genius*, he was becoming increasingly aware of what his friends and family were telling him about teaching in the underfunded schools in the US. The deprived kids that they taught – including those with English as an additional language and those with special needs – needed more one-to-one attention.[31]

The sizes of classes in secondary and elementary/primary schools are such that teachers are physically unable to give individual pupils as much attention

[31] Information about Eggers and 826 Valencia taken from Ted Talk: Eggers, D. 'Dave Eggers' Wish: Once Upon a School'. TED, 2011.

as they would like. Eggers wanted to try and help pupils with writing, and with one-to-one attention. As part of his work as a writer, he was in contact with other people who were 'interested in the primacy of the written word', and who lived near Eggers in Brooklyn. Many of them worked nonstandard work hours just as Eggers did (it appears he was more of the Kerouac school of writing routines, saying he worked from midnight to five in the morning when writing *A Heartbreaking Work*). Eggers discovered that creative and talented people who had time would be happy to come and help young people with their writing.

The first thing Eggers needed was a location for a writing centre. He found a space in San Francisco's appositely named Mission District. Because of a technicality about the street, Eggers was informed that the 'shop' must be used for retail. This first headache was solved because the physical space and the wood shapes discovered during the renovation works suggested old ships, and the idea of a pirate shop was born (although never really the intention, the shop now makes enough money to pay the rent and one full-time member of staff). Above the shop front, as part of the stone work that is the face of the building, Eggers commissioned a mural by Chris Ware.[32] The circular shape that is at the top of the stone work suggested the sun to Ware (in fact, the sun really does shine through the hole at the right time of day). The mural depicts the developments of humans, from ancient peoples battling the elements, to building the first teepee-like dwellings, and on to group communication, and finally the invention of the printed word and books. Ware explained:

> I didn't want it to make anyone 'feel good', especially in that typically moralistic 'hands across the water' sort of way, . . . I especially wanted it to be something that people living in the neighbourhood could look at day after day and hopefully not tire of too quickly. I really hoped whomever might happen to come across it would find something that showed a respect for their intelligence, and didn't force-feed them any 'message'.[33]

So the renovation was complete, and all the eager volunteers needed was children and young people. But none came. Eggers and 12 of his friends waited for weeks and weeks. He jokes, 'Maybe there was a trust gap. We were working behind a pirates supply store!'[34] So he persuaded a friend who was an educator to move from Mexico City. She made inroads with teachers, parents, and students. By 2008 Valencia had 1,400 volunteers on the roster. In addition to the drop-in workshop in Valencia 826, the organisation also works directly with schools.

[32] The shop front can be seen here: http://826valencia.org/about/history/.

[33] Thompson, Eggers, and Ware, '826 Valencia: Chris Ware's New Mural Tells the Story of the Human Race'.

[34] Eggers, 'Dave Eggers' Wish: Once Upon a School'.

Soon the idea spread. 'Brooklyn Superhero Supply' a Costco for superheroes, including 'Muscles in heavy syrup', a 'Capery' where the caped crusaders can walk up the steel steps and get the cape fanned on all sides. And in Los Angeles THE ECHO PARK TIME TRAVEL MART; WHENEVER YOU ARE, WE'RE ALREADY THEN. Like a 7–11 for time travellers, the machine that dispenses 'Time-Freezy Hyper Slush' features a sign saying, OUT OF ORDER, COME BACK YESTERDAY. Internationally, similar things were happening, for example, in Ireland *Fighting Words* started by Roddy Doyle.

The writer Nick Hornby wondered if Valencia 826 could be replicated in London so *The Ministry of Stories* (MoS) was founded in 2010 by Nick Hornby, Lucy MacNab, and Ben Payne. The MoS building is in Hoxton, London. The area is typical of many areas in London where there are significant levels of deprivation mixed with pockets of affluence, a situation that creates a dynamic mix of families from a wide range of cultural backgrounds. The MoS is located in *Hoxton Street Monster Supplies*, which has included products such as Salt made from tears of sorrow; Your Story Starts Here (a notebook with advice on writing written by children); Zombie Fresh Mints; Cubed Earwax; Milk Tooth Chocolate; and a range of Tinned Fear (stories in tins) including Escalating Panic and The Heebie-Jeebies. Behind the Monster Supplies shop-front in Hoxton Street is the writing workshop space. This includes the mysterious room where *The Chief* works, who is never seen but is occasionally heard on the Tannoy. The design replicates to some extent a kind of World War 2 bunker, including the playing of music of the period in the background giving a real nostalgic feel.

In addition to the regular drop-in sessions that happen three times a week, the MoS has a wide range of bespoke projects, including direct work with schools either in an ongoing way or as self-contained projects. One of the high-profile projects they did was called *Share More Air*, a collaboration between the MoS and *Communion Records*. The children wrote the lyrics for the songs, which were then worked on by professional musicians to produce an album that is on sale through Amazon and iTunes. The idea was inspired by Nick Hornby as a result of his collaboration with Ben Folds on their album *Lonely Avenue*, for which Hornby wrote the lyrics and Folds wrote the music. One of the children's emotional reactions to hearing their song for the first time is shown on the promotional video for the project, as is Ben Folds singing one of the songs with, amongst others, backing singing from comedian Matt Lucas.

There are various principles that underpin the approach of MoS to writing, MoS to writing, although the pedagogy of teaching writing is not formally articulated. Most of all there is an explicit focus on creativity that is largely absent from the teaching of writing in schools in England and in many other parts of the world. This creative approach manifests itself mainly in the design of innovative tasks and projects designed to engage young people's creativity.

But it is also a more implicit background to the ongoing work in workshops and bespoke projects. The approach shares some features with the writing workshop approach that I address in Chapter 6. In particular the tasks are nearly always designed to result in a published outcome. These publications vary widely and often involve professional input in a range of multimedia. Short-duration and narrow-focus tasks in MoS sessions designed to elicit creative responses in writing, and the planning for writing, are part of this but so are more ambitious projects such as *Share More Air.* The self-expression of the young people is highly valued, and alongside this comes some reservations from MoS staff about how writing has been taught in schools.

Researching the MoS

In 2012 a team of colleagues and I from the University College London, Institute of Education (IOE) were commissioned to carry out a three-year research project to evaluate creativity, writing, and the work of the MoS. The opportunity to study children's creativity and writing in this longitudinal way is not very common in writing research.

The research objectives were to analyse the impact of the work of MoS, on the young people (YP) who had involvement with MoS, in four key areas: (1) motivation for writing; (2) writing development; (3) writing attainment in relation to statutory assessment in schools; and (4) expression and communication. The research design was a mixed-methods, three-year longitudinal study comprising qualitative enquiry and quasi-experimental work on writing attainment. Two main types of research sites were the locus for investigation:

1) The MoS premises in Hoxton where voluntary attendance by YP is encouraged; 15 YP were selected (aged 8 to 9 in year one of the study and aged 10 to 11 by year three of the study), through stratified random selection, from the young people attending MoS voluntarily in out-of-school sessions. These 15 YP were used as the basis for case studies, and for creativity assessments, and as the basis for analysis of attainment data in comparison with peers of the same age who were not involved in MoS. If a case study young person stopped attending MoS, then further random selection of another YP was made to ensure a minimum of 15 case study YP in each year of the study.
2) Bespoke projects designed by MoS based in schools and other settings. Three bespoke projects per year of the research were selected in consultation with MoS as the basis for project case studies using the same research objectives, and broadly similar methods as the longitudinal design apart from statistical analyses of attainment data. Case studies of projects typically included attendance at a minimum of four full workshop sessions by members of the research team to document their observations in field notes and to interview teachers and young people.

Data Sources

The data sets for the longitudinal analyses of young people (selected as case studies) at after-school clubs and Saturday mornings included the following: a) recorded and transcribed interviews with young people (n=60+); b) portfolios of YPs' writing (n=45); c) creativity assessments based on consensual judgements of YPs' writing using a creativity assessment tool designed for the project (n=90); d) field notes from observations of workshop sessions (n=15+); e) statistical analyses of a sample of YP involved in MoS (n=25) in relation to their statutory test scores in writing compared with their school class peers (n=106). These data, and their analyses, were accumulated once per year for three years. Baseline data included interviews with YP at the start of their involvement in the research and attainment data, which included test data prior to their involvement in MoS.

The MoS permanent workshop leader and a researcher carried out all the creativity assessments and their initial analyses. A process of *consensual judgement* was undertaken for samples of writing from each of the 15 case study YP each year. The consensual judgements recorded (taking account of the processes the YP engaged in during the writing) the extent to which creativity was demonstrated: very weakly; moderately; strongly; or very strongly in relation to the following six criteria:

1) The sample of writing demonstrates imaginative adaptation of existing ideas;
2) The process of writing demonstrates imaginative adaptation of existing ideas;
3) The sample of writing demonstrates originality;
4) The process of writing demonstrates originality;
5) The sample of writing demonstrates value;
6) The process of writing demonstrates value.

Data analyses consisted of a range of qualitative data analysis and quantitative data analysis methods. Interview transcripts, examples of YPs' writing, and field notes from observations were imported to NVivo qualitative data analysis software and subject to coding in the following first level codes:

Motivation to write;

- YPs' perceptions of writing and the MoS;
- Influence of reading on writing;
- Creativity in writing;
- Expression and communication.

Sub-codes were extended from first level codes. Examples of sub-level codes included:

- Control and choice over writing;
- Composition of writing vs. transcription of writing;
- The nature of different levels of creativity;
- The influence of books and other media on writing; etc.

Statistical analyses of attainment data compared 15 case study YP with 106 of their school class peers, not involved in MoS, in order to determine writing attainment trajectories in relation to three attainment bands: low, medium, and high attainment. Standard data cleaning, tests for homogeneity of intervention and control YP, cross-tab analyses and p-value tests of statistical significance were undertaken.

Case study reports from bespoke projects were compared holistically with findings from the longitudinal elements to augment and enrich the findings in the writing of the annual reports.

The overall findings of the research, in relation to creativity and writing, were established through the main analyses: the four assessments of creativity in writing for each of the young people selected as case studies; the views of the young people expressed in interviews (including an analysis of the scores, the young people awarded, from one to ten, to rate their motivation for work of MoS versus their school); the observation of the work of MoS staff in workshops; and the analysis of the nine bespoke projects that were each detailed in project case studies.

Findings

The overarching evaluation finding was that the MoS approach to creativity and writing was having a powerful beneficial effect on the young people who engaged. This is all the more remarkable when you consider that this was only attendance at MoS for either two hours or four hours per week. I address some of the detail of the beneficial and other effects below. But it is also important to give a sense of how individual young people were directly affected by their engagement with MoS. Detailed narrative case studies, which drew on multiple data sets, were one way that the impact of MoS was studied. Mario's[35] story, one of the case study young people who attended MoS for the full three years, is a good example.

The first time we met Mario was at the first interview just at the beginning of his involvement with MoS. He was clear right from the start that attendance at MoS was to help him improve his writing: '[MoS] makes me have more ideas, so I can have more ideas when I go to school . . . It made my handwriting more neater'. Figure 5.1 shows Mario's piece of writing selected for consensual assessment of creativity in year one.

At this stage Mario was relying on the traditional story devices, such as 'One day a girl called Katie . . .'. But even in this piece there is some evidence of

[35] All names are pseudonyms.

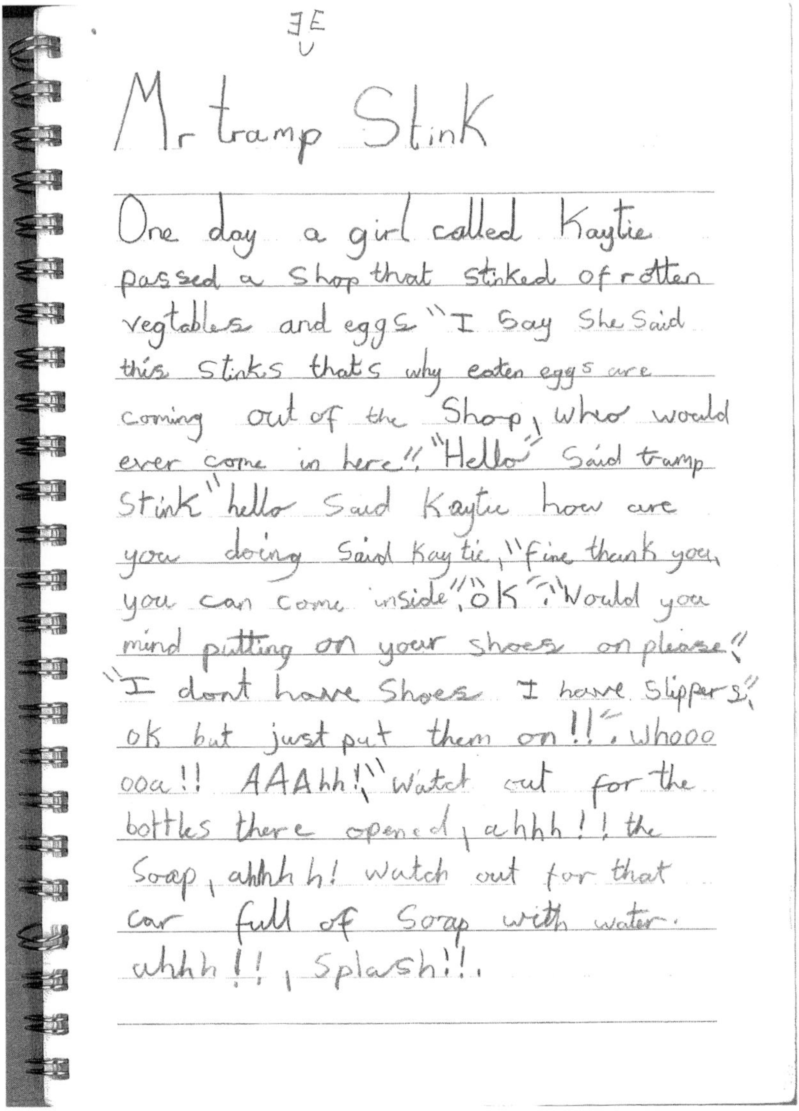

Mr tramp Stink

One day a girl called Kaytie
passed a Shop that stinked of rotten
vegtables and eggs "I Say She Said
this Stinks thats why eaten eggs are
coming out of the Shop, who would
ever come in here", "Hello" Said tramp
Stink" hello Said Kaytie how are
you doing Said Kay tie, "Fine thank you,
you can come inside", OK ". Would you
mind putting on your shoes on please"
"I dont have Shoes I have Slippers",
ok but just put them on!!", whooo
ooa!! AAAhh!, "Watch out for the
bottles there opened, ahhh!! the
Soap, ahhh h! watch out for that
car full of Soap with water.
uhhh!!, Splash!!.

Figure 5.1 An example of Mario's writing in year one of the project.

Mario's unrealised capacity for creativity in writing. The mock upper-class language of 'I say she said this stinks . . .' contrasting with the picture he painted of vegetables and eggs. The use of 'AAAhh! … Uhhh … splash!!' The curious image of cars full of soap. And the image of the face right at the top of the page. These playful ideas reflected the familiar spontaneity of some children of this age.

Compare this with one of the pieces selected for year three of the project (Figure 5.2). The writing in Figure 5.2 is more controlled. Mario was playing with some important ideas within a poetic structure and use of language: recognition of his own move way from obsession with monsters in writing; exploration of what creativity is; the final appreciation from readers or audience. The control of meaning across line breaks is equally impressive particularly given that the acrostic poetry form was imposed as a task. However, there is no simple linear development of creativity represented in the examples over the three years. Mario's development could only be understood in relation to other data such as interviews and the MoS workshop leader's knowledge of Mario's development over time. From this social perspective, there was evidence of growing confidence to experiment with different forms and ideas for writing. Mario was also able to reflect on his own areas for improvement. But, like all the young people in the study, it was writing in school that dominated conceptions of their writing selves. The school models of writing were so strong that they inhibited the young people's ability to see writing as more than a level in a test score. And the views of the teachers maintained standards just as they did in Mulcaster's day. As Mario said in his final interview summing up why he attended MoS:

> Because I want to come because I just want to make my learning better, because in school I used to be terrible, like bad levels, people still like that in my class. And I think it's improved my literacy and handwriting, yeah.

Taking all the case study young people's creativity consensual assessments over the three years of the study, there was evidence of a clear upward trend. But overall trends mask individual variation. As MoS is an institution that young people attend voluntarily, not all of the young people who were attending at the beginning of our study were attending at the end of the study. Some young people attended for two years (in years one and two of our study or in years two and three, and in one example in years one and three). Further separate analyses of groups of young people who attended for two years also showed upward trends in creativity although, not surprisingly, less marked.

Six of the case studies of young people featured those who attended for the full three years. For questions about creativity development over time, these young people are particularly important. One of the findings was that creativity was not at the same level for all young people, perhaps contrary to theories that creativity is a universally distributed trait. For example, one of the young people who attended for three years demonstrated the highest scores for originality and value at every assessment point. She joined MoS as a creative

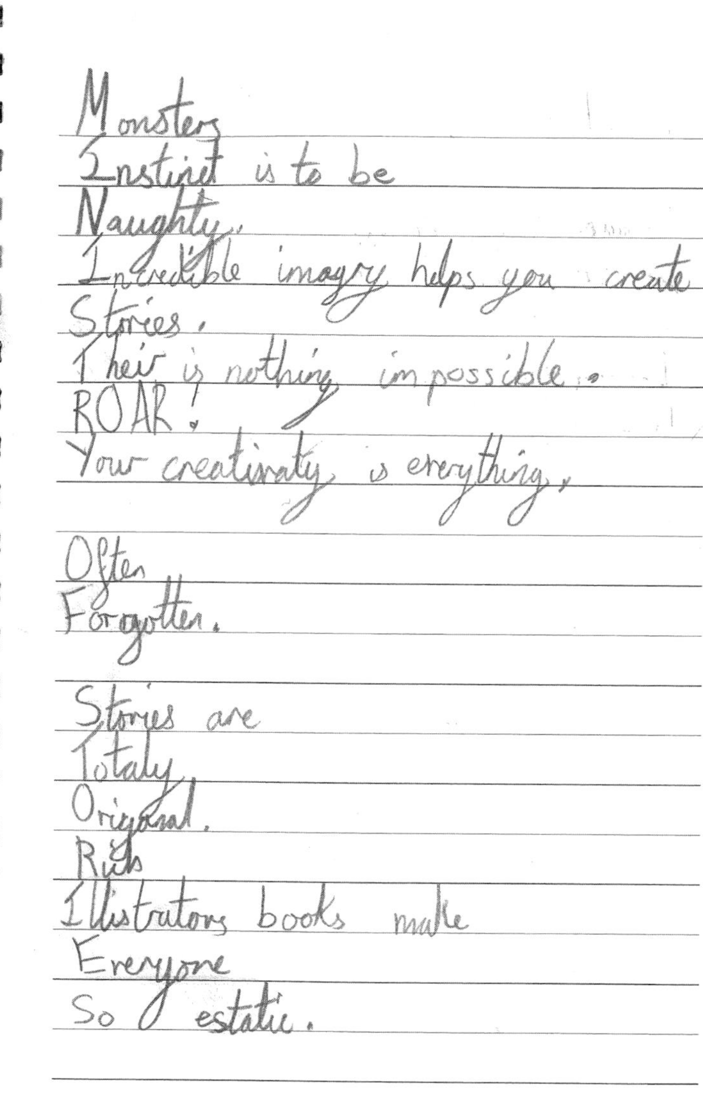

Monsters
Instinct is to be
Naughty.
Incredible imagry helps you create
Stories.
Their is nothing impossible.
ROAR!
Your creativity is everything.

Often
Forgotten.

Stories are
Totaly
Original.
Rich
Illustrators books make
Everyone
So estatic.

Figure 5.2 An example of Mario's writing in year three of the project.

and capable writer and maintained that high level. The creativity of another young person declined from year two to year three. The interview data and the experience of the workshop leader over the course of the year suggested that difficult home circumstances could have been a contributory factor for this young person's creativity demonstrated while at MoS.

As far as creativity development was concerned, two important elements were analysed in more detail in preparation for writing this chapter: *originality* and *value*. The young people's development showed that in the first year of the study their writing had more emphasis on adaptation of known influences than originality. For example, the strong reliance on favourite reading was common, such as the book series *Beast Quest* or the *Spiderwick Chronicles*. The front cover of Mario's MoS notebook revealed that gaming was important to him, especially the game *Call of Duty: Black Ops 3*, and its official interactive website. This was augmented by his favourite theme of dragons and flying sharks eating people and destroying buildings. The use of traditional story openings such as 'once upon a time' was also occasionally seen in addition to other familiar tropes of young novice writers. In the second year of the study, the young people started to use a much wider range of influences in their writing: for example, an increased awareness of the likely interests of their intended audience for their writing and beginning to deliberately 'control' the likely responses to their writing by readers.

By year three, there was evidence of much greater confidence to generate and use ideas that were personal to, and controlled by, the young person, and as a consequence more original. For example there was a much more sophisticated way of using personal knowledge to enliven writing, more akin to 'showing' rather than 'telling', or perhaps 'writing about what you know' that was a feature of the work of great writers that I explored in Chapter 4. Sophistication and experimentation with a wider range of forms and devices of writing was evident, in part explicitly prompted by MoS, and at other times developed independently. Maintaining high levels of creativity was, of course, still a challenge for the young people, which showed itself in some inconsistency across different writing tasks and outputs. For example, one young person could at times show originality through the use of particular ideas and language, but then in the same piece slip into overly descriptive, predictable, and routine writing. Greater originality was accompanied by higher levels of engagement by the young people (revealed through interviews with the young people) linked to the praise for their achievements offered by MoS staff and volunteers. Technical skills such as a good ear for the ways in which people speak and the ways that this can be represented in writing were also developing.

An important aspect of the perceived *value* of the writing was the young people's growing understanding of the ways in which writing is always for an intended readership (even as the diarist who is both writer and single reader), and the readers' needs to be engaged by writing. This is value hypothetically attributed by the writer to unknown readers. This hypothetical valuing contrasts with the real value directly attributed to writing through oral feedback by other young people who were part of the MoS workshops, the MoS staff and volunteers, and the researchers.

One starting point in their development was the extent to which the young people saw value in the process and product of their writing, and the extent to which the adults in the MoS setting recognised this same value. Engagement and motivation to write independently, as opposed to being gently coerced to write, through engaging tasks, was seen as another important element of the value that could be attributed to writing. Serious engagement with the process of writing and finishing pieces to satisfactory conclusion were other components. There was also a sense of value through informal comparison of pieces of writing with, a) the young person's other writing over time, and, b) in comparison with other young people in the cohort and over the years of the MoS.

The public-facing work of MoS also brought the work of the young people to the attention of a much wider audience, enabling the audience to attribute value. Sometimes this was very direct, for example, in a bespoke project with a school in Australia that involved sharing of autobiographical information, and other writing, over email with pen pals.

Overall, value as a concept was much harder to identify and therefore document as part of the case studies. There was no clear evidence of patterns of developmental progression in value over the three years of the study, other than the connections between the growth in the originality of the writing, and hence value attributed by MoS staff, researchers, and the young people themselves.

To sum up the most important finding from the study, the MoS approach positively contributed to the young people's development of creativity in writing from strong reliance on known texts, and derivative adaptation, towards reliance on what the young people saw as their own ideas and originality, recognised by their peers, by workshop leaders, by volunteers, and by researchers alike. This trajectory of use of personal reading as a stimulus for writing, and the due care needed to avoid derivativeness, was a feature of the development of published writers as well, as I showed in Chapter 4.

In view of Dave Egger's idea that 826 Valencia was designed to complement the work of schools, even to the degree that the centres were places where homework could be finished, the intersections between formal education and the work of the MoS were fascinating. For example Jonathan said:

> I think there's a difference because in the Ministry of Stories I have so much fun, I can write all the things I really wanted to do and I can't at school, because sometimes they tell you you have to write something about something, but at the Ministry of Stories they tell you something, but you can use anything from your imagination.

He gave an enthusiastic, reflective end-of-year interview where he related the impact of attending the MoS sessions in particular to his confidence levels: 'I think that it's a wonderful workshop so children can feel more excited about learning and writing', and 'what helps me to write is the encouragement they are giving me, and always saying that's nice and wonderful, even if I didn't write a lot'. Jonathan also perceived self-expression as a central feature of MoS writing:

RESEARCHER: What do you like most about writing at the Ministry of Stories?
JONATHAN: That I get to express myself with what I write.

The MoS approach gave the participants a feeling of freedom and choice over their writing, elements that are likely to have led to greater motivation. One of the participants, Jamal, used the words 'control' and 'power' directly: 'you have control over it [the writing process] and the MoS they give you the power to do that'. Choice motivated many of the YP to explore the conventions of writing without restraint, for example, even reflected in the seemingly unremarkable way that they could set out pages in their MoS writing books (provided by MoS) in ways that they felt were personal to them. When compared with so much school teaching of writing, where the exercise book is sacrosanct, for its titles, dates, and underlining, small elements of choice offered over the tools for writing were an important addition to the more profound choices generated as a result of the MoS emphasis on creativity.

The unique opportunity of this three-year study of creativity showed most of all that young people's creativity can be enhanced with appropriate principles, ideas, guidance, and teaching. It enabled the research team to document for the first time some of the ways in which originality and value are exhibited and are learned. The importance of choice within supportive pedagogical environments was clearly beneficial, and in this and other elements of the MoS approach there were many parallels with creative writing courses for adults, including in universities and colleges.

*

The imagination is a vital part of creative thinking, but it is not synonymous with creativity. Creativity in writing is writing that is original and that has value as judged by people with appropriate expertise. Imagination does not *necessarily* result in something original, but creativity does. The author, or other composer, begins with the search for an overall idea to guide the creation. This search is a creative process that requires unstructured time for the right idea to emerge.

Creativity is relevant to many domains of human thinking and activity. In the arts, creativity does not begin with the solving of a problem that is paramount in scientific creativity; it is a deliberate intent to create something for its own sake. Its origin is the metaphorical and literal emptiness of the blank page, the darkness of the void. Once the idea is sufficiently formed to enable the process of composition to begin, experience, knowledge, and understanding are all brought to bear on filling the page with something original, however modest that originality may be. The writers' knowledge that creativity builds in particular ways on what has gone before can release them to explore topics of interest in new ways, to play with existing ideas, in the pursuit of creating something original.

There are also many threats and barriers to creativity that the writer has to guard against. The classic problem of extrinsic motivation versus intrinsic motivation can be related to the writer's ambitions. If the main focus of the writer's ambition is genuinely to write for the pleasure and challenges of fashioning something that communicates the thoughts of the writer as well as possible, something to be proud of, this intrinsic motivation is more likely to result in successful creativity in writing than extrinsic motivation, for example the extrinsic reward of the 'bright lights of stardom'!

Writing, and creativity in writing, is a social process. Although writing involves the solitude of the writer, this solitude is punctuated by many interactions with other people. The vital interactions of volunteers and other teachers was seen in the work of the MoS. Understanding the social aspects of writing can help remove the anxiety of trying to produce the 'perfect' piece of writing, alone. If writing is done with the social in mind, the writer unconsciously opens spaces for others to contribute at some point in the writing process. For example, writers know when to leave drafts as provisional so that they can benefit from the input of others.

Time and space are vital ingredients in the creativity of writing. Structured time/unstructured time, long hours/short periods of intense activity are all part of the mix. The creativity of writing needs significant periods of time, for most writers daily: this is structured time. There also needs to be time for the thinking to be subconsciously percolating in the mind in preparation for the next day of work. I am reminded of the music composer Stravinsky who said that he kept 'bank hours'. He composed from nine o'clock in the morning until three o'clock in the afternoon daily. But, he said, the rest of the time he was nearly always thinking about what would come next.

Writing and creativity, as I argue in this book, are vital features of human existence. All adult writers were, of course, once children. How might the world of writers be effected if the experiences they had when children at school were different? 826 Valencia and The Ministry of Stories offer a new vision of education where creativity is central to writing. Schooling round the world is rarely like this vision, but it could be. Everyone experiences education for good or for bad. For that reason, most people have an interest in education and a democratic right to influence it. In her work deciding on an award for children's writing, the author Anne Fine felt that there had been 'a real drop in the standard of children's writing – not in grammar, construction or spelling, but in the untestable quality of creativity'[36] (3). Phillip Pullman described the national curriculum for young people in England as 'brutal', and suggested that we are creating a generation of children who hate reading and who 'feel nothing but hostility for literature'.[37] In his view:

> There are no rules. Anything that's any good has to be discovered in the process of writing it . . . we cannot require everything to take place under the glare of discussion and checking and testing and consultation: some things have to be private and tentative. Teaching at its best can give pupils the confidence to discover this mysterious state and to begin to explore the things that can be discovered there.

[36] Katbamna, M. 'Crisis of Creativity.' *Guardian*, 2003.
[37] Ward, L. 'Tests Are Making Children Hate Books.' *Guardian*, 2003. 2.

6 Novice Writers and Education

So far in this book I have examined writing and its processes from five major perspectives: theoretical; historical; trends in writing conventions and guidance; expert writers' perspectives; and creativity and writing. However, there remains a global arena where a great deal of writing takes place which I have not addressed in depth so far. This is the world of writing as part of education, where learning begins in the home, and continues in schools (and colleges and universities, which were a focus in Chapter 3), and becomes part of the world of work for many people. The term *lifelong learning* is one favoured by many who study education: writing is a classic example of something that can require lifelong learning, not least because there is always something more about writing that can be learned no matter how expert the writer is.

In the chapter on the history of writing, I explored the movement from oral to literate societies. Although there are still a small number of non-literate societies or communities in the world, the issue of literacy has become a global one that is linked with ideas about disadvantage and poverty. A literate society is certainly not one that is intrinsically superior to a non-literate society. However, there are opportunities that open as a result of being literate, and consequently there are opportunities that are not accessible without literacy. In statistics reported by the United Nations Educational, Scientific and Cultural Organisation (UNESCO) in 2015, it was estimated that world-wide 86% of people age 15 or above were literate, and that 91% of people aged from 15 to 24 years were literate.[1] But this also meant that '758 million adults 15 years and older still cannot read or write a simple sentence. Roughly two-thirds of them are female'.[2]

One of the key places that literacy is learned is in formal education, in early years settings and in schools, so first and foremost it is important that children have *access* to education. The *Millennium Development Goals* (MDGs) report published in 2015 noted progress in increasing children's attendance at schools but also some severe challenges:

[1] UNESCO Institute for Statistics, 'Literacy', UNESCO, 2016.
[2] UNESCO Institute for Statistics, 'Literacy', UNESCO, 2016.

- Half of the 58 million out-of-school children of primary school age live in conflict-affected areas.
- More than one in four children in developing regions entering primary school is likely to drop out.

In spite of impressive increases in the net enrolment rates of primary school children, in the early years of the MDGs, this progress appeared to have stagnated by 2012, particularly in the countries of Sub-Saharan Africa where the enrolment was 78% of all children of primary school age. In addition, the tensions over funding for the countries in most need could be seen in the statistics about education:

> Donor aid to education had risen steadily after 2002, peaked in 2010 then declined by 7 per cent between 2010 and 2011. Alarmingly, for the first time since 2002, aid to basic education fell: from $6.2 billion in 2010 to $5.8 billion in 2011. Low-income countries – which received one third of total educational aid to basic education – witnessed a decrease in aid to basic education, in contrast to middle-income countries where aid to basic education increased. Aid fell by 9 per cent in low-income countries between 2010 and 2011, from $2.1 billion to $1.9 billion. In sub-Saharan Africa, home to over half of the world's out-of-school population, aid to basic education declined by 7 per cent between 2010 and 2011.[3]

The issue of attendance at school is particularly important because children's access to learning is limited if they are unable to attend school. However, there are also questions about the quality of education that children receive once they are attending school.

A feature of the global statistics is that literacy often means reading, as this is easier to assess than writing. However, writing is important not just for its own sake but also because it contributes positively to children's reading development as well. The statistics that I have described so far in this chapter underline the importance of literacy, and the challenges that are faced worldwide in helping the learning and teaching of writing.

For any learner, adult or child, teaching needs to be matched to development. This requires teachers, and others who support writing, to know what typical features of writing development are, so they are able to anticipate and plan for optimal teaching related to learning. Hence the first section in the chapter begins by looking briefly at some features of children's development as writers from the very earliest stages. Next a review of rigorous research showing the most effective methods of teaching writing is presented. Most of this research has been carried out in high income nations, so I next explore some of the implications for low income nations that are the focus of the *Sustainable Development Goals* that replaced the MDGs. The teaching of English in these country contexts, where English is an additional language to one or

[3] United Nations, *Millennium Development Goals Report 2014*, 19.

more home languages, is an important aspect of the global picture, so a report on some research I was involved with in Tanzania is included as an example of the opportunities and challenges. The final part of the chapter reflects on the teaching of writing in England's schools, a country where, as the birth place of the English language, you might expect that national policies on literacy would result in the very best of teaching and learning of English.

The Development of Writing

From the moment children are born they develop in ways that will eventually contribute to their development as writers. For example, the eyes learn to focus and discriminate, something that will be essential for distinguishing between subtle differences in letters. When a child first sees objects, they begin to be curious about their properties. When they start naming objects, from about 18 months onwards, they see that objects can be moved, for example, by inverting them, and that this inversion does not change them fundamentally as an object. But from about age three onwards children will begin the process of learning that that there are entities in their world that can appear to change if inverted or transformed in some other way: letters and numbers, or what are called graphemes. We can try and imagine the child's first encounters with graphemes:

I

The example 'I' could be a lower case 'L', or a number one, but it is in fact an upper case letter 'i'.

Il1

The upper case letter 'i' and the lower case letter 'L' are almost indistinguishable in the Arial font on my computer (I was curious what the font of this book would finally be, and if this would make the two letters more distinguishable. At copy edit stage, of the text for the book, the Cambria Math font showed the upper case 'I' with a serif that extends to left and right of the top of the letter, whereas the lower case 'L' only has the serif extending to the left side), but if I increase the font size to more than 70 the 'L' is very slightly thicker than the capital 'i'. The number 1 is distinguishable because it has a serif at the top, but in many people's handwriting it may not have the serif. The only way to really clearly distinguish between the 'I' and the 'l' is to put them into a meaningful context, for example: 'I am going to learn'. So the young child has to learn that the shape that looks like a number one can represent a number, a phoneme in a word (e.g. 'Indeed'), or a whole word itself, as in singular person (I' went home.'). Young children encounter these mysteries of language and are predisposed to working out their meanings, with the social support of more expert adults.

The semantic context that a sentence provides is a fundamental aspect of written language, in so many ways. A good example is the word 'read'. We only can confirm the middle phoneme (sound) of the word 'read' if it is in a sentence context. If the sentence context was, 'I will read a book', then the phoneme represented by the letters 'ea' is the longer /ee/ sound, the same phoneme as in the word 'need'. But in another contexts, such as 'Last Tuesday I read the book', the shorter /eh/ sound, the same phoneme as in the word 'red'. My favourite example was *The Centre for Reading at Reading* (at the University of Reading, the city in England).

So when children are very young they use their eyes to distinguish between shapes. At the same time, their ability to point, touch, and grab things develops. Before too long the dexterity of their hands develops enough to allow them to hold a pencil, crayon, or felt pen, or to touch a digital screen. At first there is no differentiation by the child between what we call drawing and what we call writing, but one of the earliest stages of writing development is to start to understand that distinction. Children's behaviour from a very young age shows their genetic capacity to engage with written language and increasingly to seek to express themselves through this language.

One source of research of relevance to understanding writing development is in-depth longitudinal case studies of the ways in which individual children develop their writing and reading. A seminal study of this kind was Glenda Bissex's study of her son Paul that she carried out for her PhD, and that was published by Harvard University Press in her book called GNYS AT WRK.[4] The title of the book is part of a sign that her son wrote: DO NAT DSTRB GNYS AT WRK [do not disturb genius at work]. A range of studies of this kind have been published.[5] Part of my own work has included analysis of the development of my children's reading and writing.[6] To give an example here is one brief account of some of the evidence I collected in relation to the first signs of writing development.

Aged 12 months Esther's[7] first marks on paper with a writing implement, as opposed to marks made in another medium such as sand with her fingers, were noted. At age one year and ten months she was beginning to realise that she could communicate meaning through pictures. At breakfast time one morning she said, 'Cow', in relation to a drawing that she had done. One of us misheard her and asked her if she said, 'Car', to which she replied, 'yeah!'. Her answer revealed her general understanding that pictures could carry meanings but not that meaning has specific attributions that do not change on subsequent viewing or reading. When Esther was 2 years 1 month she started to draw what she called a 'tick tock' but by the time she had finished she said it was a 'banana' because it did look more like a banana than a clock. Now she had some understanding of the permanence of meaning. Her understanding that print carries meaning was shown in the same month, when she saw a shopping list and asked, 'What does it say?' At 2 years 3 months a letter from Grandma to Esther was read aloud. When encouraged to reply Esther drew several diagonal lines which

4 Bissex, *Gnys at Wrk: A Child Learns to Read and Write.*
5 Summarised in Wyse and Jones. *Teaching English, Language and Literacy.*
6 Wyse, *How to Help Your Child Read and Write.*
7 Esther's writing was also seen in the first chapter of this book.

ran from left to write and said that it meant, 'I would like one'. Her name was represented by some smaller lines that she drew. Orientation on the page, and relative sizes are important basic concepts in relation to the conventions of writing, all of which young children have to learn.

In-depth case studies such as these can be analysed to identify common patterns of development in different aspects of writing. For example, the development of spelling has attracted a range of analyses. The young child learning the spelling system of the English language passes through several recognisable stages. In a way each young child reinvents the alphabet, perhaps in some ways similar to the historical invention of alphabetic writing.[8] Indeed there is a rather interesting symmetry between the stages of spelling development and the key moments in the development of the alphabet that I outlined in Chapter 2 (see Figures 6.1 to 6.5 and Table 6.1).

The sophistication of the rebus, and hence children's much later understanding of the way the rebus works, is perhaps another signal of how profound the rebus was because it made the important link between sounds and a system of more abstract symbols.

Just as the alphabet was a fundamental invention for humans, children's development of the understanding of the alphabetic code is one of the most fundamental things that they must learn if they are to learn to write and read. As a result, the attention to *phonological understanding* as part of learning to be literate, and the teaching of *phonics*, has probably attracted more attention in education across the world than any other single education topic. The debates about learning to read the alphabetic code have been so strong that they have been described as the 'reading wars'. There have been some highly dubious politics and ideology connected with these debates[9] at the expense of robust evidence that clearly shows how reading should be taught.[10] The reading wars have even brought extreme views of links between conservatism, religious belief and advocacy of the 'bottom-up' *synthetic* teaching of phonics 'first and fast', versus liberalism and atheism linked with the advocacy of approaching the teaching of reading in a top-down way. Top-down approaches advocate motivating children to read through engaging them with exciting books first and foremost, then linking this with the teaching of words, letters and phonemes. The momentous invention of the alphabet, that is part of human history, not only enables us to communicate in writing but also still resonates very strongly in modern societies as an aspect of fundamental concern.

[8] Olson, *The Mind on Paper.*

[9] Cummins, 'Pedagogies for the Poor? Realigning Reading Instruction for Low-Income Students with Scientifically Based Reading Instruction', 564–572.

[10] Wyse and Goswami, 'Synthetic Phonics and the Teaching of Reading', 691–710.

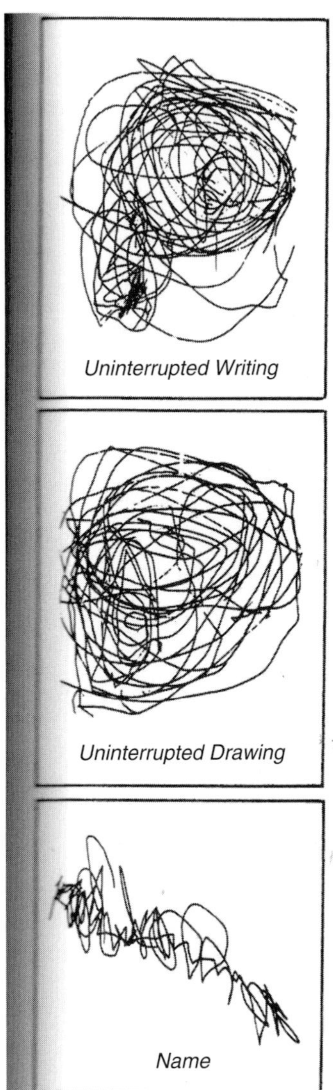

Figure 6.1 Mark making stage. Harste, Woodward, Burke, *Language Stories and Literacy Lessons*. By permission of Heinemann.

Figure 6.2 Pre-phonetic stage.

Figure 6.3 Semi-phonetic stage.

Figure 6.4 Phonetic stage.

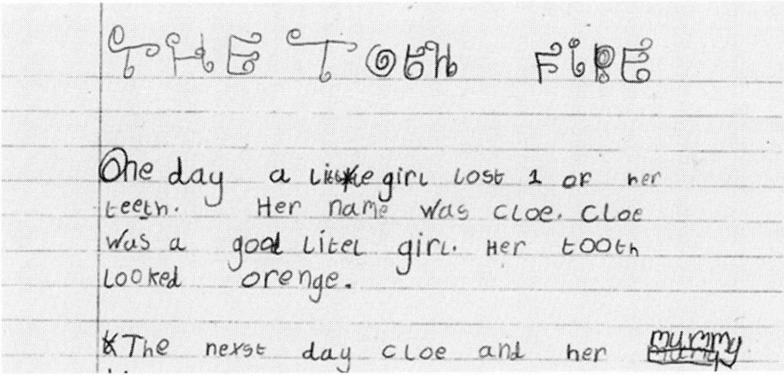

Figure 6.5 Transitional stage.

In summary, individual child case studies, and the experience and knowledge of teachers who may teach the same ages of children for several years, have enabled general milestones of development to be recognised[11]:

Milestones by age four

- Knows that pictures are different from writing. Can express messages and meaning using non-conventional written marks.

[11] Wyse and Jones, *Teaching English, Language and Literacy.*

Table 6.1 *Children's spelling stages compared with historical developments of writing*

Spelling stage of children	Approximate age	Description of children's development	Parallel historical development	Approximate date
Mark-making	2 years to 3 years	No use of letters. Communicative meaning unclear. Meaning not permanent, so children will give different interpretations on different occasions.	Cave art	
Pre-phonetic	3 years to 4 years	The first stage is the pre-communicative stage, when young children are making their first attempts at communicating through writing. The writing may contain a mixture of actual letters, numerals and invented symbols and, as such, it will be unreadable though the writer might be able to explain what he or she intended to write.	Clay tablets – cuniform	4000 to 2600 BC
No equivalence		Language play of the sophistication of the rebus only happens from about age eight onwards.	Rebus	3,100
Semi-phonetic	4 years to 5 years	When children are at the second stage, that is the semi-phonetic stage, they are beginning to understand that letters represent sounds and show some knowledge of the alphabet and of letter formation. Some words will be abbreviated or the initial letter might be used to indicate the whole word. Consonants are used more frequently than vowels.	Phoenecian/Proto-Canaanite alphabet	1,050

Phonetic	5 years to 6 years	At the phonetic stage, children concentrate on the sound–symbol correspondences, their words become more complete and they gain an understanding of word division. They can cope with simple letter strings such as -nd, -ing, and -ed but have trouble with less regular strings such as -er, -ll, and -gh.	First alphabetic writing: in Greece	800
Transitional	6 years to 8 years	During the transitional stage children become less dependent on sound–symbol strategies. With the experience of reading and direct spelling instruction, they become more aware of the visual aspects of words. They indicate an awareness of the accepted letter strings and basic writing conventions of the English writing system and have an increasing number of correctly spelt words to draw upon.	First English writing	400 AD
Conventional	7 years onwards	Finally, the fully competent speller emerges at the conventional (or correct) stage.	Beginnings of standard English	675–975 AD

- Uses *invented spelling* which combines letters in both non-conventional and conventional ways, reflecting emergent understanding of the links between phonemes (sounds) and graphemes (letters).
- Has a concept of what a written word is and so will insert spaces between words.
- Knows the conventional direction of print relevant to the language being written, e.g. left to right – top to bottom.
- Can form some or all of the letters of the alphabet without full understanding of their linguistic properties.

Milestones by age seven

- Has awareness that writing exists in a range of forms, such as story, poem, newspaper article, etc. Will be more confident with narrative writing than other forms.
- Writing is comprised of sentences in conventional grammar.
- Many words spelled using conventional English spelling but some words still represented using invented spellings.
- Some basic punctuation marks used conventionally (e.g. full stops) in line with understanding that punctuation is used in specific ways related to the meaning being expressed in writing.
- Upper case and lower case letter formation secure.

Milestones by age eleven

- Greater understanding of the features of some different forms of writing and capacity to write in a range of forms. Constructing lines of argument in writing still to be developed.
- Writing used to support learning, in a range of school subjects, including for note-taking.
- Understanding that writing requires editing and revision so can consist of one of more drafts.
- Grammar and spelling mainly conventional. Able to use dictionaries and computer spell checkers.

The first half of this chapter has indicated some of the ways in which children's development of writing begins. But it is the systematic teaching of reading and writing that is necessary for nearly all children if they are to develop fully. This is the domain of different kinds of research, such as experimental trials, that can inform effective teaching.

Research on Effective Teaching of Writing

The importance of reading and writing in order to gain access to opportunities in society has resulted in schools (early years settings and primary/elementary schools in particular) having the responsibility to ensure that children and young people learn to write. This prompts the question, what is the best way to teach writing? The answer to this question may seem remote from some of the other aspects of how writing works that have been addressed so far in this book. For example, it is not immediately obvious how the reflections of eminent writers' processes might translate into how writing is taught in schools. However, there is an approach to the teaching of writing that has some strong parallels with the world of professional writing.

In the 1980s, a book by Donald Graves, a teacher and researcher born in Fall River, Massachusetts, stimulated high levels of interest in Australia, the US, New Zealand and the UK about what was a new approach to teaching writing in schools. The impact internationally of a single approach to teaching writing in schools has not been surpassed to this day. Donald Graves' approach became known as the *process approach* to writing.

The main connection between the process approach to writing and the world of professional writing was the way the process approach set writing within a classroom publication process. The products of the writing that children undertake are 'published' books that are made in the classroom. In the 1980s, these books would be constructed from print materials, with computers used mainly to improve presentation of print. These days publication is possible in many more ways via digital media and in classroom e-books. The published books become part of the classroom reading materials along with professionally published books. The books then become part of the literate environment of the classroom and as such are subject to both formal and informal review by the members of the class, and can be further used as teaching resources, as the basis of discussion and analysis.

Unlike traditional methods of teaching writing that involve teachers setting writing exercises, for example in grammar, the process approach begins with children identifying a range of possible ideas for a piece of writing (e.g. a simple list of five ideas), choosing one, and beginning work (consistent with Tolstoy's theory of writing teaching in Chapter 5 and with research on the importance of choice as part of creativity). This idea of children making choices over the topic, form, and other features of the writing that they want to do is one of the most important elements of the process approach. In more traditional teaching, children do not encounter the decisions that need to be made in relation to what to write about, and the kind of form of writing to be done. Choice, as conception of the idea for a book, is of course fundamental to the work of expert writers.

The writing takes place in a classroom writing workshop at last once per week. Writing not finished in one workshop is simply continued in the next workshop until it is finally published, or the child and teacher decide the piece is not working, so it is discarded and a different piece of writing started. The teacher works to help each child develop by discussing and helping them improve the writing in relation to both composition and transcription (spelling, punctuation, etc.) aspects. The teacher also plans what are called 'mini lessons'. Having done ongoing assessments of the children's writing in the class, the teacher identifies common problems and issues that need input. Either the whole class or a small group from the class have short lessons, perhaps about 20 minutes, where they learn about key features of writing that they could improve by reflecting on examples of writing in progress in the class.

I have outlined some of the key features of the process approach but as Graves's book on the approach shows, there is much more detail to the process approach than can be covered here.[12] Also there were key differences between the way it was originally conceived and the way it was taken up in England, including greater emphasis on teacher-planned tasks to augment the writing workshop approach, as I documented in the first research project I carried out.[13]

So Donald Graves, a persuasive writer, motivated teachers to use his approach. But beyond the important recognition by teachers, a key question is what is the objective evidence that the process approach has a positive impact on children's writing? One way to know whether a teaching approach is effective is to carry out a *randomised controlled trial* or RCT. An RCT in education will for example compare one approach to teaching with at least one other approach. The method under investigation is the *intervention*, and its comparator is the *control*. The methods of the RCT include random allocation of the participants (pupils in this case) to intervention or control groups. All the participants are tested using the most appropriate tests possible, which ideally have been 'standardised' against a large population of similar participants as part of the development of the test.[14] Then, after the interventions have been carried out, the tests results are compared through statistical analyses that determine whether the outcomes of the tests could have been due to chance or whether the outcomes are, on the basis of statistical probability, the direct result of the intervention.

There are a growing number of RCTs being carried out to examine effectiveness of teaching in schools, including in the teaching of writing. Steve Graham has pioneered this kind of research in relation to writing teaching, including not only carrying out RCTs but also systematic reviews and meta-analyses that systematically accumulate the findings from multiple experimental trials, that address the same research questions, to see across more than one study how effective a particular approach is. In his most recent work he has compiled systematic reviews of systematic reviews which give very clear indications of how writing can best be taught in schools. I summarise below and provide further explanation of Graham's series of main recommendations that simplify much complexity across multiple experimental studies.

1. The first recommendation is the simple but powerful idea that young people must write regularly, and hence increasing the amount of time actually

[12] Graves, *Writing*. [13] Wyse, *Primary Writing*.

[14] In 2017, when this book was written, the availability of rigorous and valid tests of young children's writing was very limited.

writing improves outcomes. This appears obvious, and is entirely consistent with the views of expert writers that I presented in Chapter 4, but sometimes simply doing more of an activity doesn't necessarily result in optimal gains in achievement. As part of having pupils write more, studies have shown that the process approach in particular has important elements that support writing development, with a moderate overall *effect size* of 0.34, and a high effect size for primary/elementary pupils of 0.48 (as opposed to 0.25 for secondary pupils).

Effect sizes go beyond simply establishing whether an approach has worked or not, to an indication of how well it worked, through their measure of the *extent of difference* between comparison groups in experimental studies. An effect size from 0.01 to 0.1 is considered low effect and equivalent to between zero and 2 months of education progress as measured by standardised tests appropriate to the nature of learning measured. An effect size from 0.26 to 0.44, equivalent to a range of three to six months progress, is considered moderate. An effect size of 0.5 to 1.0 is described as high effect to very high effect, within the range of six months progress to one year's progress.[15]

2. The second Graham recommendation is that teachers need to create an appropriately supportive writing environment in the classroom. A supportive writing environment is one that includes teachers communicating enthusiasm about writing and providing specific positive feedback about students' efforts. Support from teachers should be just enough to help students succeed but not so much that students' independent thinking is compromised. Teachers also set clear goals for writing, and have high expectations, but also adopt teaching to meet the different needs of individual students.
3. Evidence-based practice in the teaching of writing also requires pupils' skills, strategies and knowledge to be developed. The knowledge required includes the important high-level aspects such as creativity. Consistent with one of the features of the process approach, it has been shown that teaching about planning, revising and editing text is important but also the lower-level details such as how paragraphs work.
4. Not only do students need to learn about strategies but they also need to 'self-regulate' by being able to reflect on their own writing and their success or otherwise at using the strategies that they have been taught. In addition to compositional knowledge and skills, transcription aspects also need teaching, such as handwriting and typing, spelling, and vocabulary linked with particular types of writing. Attention to sentence construction, for example through sentence-combining exercises where simple sentences are combined to produce complex sentences has been shown to be effective. Traditional grammar teaching has *not* been shown to be effective in enhancing writing

[15] Higgins, Kokotsaki, and Coe, *The Teaching and Learning Toolkit.*

development. But teachers work constantly with children, including with the use of feedback and marking, to help children and young people use sentences to communicate effectively.

5. One important evidence-based practice that applies not just to writing but to high-quality teaching more generally is effective assessment of pupils' learning by teachers to inform teaching. This has become known as *assessment for learning*. The reason for the specification of 'for learning' is that assessment is used for a range of purposes in education: for example, it is sometimes used to hold teachers to account on the basis of correlations between pupil test scores and teacher performance. Research on the use of assessment information to hold teachers to account, known as high stakes assessment, has shown a number of problems for education, whereas assessment for learning has shown clear benefits. Consistent with assessment for learning there is evidence from writing teaching research that teacher feedback to their pupils about their writing is a vital part of learning to write. This feedback needs to include positive specific feedback not just bland general praise. Writing is also improved when students are taught to evaluate their own writing, and when peers are taught to give each other appropriate feedback about their writing. There is also some evidence that in limited ways computers can give feedback about writing and that this can be beneficial.
6. Computer software such as word processing software has been shown to enhance writing. Yet in spite of this evidence, and in spite of the proliferation of computer devices in society, the bulk of writing in schools is still pencil or pen and paper. And particularly rare is the practice of starting a first draft of writing on a computer and then continuing this through to completion.
7. Steve Graham's final main recommendation is that pupils' writing benefits not only from pupils experiencing writing, supported by teachers, and by pupils' own reflections on their writing, but also using writing to learn as part of all the subjects of the school curriculum. Part of the benefit in this case is in writing for a variety of purposes and hence meeting the need to experience different forms of writing associated with different subject areas, such as the science experiment report or the history essay.

Teaching in Low-Income Countries

The experimental trials that informed the recommendations above were all carried out in high-income country contexts. When we turn to low-income countries, there are far fewer experimental studies that have been carried out. A systematic review by Sonali Nag and colleagues reviewed experimental trials, of high quality and moderate quality, carried out in low-income country contexts. The main finding of their work was that oral language skills are of prime importance in both low-income and high-income countries. Oral language proficiency and fluency is the foundation for the development of literacy (although many more studies have focused on reading rather than writing). They also noted that a particular complexity in many low-income countries is that the language of school instruction is not necessarily the language children speak at home.

In addition to experimental work in low-income countries, a range of qualitative research has been carried out which Nag and colleagues also reviewed. There was evidence from qualitative studies that the quality of teaching is a major issue in relation to problems with children's learning of literacy. One key problem that the review identified was that teachers often do not understand how meaning and understanding are at the heart of learning to read and write, and therefore teaching should reflect this. The training of teachers in low-income countries often did not equip them to appreciate and understand elements such as the centrality of meaning to written language. As a result they naturally fell back on their own experiences as pupils, which often involved rote learning, including unison repetitive chanting as the main teaching approach.

One of the studies cited in the Nag et al. review is one that I undertook with colleagues at the University of Cambridge. Our research was a study of the teaching of English in primary education in Tanzania. The fieldwork took place in the capital city of Tanzania, Dar es Salaam. The English language, writing, reading and speaking, is regarded by the Tanzanian government as particularly important for economic prosperity because it is seen as the language of global trade.[16] In Tanzania, English is also a legacy of British colonial power. These two issues, English as a language of economic prosperity, and language as emblematic of colonialism, are the site for intense debates about the desirability of encouraging English, or other colonial languages, in the face of perceived threats to indigenous languages. The history of language in Tanzania reveals a fascinating picture of compromise and complexity for learners and teachers. In 1967, Kiswahili was made the medium of instruction in primary schools, but in spite of plans to do the same in secondary schools, the medium of instruction remained English. For that reason, in Tanzania English is typically taught as a subject of the primary curriculum by teachers with greater language skills in English, but children do not benefit from the daily exposure to a language that English as a medium of instruction would bring.[17] They do, however, experience

[16] United Republic of Tanzania Ministry of Education and Culture, *English Language Syllabus for Primary Schools*.

[17] Another line of argument is that teaching in an African language such as Kiswahili would be more appropriate as this language is better known by many teachers and children. Media reports in 2016 suggested that the medium of instruction in secondary schools was to change to Kiswahili.

Tanzania's second official language Kiswahili, and children also experience the many other tribal languages that are part of Tanzanian culture, and the lives of most African people.

Tanzania is a relatively settled African country: for example, it is not subject to ongoing major conflict. The formal education system on the Tanzanian mainland is based on seven years of primary school. Official entry to school is when the child is age seven. Primary schooling is organised into classes of *standards* from standard one to seven. This is followed by four years of lower secondary school, two years of senior secondary school, and three years of tertiary education. If children enrol at the government-prescribed age of seven, and if they progress without repetition, they should be age thirteen to fourteen years in standard seven. The transition from primary school to secondary school depends on the performance in the Primary School Leaving Examination, an examination that includes the subject of English.

Although generalisation on the basis of statistical significance was not a requirement for the study, great care was taken to select a primary school where its socio-economic context would share characteristics with many of the urban schools in Tanzania. As a result of discussions with an educational expert at the University of Dar-es-Salaam and with District and Ward Education Officers, a primary school in Manzese Ward in Kinondoni District in Dar-es-Salaam, which was typical of economically deprived areas in the city, was selected. Access to the school for the research was only possible as a result of establishing supportive partnerships with the national government ministry, the local district and the ward. The school was located about eight km from the centre of Dar es Salaam. The area was highly populated with over 5,000 households, and an estimated population of approximately 67,000 people (32,613 females; 34,389 males). The ward was divided into six sub-wards, which were administrative units within the ward. Manzese ward is described as an 'informal settlement' where there has been very little planning in relation to building regulations, sanitation and infrastructure.[18]

On initial contact with the case study school, it had a total enrolment of 1785 pupils (904 males; 881 females) with forty-three teachers (36 female; 7 male). Registration data showed that a high proportion of children transferred in and out of the school, which is consistent with peripatetic life in an urban environment. In 2010, the school records indicated the following primary school leaving examination scores averaged across all subjects: 1 to 50 marks = 8.33% pupils; 51–99 = 24.16%; 100–150 = 38.01%; 151–200 = 25.70%; 201–250 = 1.54%. In subsequent years, the government published national statistics that indicated the following in 2011: number of students passed A to C = 53%; average total marks per pupil out of 250 = 185.84.

[18] Ramadhani, 'Effect of tenure regularization program on building investment in Manzese ward in Dar es Salaam, Tanzania. (MSc)', Enschede, Netherlands: 2007.

Forty teachers in the case study school had completed the traditional teaching certificate (also known as 'Grade A' teachers) which is a two-year full-time course of study, two teachers had diplomas (two years duration), and one teacher had a degree (three to four years duration). All teachers in the school had a responsibility to support the development of pupils' English language proficiency. Some of the teachers in standards five to seven were designated as subject specialists, including some for English teaching; however, a teacher's designation could change according to the school's need each year and the balance of different subject expertise amongst the teachers. Teachers in standards one to three also had responsibility to support the teaching of English but typically did not regard themselves as specialists. Each standard had 3 classes, with each class typically exceeding 50 pupils.

The research had two main aims: to support the whole school to develop its capacity to help children learn English; to better understand the key issues that teachers in this kind of context face when they try and improve their teaching of English.

The physical conditions of all classrooms observed were similar throughout the school from standard one to standard seven. The walls of the classrooms were bare, with only very occasional use of posters or wall charts. Walls were punctuated by windows without glass. An electricity supply was not present in most classrooms. In the first few standards, there were not enough chairs or desks so some children were obliged to sit on the floor.

The main teaching resources were blackboard and chalk. Teachers also relied on textbooks produced commercially by western publishers approved by the Tanzanian education ministry. One or two textbooks were shared amongst eight or nine pupils across the standards, and in many lessons the textbooks were not given to the pupils for the entire lesson. Overall, pupils were attentive, and the classes were well managed by the teachers. Lessons that were observed by the researchers often began with all pupils singing a song together and clapping hands followed by a teacher's greeting. Then the teachers gave a short introduction to the topic of the lesson, and wrote the contents of the lesson and/or questions on the blackboard for the pupils to copy. Teacher explanation and questions followed with pupils answering and repeating answers in chorus. The main lesson task would often require copying what was written on the blackboard. The lessons finished with teachers walking around the class to check pupils' writing in their workbooks. It was very rare for teachers to review the previous lesson or conclude with a summary of the lesson. In many classes, pupils spent a great amount of time listening to the teacher's explanations and repeating the same sentences many times.

A common approach to teaching English in the school, and one that was the norm when we started working with the school, featured formal grammar teaching. For example, teachers' explanation of grammatical terms such as 'preposition', and a focus on the 'rules' of English grammar. During this teaching, the pupils usually contributed one-word answers in unison. The questions by the teacher prompted single word answers by the children, and frequently included repetition by the whole class of a model answer given by teachers, or repetition by the whole class of correct answers given by an individual pupil. These introductory whole class aspects of the lessons were followed by written exercises often involving the pupils copying sentences written on the blackboard into their exercise books. The English teacher, Ms Towo's[19] standard seven lesson on active and passive grammar was typical of this kind of grammar-oriented lesson (the mixing of English language and Kiswahili that is a feature of this lesson was common to all lessons).

'The monkey eats a mango (active voice)' [written on the blackboard]

MS TOWO: This is active voice. So, as usual, we take the last wordie to become the first wordie. This 'a mango' comes first. Is 'mango' singular or plural? Ugh?
PUPILS: Singular! *In chorus.*
MS TOWO: If it is singular, so how do you . . . the auxiliary verb is, which one?
PUPILS: Is. *In chorus.*
MS TOWO: Past participle of it is what?
A FEW PUPILS: . . . eaten!.
MS TOWO: Then, the past participle of the verb 'eat' is what?
MS TOWO AND PUPILS: Eaten! *In chorus.*
MS TOWO: So, as usual, don't forget to write the word 'by' in front of 'the monkey'. Then this first wordie become the last wordie.
MS TOWO: Uhaona? [Do you get it?]. Imeeleweka hapo? [Have you understood that?]
PUPILS: Ndiyo, ndiyo! [Yes] *loudly*
MS TOWO *then reads out a sentence written on the blackboard.*
MS TOWO: 'A mango is eaten by the monkey.' This is passive voice. So, change the following sentences into passive voice . . .

As someone regarded as a specialist in the school, this teacher's command of English was strong relative to the majority of teachers in the school (many of whom spoke very little English at all). But the lesson raises a number of questions. The only writing that we saw was short exercises written into exercise books, if the pupils' parents had provided them, completed by the children sometimes sharing one pupil book between as many as 10 children, or simply copying from the blackboard. The importance of regularly practising writing as one of the most effective ways to improve writing was a major challenge in this context. The other question the extract raised was whether the learning of active and passive forms of language was the most relevant teaching for these children. The short answer is no.[20] And if the answer is no, then why

[19] All names are pseudonyms. [20] The longer answer can be found in Wyse et al., 2014.

were the teachers teaching in this way? One reason was that because of the intense resource problems in the education system caused by the weak economy the teachers had never had the opportunity to meet, as part of planned professional development together, to discuss teaching. Time to meet like this has a number of logistical difficulties if organised during school hours because, a) money for cover teachers would need to be found (even if this was a realistic possibility); and b), because the teachers were needed at home for other work, paid or unpaid, so were understandably reluctant to stay beyond the end of the school day. Hence perhaps the main reason for the kinds of teaching was as a result of the custom and practice that schools build up over many years.

As a result of our interventions, we did find some modest developments. The following example from one of the lesson videos we collected is indicative of a teacher, with greater knowledge of English than many of the other teachers, demonstrating her capacity to engage with the new educational ideas we introduced. The extract also indicates the challenges that all the teachers faced.

The teacher was holding a large-format copy of the English language children's book Peace at Last *by Jill Murphy.*

Ms SAIDI: Last week, we already read about this book, yeah? Are we?
PUPILS: Yeah . . .
Ms SAIDI: Have you read about this book? All of you, yeah?
PUPILS: Yes.
Ms SAIDI: I want to ask the question about this book. Because we're already read this. So mshasoma kwenye kitabu? [So you have already read from the book?] Are we together? Tell me the story about this book. What have you learn about this book? Mlisoma nini mkaelewa kutoka hiki kitabu? [What did you understand when you read from this book?]
PUPIL A: Nimeelewa Mr Bear hapendi kelele. [What she has said is My Bear does not like noise.]
Ms SAIDI: Mr Bear don't want noise. Is she right?
PUPILS: Yes.
Ms SAIDI: Yes, Mr Bear don't want noise. What else? Nini kingine mumesoma katika hiki kitabu? [What else have you read in this book?]
PUPIL B: Kulikuwa hakuna maelewano kati ya Mr Bear na family yake. [There was argument between Mr Bear and his family.] *Ms Saidi repeats what the pupil B has said.*
Ms SAIDI: Is she right?
PUPILS: Yes!
Ms SAIDI: Ehe nani mwingine ataniambia ameelewa nini kwenye kitabu? [Who else will tell me what they have understood from the book?] Kulikuwa kuna makundi mangapi? [How many groups were there?] *The class must have previously read this book in groups. The whole class reply in chorus:* 'nane' [eight].
Ms SAIDI: Haya kundi la nane liko wapi? [Ok, where is the eighth group?] Milielewa nini kutoka hiki kitabu? [What did you understand from this book?]
Ms SAIDI: Do you wanna read again?
PUPILS: Yes. [Loudly]

This lesson had been preceded by another lesson in which for the first time in her career this teacher had read a story aloud to a class. The reason that the teachers had access to books was because we had organised to bring as many children's books written in English that we could to give to the school. Towards the end of the project, we were successful in linking the school with a non-government organisation who provided books for schools, in Kiswahili and in English. Even the very first question the teacher asks the class was part of a completely new approach for her. She began with a reminder of the last lesson, and then asked the open question 'Tell me the story about this book. What have you learn about this book?' This prompted the children to recollect events and ideas from the story. For pupils who were used to responding with single-word answers in unison, this also was very new to them. The teacher pragmatically used Kiswahili to back up the English to ensure that as many children as possible were able to follow the lesson.

In addition to teacher knowledge, teacher experience, and lack of opportunities for professional development, another possibility was that Tanzania's national curriculum policy would influence teaching. The *English Language Syllabus for Primary Schools, Standard I–VII*,[21] which prescribed teaching objectives, included a strong emphasis on the teaching of formal grammar in a way not sufficiently consistent with research evidence on effective teaching of English. However, the government syllabus also included the requirement for contextualised English teaching:

> throughout the course you need to present new language in a meaningful context using pictures, realia, gestures or demonstration to make meaning clear to learners. Always involve your learners when teaching. Participatory, learner-centred and activity-based teaching will give better language results than non-participatory or teacher centred teaching.[22]

Although this overarching requirement appeared to be somewhat rhetorical, in view of the heavy emphasis on formal grammar teaching in the syllabus, it is clear from the recommended activities that teachers were expected, for example, to use real objects in the classroom, and put pupils in pairs for role-play; etc. Our research revealed that the teachers only had limited knowledge of the English Language Syllabus hence their confidence and competence, linked with their limited knowledge and experience of the English language (within a wide range of knowledge between individual teachers), combined with custom and practice in the school, were the main reasons for the practice we observed.

[21] United Republic of Tanzania Ministry of Education and Culture, *English Language Syllabus for Primary Schools*.

[22] United Republic of Tanzania Ministry of Education and Culture, *English Language Syllabus for Primary Schools*, 1.

Research has shown that the quality of teaching, and hence the training of teachers, is a vital part of improving literacy in both low-income and high-income country contexts. While the challenges in low-income nations are extensive, progress has been made, particularly in relation to more children being present in primary education. But the quality of teaching they encounter when in school is too often of insufficient quality. However, high-income nations are not without problems in relation to the level of pupils' literacy, nor without problems of questionable government school curriculum and assessment policies.

English Teaching in England

In the country where the English language first emerged, one where English is by far the dominant language and the language that nearly all citizens speak, it is a reasonable expectation that it is well taught in schools. While there is a great deal of excellent teaching and learning, there are also some significant challenges.

A government-commissioned report in the UK found evidence that general learning difficulties affect up to 10% of children, and 4% to 8% of children are affected by specific learning disability or dyslexia. The long-lasting effects of dyslexia contribute to individuals' reduced well-being, self-esteem and mental capital, and even produce a predicted reduction in lifetime earnings to the individual of more than £80,000.[23] As part of the challenge of supporting children with Special Educational Needs, and all children, there is evidence that too many young people do not acquire the reading and writing levels that they need for work and to benefit fully from life's opportunities. Learning to write happens for most people during their school years. Consequently, most people in high income countries are literate, but there are significant numbers of adults who struggle with reading and writing.

The term 'functional literacy' is used to describe the level of literacy required by people to cope with the typical demands of lives in literate societies. In the UK the definition of functional literacy was set by a government review of adult skills. This level was described as level 1, and the levels below this called 'entry levels'. Level 1 literacy is equivalent to a marginal pass in the exam that most people sit when aged 16, the General Certificate of School Education (GCSE).[24] This is still a very low level of literacy. For

[23] Government Office for Science, *Foresight Mental Capital and Wellbeing Project.*

[24] A marginal pass is graded at D, E, F, or G, on a scale from A to G. The quoted examples of the consequences of not meeting levels are published in Department for Business, Innovation & Skills (2011). *BIS Research Paper Number 57.* 'The 2011 Skills for Life Survey: Headline Findings', 20.

example, this would not be enough to progress to the A Level examinations that some people study for when aged 17 to 18, although it would be enough to enter some vocational courses.

As part of the government-commissioned survey of adult skills in England, 14.9% of the people who were interviewed and tested were assessed as below 'level 1', which means that they 'may not be able to read bus or train timetables or check the pay and deductions on a wage slip'.[25] If this is extrapolated to the approximately 30 million working population[26] in the whole of the UK this means that 4,500,000 people may not be able to read a time table; 1,500,000 people, at 'entry level 1' or below may not be able to, 'write short messages to family or select floor numbers in lifts '. Entry level 1 is equivalent to the level of the school national curriculum for children aged five to seven.[27] Life for these 4,500,000 people is not only restricted because they can't access so many jobs that require higher levels of writing skills, but also the day-to-day difficulties of surviving in a world that is dominated by print must be severe. The constant need to hide the lack of understanding from friends and colleagues is bound to have a damaging effect on self-esteem.

There is much less research on what kind of teaching is effective for adults compared with that for school-age learners, but it is instructive to see what the key messages are. One of very few studies to focus on writing, as opposed to literacy more generally, studied 199 learners, in 40 classrooms, in 20 organisations who were working to improve writing in the UK. Small but significant improvements in writing were attributed to a range of theories and practices. Consistent with experimental trial evidence with younger learners, having plenty of opportunity to write was vital, and for the learners in this study it was estimated that 150 to 200 hours of teaching and learning was required in order to progress one level. That equates to between 1 month and 2 months of full-time education; or 20 to 30 weeks for one full day per week; or more than one year of classes of two hours per week. This is powerful evidence indicating why improving literacy for those who have not succeeded at school is so costly for society, and how challenging it is, in relation to amount of time, for those people affected.

The research found that if meaningful contexts for writing activities using a range of different forms of writing were provided, and if these were clearly linked with the learners' experiences in their lives, adults' writing improved. In addition, time was needed for discussion between teachers and learners about writing and the tasks, and individual feedback and support was needed while learners were writing, through teachers who were responsive to their learners'

[25] Department for Business Innovation & Skills, 'The 2011 Skills for Life Survey', xxvii.
[26] Office for National Statistics, 'UK Labour Market, February 2015'.
[27] Entry levels 3, 2, and 1 are below level 1.

needs and flexible to adapt the planned session according to those needs. Overall the findings emphasised that 'teaching should approach the technical aspects of writing: spelling, grammatical correctness and punctuation, within the contexts of meaningful writing tasks rather than through decontextualised exercises'.[28] It appears then that the key elements of the process approach to writing that work for young writers also work for adult learners.

The evidence from studies of children's development, from studies of effective teaching of writing (with both child and adult learners), and indeed the range of evidence of the nature of written language that I have addressed in the different chapters of this book provides a significant basis for planning literacy policy in education systems. The final part of this chapter explores the extent to which evidence appears to have been part of England's national curriculum for schools.

England's National Curriculum

The national curriculum requirements determine to a large extent how writing, and all the subjects of the curriculum, are taught in most schools in England,[29] and hence have an important influence on children's learning and lives. In addition to their practical significance, national curricula are also symbolically important because they represent a statement of the expectations that a society has for its citizens, and in various ways articulate a vision for the kinds of knowledge that the society values.

Prior to 1988 the countries of the UK – Northern Ireland, Scotland, Wales and England – did not have national curricula. The Education Reform Act 1988 established the need for the Secretary of State for Education to establish a national curriculum and associated national assessment system. It is far from clear that this legal requirement has resulted in demonstrable, sustained improvements in children's learning since its inception, in fact there is troubling evidence of problems in spite of the significant expenditure of public funds.[30] One of the enduring areas of debate, since 1988, has been about the way in which language, and particularly what is called 'Standard English', is specified in the national curriculum. This is also one of the recurrent considerations of this book: how standardised forms of the English language emerge and how they are maintained and perceived through social groupings and the published outputs of these groups, including language conventions and guides.

[28] Grief, Meyer, and Burgess, *Effective Teaching and Learning: Writing*, 11.

[29] Independent schools, academy schools, and free schools are not required to follow the national curriculum, although many do because the statutory assessment system creates pressure to cover aspects of the national curriculum.

[30] Wyse and Torrance, 'The Development and Consequences of National Curriculum Assessment for Primary Education in England', 213–228; Alexander, *Children, Their World.*

There have been a series of changes to England's national curriculum over the decades since its inception, and the 2014 version brought some fairly radical developments. The introduction to the national curriculum sets out a framework that includes overarching principles about 'Language and literacy'. One of the opening statements in this section is, 'Pupils should be taught to speak clearly and convey ideas confidently using Standard English.' An alternative to this that represents a better fit with evidence from linguistics might be, 'Pupils should be encouraged to speak using language forms appropriate for the context of interaction.' This statement accounts for the fact that levels of formality require different kinds of language use. A classic example being the difference in language required for many job interviews versus an informal conversation with a friend.

The statement raises another linguistic consideration: how does the national curriculum define 'Standard English'?:

> Standard English can be recognised by the use of a very small range of forms such as those books, I did it and I wasn't doing anything (rather than their non-Standard equivalents); it is not limited to any particular accent. It is the variety of English which is used, with only minor variation, as a major world language. Some people use Standard English all the time, in all situations from the most casual to the most formal, so it covers most registers. The aim of the national curriculum is that everyone should be able to use Standard English as needed in writing and in relatively formal speaking.[31]

The idea that standard English is used only with 'minor variation' throughout the world is simply untenable, particularly in relation to spoken English. In every country in the world where English is used the local contexts result in modifications to what some claim is standard English. The very existence of different dictionaries for different versions of English is proof of this (e.g. American English, see Chapter 3). And the suggestion that some people use standard English 'all the time' is very dubious. Standard English is technically a dialect. In 2007 it was estimated that it was spoken natively by 12% to 15% of the population in England, with use more common in speakers with higher socio-economic status.[32] This means that for 85% to 88% of the population standard English is not spoken natively by them. A more appropriate aim of the national curriculum would be: 'Children and young people should be able to use spoken and written language that communicates most effectively in relation to the context they are in.' This implies that young people should take account of the fact that language use will differ significantly according to whether that context is spoken language or written language.

[31] Department for Education, 'The National Curriculum in England', 99

[32] Kerswill, 'Standard and Non-Standard English'.

Turning again to the introductory framework of the national curriculum, the main driver for the teaching of reading and writing is the acquisition of *knowledge* in all subjects. The intrinsic rewards of writing or the fundamental need to communicate meaning are not specified first and foremost. Instead, stamina and skills are specified, and that pupils 'should be taught the correct use of grammar'. Had the national curriculum been more appropriate, linguistically, it would have specified that 'pupils should be taught to use grammar appropriately for the context of language use'. Some use of non-standard grammar, e.g. for talking to friends, is more appropriate, will facilitate more efficient sharing of meanings, and is necessary for maintaining peer-group dynamics in the best interests of the speaker. Standard English use is necessary for most forms of writing, although text and internet message forms are often closer to informal spoken language.

But particularly problematic is the emphasis on traditional grammar in the specifications for primary education. This has been one of a number of divisive elements that are part of the history of debate about literacy and schooling since 1988. The requirements include an appendix of 6 pages specifying the teaching of grammar (on top of the 'vocabulary, grammar and punctuation' section in the programme of study for each year group; and 25 pages of requirements for the teaching of spelling including word lists for every year of the primary school). Evidence that the expected teaching should be traditional grammar teaching, rather than teaching based on modern linguistic knowledge, can be seen clearly in the relationship between the curriculum and the national tests that pupils have to sit when they are aged ten or eleven. In 2016 the questions, that mainly attracted one mark, included the following:

3. Circle the **object** [grammatical not physical] in the sentence below.
4. Draw a line to match each sentence to the correct **determiner**.
10. Pick one box in each row to show if the sentence is in the **present progressive** or the **past progressive**.
27. Underline the **subordinate clause** in each sentence below.

The rationale for the teaching of formal grammar is explained like this:

> The grammar of our first language is learnt naturally and implicitly through interactions with other speakers and from reading. Explicit knowledge of grammar is, however, very important, as it gives us more conscious control and choice in our language. Building this knowledge is best achieved through a focus on grammar within the teaching of reading, writing and speaking. Once pupils are familiar with a grammatical concept [for example 'modal verb'], they should be encouraged to apply and explore this concept in the grammar of their own speech and writing and to note where it is used by others. Young pupils, in particular, use more complex language in speech than in writing, and teachers should build on this, aiming for a smooth transition to sophisticated writing.[33]

[33] Department for Education, 'The National Curriculum in England', 75.

'Explicit knowledge of grammar' (such as being able to name a subordinate clause, or verb, or split infinitive) is *not* according to the evidence 'very important'.[34] What *is* very important is that children and adults of all abilities can use sentences and words effectively to communicate their intended messages in the way most appropriate for their listeners or readers. This is a craft knowledge, and an experiential knowledge, not an explicit knowledge in the way it is prescribed in England's national curriculum. There is no evidence that the use of knowing what the term 'modal verb' means helps writing. Nor is there evidence to support the idea that 7-year-old children should know the term 'subordinate clause'; 8-year-old children 'determiner'; 9-year-old children 'modal verb'; 10-year-old children 'active/passive'. It could be knowledge appropriate for teachers, although even that is debateable, but it is absolutely not of use for children learning to write. The further one analyses the specifications for English in the national curriculum, the more the Ministers' ideology, at the expense of evidence, is clear. The overall framing and conception of the national curriculum as a whole at primary education level is not appropriate for a twenty-first-century curriculum that could have been built more carefully on the wealth of robust evidence available.

My critique perhaps inevitably leads to one final question: what might the current national curriculum requirements for English in England be replaced with? To conclude this section I use one final comparison with music. The specifications for the subject of music in England's national curriculum occupy just 3 pages, unlike for English which has 88 pages. But in my view the overall framing for the music curriculum, and much of the detail, is just as appropriate for an English curriculum, as I have shown in Table 6.2 by doing little more than replacing the word 'music' with the word 'language'.

If political leaders were to change England's national curriculum in such a way, and support this change with significant professional development opportunities for teachers, it is likely that we might see some improvements in children and young people's use of and understanding of writing, language and literature. It is also possible that the worrying consequences of the literacy levels of many adults, addressed earlier in this chapter, could be substantially ameliorated.

*

The youngest children's early writing behaviour is driven by their general curiosity about things in their lives. They learn that if they express themselves in particular ways, through appropriate language, they are better able to fulfil their needs and desires. For example, the young baby's cry for food becomes the ability to point at the food it wants, which eventually transforms into the

[34] Andrews, Torgerson, Beverton, et al., 'The Effect of Grammar Teaching (Syntax) in English on 5 to 16 Year Olds' Accuracy and Quality in Written Composition'; Graham and Harris, K. 'Evidence-Based Writing Practices'; Wyse, 'Grammar. For Writing?', 411–427.

Table 6.2 *How English could be represented in the national curriculum of England*

Language
Purpose of study Language is a universal medium that embodies one of the highest forms of creativity. A high-quality language education should engage and inspire pupils to develop a love of reading and writing, and their talent as language users, and so increase their self-confidence, creativity and sense of achievement. As pupils progress, they should develop a critical engagement with language and literature, allowing them to compose, and to read with discrimination, a range of texts both digital and printed.
Aims The national curriculum for language aims to ensure that all pupils: • Perform, read and listen to, review and evaluate texts across a range of historical periods, genres, styles and traditions, including the works of the great authors. • Learn to use talk effectively, to create and compose texts on their own and with others, and to use technology appropriately. • Understand and explore how text is created, produced and communicated, including through the inter-related dimensions: language structures, grammar, punctuation, spelling, and phoneme-letter links, and a range of formatting styles.
Attainment targets By the end of each key stage, pupils are expected to know, apply and understand the matters, skills and processes specified in the relevant programme of study.
Subject content
Key stage 1 [age 5 to 7] Pupils should be taught to: • Use language expressively and creatively by composing and reading texts. • Use writing tools effectively. • Read and listen with concentration and understanding to a range of high-quality texts. • Experiment with, create, select and combine sentences and words using the inter-related dimensions of language.
Key stage 2 [age 7 to 11] Pupils should be taught to read and write with increasing confidence and control. They should develop an understanding of textual composition, organising and manipulating ideas within text structures and sometimes reproducing texts from memory. Pupils should be taught to: • Perform poetry and plays in solo and ensemble contexts, using their voices with increasing accuracy, fluency, control and expression. • Improvise and compose texts for a range of purposes using the inter-related dimensions of language. • Listen with attention to detail and recall texts with increasing memory. • Use and understand the conventions of written language. • Appreciate and understand a wide range of high-quality texts drawn from different traditions and from great authors. • Develop some understanding of the history of language and literature.

ability to say in words what it wants. As children grow older their ability to control written language develops, giving them even greater capacity to compose messages meaningful to them and increasingly understandable by others.

In relation to the school years, we now have strong research evidence about what works in the teaching of writing yet too many young people do not learn to write adequately for the requirements and pleasures of life. An approach to writing that emphasises the processes of writing – rather than decontextualising teaching into exercises such as on grammar – is more effective. Creativity should often be at the heart of good writing teaching, and a supportive environment for writing where skills are taught and where students collaborate. The right kind of feedback from teachers and peers is vital, as is the writer's ability to be self-critical.

The consequences of not learning to write, and to be literate more generally are serious. For adults in any part of the world they are denied access to both employment and full enjoyment of the many possibilities in life. This is true in wealthy nations and poorer nations alike. But the consequences for regions such as sub-Saharan Africa are particularly worrying. Yet there is much to be optimistic about. On a global scale it has been shown that real progress towards goals on development has been seen. We also have some promising approaches to helping teachers in these countries help their students, but more research is needed in these areas. Not least because most research has been carried out in western nations rather than the Global South.

To varying degrees, teachers in different countries in the world have professional autonomy to approach the teaching of writing in the ways they see fit. But whether people learn to write, and how successfully they learn to write, is also strongly influenced by wider society. All societies have means to pass down the knowledge of older generations to younger generations. In oral societies this happens, and has happened, through processes such as oral storytelling, and in ancient Greece the work of the teachers and pedagogues. In modern literate societies, learning is formally organised through education systems, in addition to the personal learning that arises in homes and communities. An important part of society's influence is the way governments structure education systems, and the extent to which these governments' policies are true democratic representations of what people want, and that reflect the best knowledge about how to teach and how people learn.

This chapter's broad review of the writing lives of children in homes, schools and communities, of adults who struggle with society's demands, of the work of teachers and children in different countries of the world, has shown overall that abundant evidence and knowledge already exists about how writing works. Not only does the evidence show that meaning is at the heart of writing but also that it should be at the heart of teaching. When meaning is understood in the ways analysed in this book, and when the technical aspects of writing are seen to serve the drive for meaning, rather than these technical elements unduly dominating teaching, then the craft of writing is learned. As a result, politicians with responsibility for literacy should ensure that their policies reflect this evidence, rather than unduly base policies on personal ideology that leads to practices that are at best far from optimum, and at worst damaging to learners' and societies' best interests.

7 The Process of Writing

Throughout this book, I have shown that understanding how writing works requires, most of all, understanding of the processes of writing. In order to make these arguments, as the writer of the book, I was necessarily embedded in a process of writing myself. Reflections on this process provided a final source of data for analysis: a diary of reflections on the process of writing the book. The diary entries were reflections that I recorded periodically when events and thoughts related to the writing seemed important. I began writing the diary in July 2013. In the early stages of the book, the work was focused more on research, analysis and recording. The writing was more provisional and speculative. In these phases, I recorded observations when I felt something significant related to my processes of writing, and to my thinking about the book, had occurred. During more concentrated periods of writing I noted my thoughts a minimum of once per week and sometimes daily. So, for example, between October and December 2016, when I had some study leave, the frequency of observations increased.

Consistent with the analysis of expert writers in Chapter 4, I've used the same categories/subheadings to structure the first part of this chapter. The final part of the chapter concludes the book by summarising how writing works and, consequently, how it might be taught.

You Throw the Rock and You Get the Splash

I describe the stimulus for the book overall as having a broadly educational intent. By the end of the book, it also deals with education quite specifically. However, beyond knowing that the book would have some broad educational purpose, more than three years ago I still faced the starting point for any writer: the blank page and the question, what will I write? This connects with the search for inspiration for writing. My reason for writing this book in the first place was to try and make a significant contribution to knowledge. During my career, I have written about writing many times, in research papers, research reports and two books. I decided that a full book was needed if I was to have sufficient space to address the topic from the multidisciplinary perspective that I wanted to adopt. I also wanted to write a sole-authored book because if written well such a book can enable a different, more coherent and sometimes more significant and weighty contribution from other kinds of texts such as journal articles or edited books.

Beside the Clock's Loneliness

The question of what to write was related to my interests and expertise as a researcher. The professional writers' advice to write what you know about was obviously relevant here, although it is one thing to decide on a broad topic but quite another to think how that topic needs addressing in a way that is original and of value. Perhaps it wasn't a blank page after all, perhaps I was faced with an infinite notebook with a mixture of blank pages, not entirely coherent notes on some pages, and occasional pages full of text almost ready to be imported. My prior experience as a writer clearly was important because it gave me the confidence to go for what I most wanted to write. There was also a sense of my returning to where I began my academic career. Was this a stage-of-life feeling? Maybe.

More than twenty years ago, following my round of rejections by publishers for a first book proposal, my second proposal, a book about the teaching of writing attracted the attention of two publishers. The idea for the book arose as a result of my first research degree, which was a study of the teaching of writing. In the end I opted for Open University Press. Self-critically I can now look back with the benefit of hindsight and more experience and see that I could have done a different research project, better than the one I did that informed the book. However to counter-balance that critical thought, getting an MPhil published at all is positive because it is rare. So in a sense the inspiration for *How Writing Works* began more than twenty years ago.

Another important influence on *How Writing Works* was my epistemological orientation. I see great value in post-positivist *and* interpretivist orientations to knowledge. The scientific method, with its use of random allocation to intervention and control groups, robust measurement, and outcomes interpreted on the basis of statistical probability, does in my view have an important role to play in education and social science, not least in the comparison of teaching methods. At the same time, there is much that can be discovered through the qualitative methods so often aligned with interpretivism. The epistemology of positivism vs interpretivism, in the context of research, has been the heart of intense philosophical debates. My reliance to some degree on philosophy, and particularly the philosophy of pragmatism, is one way I have found to bridge these orientations Pragmatism has been linked in some ways with the mixed-methods approaches to research problems, approaches that combine the best of quantitative and qualitative methods. Pragmatism is also important in relation to education because its focus includes attention to the relevance of theory for the work of learners and teachers, and in some cases for educational policy. There is also in my view a link between pragmatism, mixed methods and multidisciplinary perspectives.

Throughout the book, I have drawn on work from a range of relevant disciplines. Each of these disciplines has its favoured epistemological and ontological positions, and each to some degree will often suggest that other disciplines are unable to address research problems in the ways that are necessary. Education as a relatively young academic discipline has an interesting internal debate about its own status as a discipline and/or a field. Indeed for part of the time I was researching for this book, I completed the editing of a significant new work that is intended as state-of-the-art (and/or science!) publication in relation to the progress of education as a discipline.[1]

A Tenor Man Drawing a Breath

And then there is music. My first degree was at the Royal Academy of Music in London. Although I was offered places at universities, for example a place at the University of East Anglia and a choral scholarship (baritone, though, not 'tenor man'), my early preference was for the *performance* of music. I see some links between this interest in performance and my interest not only in the theoretical aspects of writing but also in the practical aspects. Ever since a friend and professional composer, Alastair Greig, raised the question of whether a playing musician could be a genius the way a composer could, I have wrestled with the ideas of creativity in composing versus creativity in performance. My professorial lecture at the Institute of Education in London (now merged with UCL) brought together my interest in music with my interest in education, including my short performance on the viola of some unaccompanied Bach and some unaccompanied Reger as an introduction to some definitional concepts of creativity.[2] My understanding of music clearly is an influence on my academic thinking both implicitly, for example in an aesthetic sensibility to research, and at times explicitly, such as the use of music as a comparator in this book.

Voices Heard in the Darkness

The overall orientations for the book drew on my life history as a writer, my ambitions to contribute to knowledge, and my interest in writing as a subject of research. The decision on topic and type of book then brought me to the more

[1] Wyse, D. et al. *BERA/SAGE Handbook.* [2] Wyse, *Creativity and the Curriculum.*

specific influences. This raises the question, to plan or not to plan? In narrative fiction writing there are writers who say they simply set off writing without any written planning. However, this pre-supposes that they have not had to pitch the idea to a publisher. Any pitch requires the articulation of a vision and varying degrees of detail. But the idea of writing without detailed planning seems to be rare for non-fiction writers, and differs for those who prefer to write a whole book first and then try to get a contract, rather than to write the pitch first. In order to get a contract, I had to construct a proposal that I knew would be peer-reviewed by experts in the field internationally. This required me to address several issues: reasons for writing the book; general overall account of content; list of chapters and indication of content of each chapter; credentials of the author; readership and market; and to show knowledge of other published texts addressing the same topic. So in this thirteen-page document was the first stage of more detailed planning.

My influences were not only topic and subject influences but also an interaction between planning, researching and the selection and rejection of topics, which continued throughout the writing process. In another book I have published about writing, aimed particularly at students of education in colleges and universities, I proposed the idea of *retrospective planning*.[3] This is the idea that there is a reciprocal relationship between planning and writing. Planning a piece of writing is always necessary (however unstructured that planning may be), but any initial plans need to be modified *as* the writing progresses, and the ongoing changes to the plan should modify *how* the writing progresses. In my experience, modification of original plans is an entirely natural consequence of the writing, its challenges and what Dewey called the surprise of the consummatory aspects of language. If the writing planning is adhered to too closely, it might impede some of the creative discoveries that are part of the writing process. At the same time, flights of fancy that take the writer too far away from the core of the task are also risky. The plan acts like a *sounding* board: and as I write that phrase, how aptly is seems to link the writers' ear with the ongoing planning.

My recognition of retrospective planning resulted in the book proposal synopsis being recast as an ongoing plan of the overall structure, modified as necessary as the writing progressed. No further chapters were added, nor were any deleted, but the order of three of the chapters did change. Quite late in the process, I decided to move the chapter on creativity and writing and place it straight after the chapter on expert writers because creativity was an important theme in the expert writers chapter, and hence it seemed to lead more naturally into the chapter on creativity. In addition, the chapter on creativity ends with the report of my research study with children and young people, which led appropriately into the novice writers chapter. These

[3] Wyse & Cowan, *Good Writing Guide*.

kinds of large structural changes were only made when drafts of chapters were almost complete, and hence clearer in my mind about what their main lines of argument were.

Taking planning as a form of preparation for writing, there were a few other aspects. For some chapters, additional documents were developed that supported the writing of the chapter. The chapter on thinking about writing was informed by a spreadsheet that recorded quotes and my key points resulting from new areas of reading. Although my attention to philosophy had increased over the course of my career, the research for this book required extending my knowledge, particularly in relation to the span of philosophy from the ancient Greeks to more modern philosophy, but also in relation to pragmatism. And for all of this I sought to read, first-hand, original philosophical works (including high-quality translations) but also up-to-date academic commentaries. The more rigorous approach in the spreadsheet was supported by the more free-flowing 'planning and quotes' document I had for all the chapters in the book. This allowed me to note topics and sources to follow up and to record my reflections on these sources. The origins of this began with a simple table of what I thought might be the table of contents, which was added to until it became transformed into the planning and quotes document. For the history chapter, in addition to the free-flowing planning and quotes document, I also constructed a timeline spreadsheet so that I could be checking the chronology of key events in the history of writing, key authors and key writing-process developments. The computer folder that held all the material for the book included a sources folder containing a wealth of documents that were referred to in the book. These multiple sources were also reflected in the internet browser bookmarks folder that was established.

An additional planning document was a one-page outline of the key questions and theoretical framing for the book. This was used as an aide-memoire to check the relationship between the framing for the book as a whole and my unfolding writing of individual chapters. I didn't want to feel constrained by the theoretical framework because I saw the framing as a tool to unify and enrich a text, but I also did not want to stray too far from my framing, which was both theoretical and also based on a line of argument within the aims of the book as a whole.

Additional planning was represented by a systematic analysis of the texts that informed the writing guides chapter, recorded in a spreadsheet. Basic bibliographic information was recorded alongside columns for author/editor disciplinary background, overall approach to the topic, the category that I assigned, and my analytic notes. Selection of texts to feature prominently in the chapter was made on the basis of this initial overall analysis. The fine-grained analysis of the advice in the guides then emerged as part of the writing process of the chapter.

The most rigorous and time-consuming new analysis for the book was of the *Paris Review Interviews* in preparation for the expert writers chapter. This began with a pilot analysis where I selected authors, such as Philip Roth, whose books I had read in significant numbers. The pilot analysis progressed to the careful reading of volumes one to three of the *Paris Review* books. By the time I reached the fourth volume, my main findings were clear and had coalesced around five or six categories that became the subheadings of the chapter. My analysis techniques were informed by an approach that originated in the 1960s in the sociology department of the University of Chicago. *Grounded Theory* is a qualitative research design or approach that seeks in-depth investigation of cases that typically are cases of people's experiences in particular settings. The idea is that new theory is developed, where to a large degree there has been no previous theory, and that this theory is closely aligned with the language of the participants. One feature of grounded theory analysis is that the analysis of data reaches a point described as *saturation*. I reached that point in February 2015 as I continued analysis of the fourth volume. However, in late 2016 (I didn't record this but probably October) I returned to the *Paris Review* volumes because I had discovered the online resource which allows digital import to data-analysis software. There was not sufficient time to analyse the whole digital archive, so I switched to using a random number generator that I developed to identify a stratified random sample of new interview reports, which I then duly analysed. The analysis, which is a process of identifying key ideas in the interview transcripts and 'coding' and organising these in ways that help the analyst to theorise their meanings, is a classic approach for qualitative research.

The final planning elements were related to the chapter on creativity. The first half of the chapter required me to update my knowledge of creativity research, particularly new findings from neuroscience. During the research for this chapter, I had one of those wonderful moments where I discovered a paper, published in 1953, which so beautifully anticipated the debates of the creativity field up until the present day. The second half of the chapter benefitted from the work already done on a three-year study of young people's creativity. Having led the project team, with my colleague Andrew Burn, including leading the writing of the final report, I had some material, including data, to work with. But this needed rewriting to fit the shape of the chapter and to be relevant to the book as a whole. It also required some new analyses, not previously part of the research project, of the ways in which the young people's writing was judged to represent originality and value, and to investigate the extent to which this could be seen as developmental progression or not.

Keeping the Machine Running

Another major factor in the writing of the book was time. In view of the pressure on academics to publish, it is paradoxical that sufficient periods of time to support new writing are not at all easy to find. Like most professional people, I need to engage with multiple tasks, including leading a department of more than 110 academic staff, carrying out research projects, teaching, assessing, reviewing, speaking at conferences, supporting the academic community, and many more. My promotion to head of an academic department meant that my time for research and writing would need even more careful planning. I was due a study leave period; typically these last for one term of three months although some non-writing work always continues, particularly work with PhD students and work on research projects. This study leave was essential for the work on the book.

There is one more observation I have about time, and about location. In December 2016, I visited David Olson at the Ontario Institute for Studies in Education. I did not know David until that visit, but I had hoped to meet him because his book *The World on Paper* has some important similarities with what I wanted to do: it was multidisciplinary; it included a focus on the history of writing; it included philosophical attention to its subject; but most of all it was a book I really admired. The meetings with David were an inspiration. I also met with a range of other colleagues, and visited the site where Marshall McLuhan worked on *The Gutenberg Galaxy*. But the visit also meant I was on my own in a hotel room for extended periods where *all* I had to do was write. Jet lag meant I started to keep some of Kerouac's working hours! It would be remiss not to mention that I was, of course, also working to a deadline for the manuscript to be sent to the publisher.

The structural work on the book came before the editing. That is not to say that sentence-level changes weren't made all the time. But much of the text was left in rough state while I worked on the main structural blocks, the chapters, the sub headed sections, the sequences of paragraphs. In the final weeks, including my time in the Toronto hotel, the detailed work of sentence-level and word-level changes intensified. In part this was as a result of growing confidence that the structure was settled, and as a result of the urge to further shape the coherence of the lines of argument. A curious reaction that I experienced a couple of times was returning, after a lapse of time, to a chapter that I had thought was largely finished, only to feel that it was really not finished because the overall shape of the book had moved on. At other times, there were occasional pleasant surprises: namely the anticipation, and slight fear, that I had to read a section that was not sufficiently formed turned out to be misplaced.

It was not possible to do justice to the endless editing of words, phrases and sentences that goes on throughout the writing, and particularly once the overall structure is settled. As one indication of the multiple edits, I have a file called 'cuts' that is more than 27,000 words. These cuts were made for two main reasons: (1) the material was not right for the overall lines of argument in the book; (2) the tone of the material was wrong, or in other words my writer's ear detected that something was 'out of tune'.

There were also various comments I made in my diary of the writing process (which informs this chapter) about these smaller details. One of these observations concerned what I thought would be the first paragraph of the first main chapter of the book, on thinking about writing. At that stage, I only envisaged a short introduction: this introduction became a full chapter; hence the thinking-about-writing chapter became the second chapter of the book (but titled finally as Chapter 1!). On 4 March 2014, I recorded my reflection that the first paragraph of the thinking about writing chapter, which at that point was possibly going to be philosophy only, had required excessive revisions each time I returned to it. I recognised the value of reading from the beginning of a section written at the previous writing session, to remind oneself of progress but also to check that the writing was as intended. I also recognised the importance of beginnings: beginning of a whole book, a chapter, a section. In the end, though, in spite of all the revisions the paragraph did not survive because it suffered from some other good advice – that sometimes we need to write ourselves into a work then delete a lot of early writing. I couldn't help but think about Oscar Wilde's comic remark in answer to a question about what he did in the morning. He said,

> 'In the morning, after hard work, I took a comma out of one sentence.'
> 'And in the afternoon?'
> 'In the afternoon I put it back again.'[4]

Another example of sentence-level editing, which also has wider relevance to the writing at text-level, was moving a particular sentence. The sentence in question was the first sentence of a paragraph in the chapter on guides to writing: 'The wealth of information surrounding this example of "meaning", and all entries in OED, renders the description "dictionary definition" rather limited.' I moved the sentence because it made the point before the reader had seen the evidence to support it. The sentence pre-empted the presentation of information that supported the point being made. It worked far better in a final summary paragraph after the reader had read the evidence. This is the kind of advice I regularly offer PhD students when reading drafts of their writing, yet in the heat of the first draft I didn't spot this. It was only with editing that I noticed and changed this. It is also important to note that my early drafts are littered with errors that I only correct later. For that reason, I dislike having the spell check on while writing. When I write, composition is entirely separate from editing.

The first words of the first draft of the first chapter were written sometime in January 2014. I wrote this final sentence of the first full draft of the book on 22 November 2016 (and yet another draft on 10 December 2016; and worked on the version created by the copy editor on 23 June 2017). The final half of this chapter, the conclusions to the book, was not written until the major work of

[4] Cooper, 'Quotations by Oscar Wilde'.

discussing drafts of chapters with selected colleagues in the UK and abroad, and the subsequent modifications to the book, had been completed. And on the 2nd of August 2017 at 06:48 I added this sentence to the digital proof copy of the book. The day before, I had been emailed the front cover design for the book, based on an image I had been asked to select from a collection of images. My work on the copy edited MS Word version, and then on the Adobe Reader version of the proofs, required many word and sentence edits as a result of the excellent work that the copy editor and proof reader did.

How Writing Works

The innate human desire to make and communicate meaning drives written language. All other aspects of writing are subservient to this desire. Understanding the processes of writing is paramount if the products of writing are to satisfy writers and their readers. The ear of the writer is her most precious attribute. When well developed, this ear brings analytic precision, compositional fluency, and technical skills that are necessary to create and craft writing.

At this point, it may be tempting for some writers to use the succinct structure of a list to communicate the main ideas that have been revealed through the book's analyses. For example,

Maxims for Writers

- Descriptivism rules!
- Acquire the wisdom of conventions, not conventional wisdom.
- The solitude of the writer is nothing without the friendship of readers.
- Those who write well, teach.
- Write now.

Or:

Six Tips for Writers

1. Create time for free-flowing thinking to generate ideas for writing.
2. Create space and a place for writing.
3. Write 1,000 words every working day.
4. Think about the concept of the writer's voice, and establish your voice.
5. Seek feedback on your writing. Be selective with advice, and integrate it with your own critical reflections.
6. 'Teach' others about writing, in order to write better yourself.

But these maxims and tips cannot capture the elusive ear of the writer, and cannot reflect the need for guidance to be individualised. Most of all, they fail to capture the nuances that are a necessary part of understanding writing. A more complex summation is that writing works as a result of the following interconnected conditions, which are a theoretical frame that underpins the learning and teaching of writing:

1. Efficiency of communication, minimisation of ambiguity, and constant growth in speed and range of communication drive the development of writing in an organic way.
2. Written language is most appropriately understood as cognitive processes directly altered by social factors realised in pragmatic contexts.
3. Creating meaning in writing is linked holistically with form, structure and orthographical elements.
4. Oral language and written language share linguistic elements but are significantly different forms.
5. Accounts based on analysis of language in use, more powerfully, accurately and usefully, explain written language than prescriptive accounts.
6. Creativity is a fundamental characteristic of writing, and consists of the key concepts of originality and value as determined through consensual judgement.

Writing is a combination of the individual's thinking inextricably and directly shaped by the social context. Language is the cherishing mother of all significance because it is inner experience and it is social interaction. All artefacts, including the artefacts of writing, are only given meaning, and hence only fully exist, as a result of language.

Learning and teaching writing at any level require understanding and active consideration of individual writers and the social context for their writing. The beginning of the writing process, the decision to write at all and the selection of ideas for writing are to varying degrees in the control of the individual. However, the individual's decisions and ideas are influenced by his history as a writer, however modest, his social networks, and his engagement with writing around him. Selection of words, sentences, structures, while maintaining a coherent vision of the overall purpose for the writing, is the writer's challenge.

Cognitive processes drive the continual reinterpretation that is inherent in the writing process, for example, a) when the natural emphasis of the process is on the urgent catching and encoding of ideas or b) when the process requires more detached reading and editing after the initial drafts. The misunderstanding that writing is usually correct or complete in the first draft is a barrier to proficient writing. Even the more immediate forms of communication that digital communications have brought often benefit, at the very least, from some careful scrutiny of the particular message and how it might cause the recipient to react prior to the finger tap that sends the message. The cognitive processes of writing are largely subconscious, but understanding writing as a series of events that begins with fragments, pages and more generally drafts, where the mental load can be lessened through free-flow writing in each early stage, may be a means to have some level of control of cognition. Just as breathing is the only conscious way to control other non-controllable physiological processes, then perhaps controlling the writing process is the way to control writing cognition.

The most important social interaction is the writer's interaction with the first readers. Their reactions to the writing and the writer will be key – something that places a burden of responsibility on them as 'critical friends' and as 'educators'. The favoured first reader could be a close and trusted friend or partner, or it could be a teacher, who could herself orchestrate that first encounter with others on behalf of her students. Novice writers, including those learning in schools, encounter teachers as gatekeepers of topics, forms, meanings and processes. But those teachers are themselves often constrained by systems, including the accountability that tests and examinations required by governments engender. For professional writers, the first contact with an individual is followed by the interaction of networks that are part of authors' lives. The social milieu and influences of the professional writer are set in the context of gatekeepers of writing, such as journal and magazine reviewers, agents and commissioning editors. Writing requires writers who understand the links with the social context and are able to respond appropriately to that context by understanding when to engage with others and when to protect the writer's solitude.

The history of writing demonstrates the paradox of two dominant phenomena: stability and change. The human drive to create and respond to meaning in language, which began with the songs of apes and continues in the digital media of the twenty-first century, remains paramount, universal, and constant. The kinds of changes signalled by the invention of the alphabet and the developments in printing of books are now unfolding in the digital age. There is more writing now than ever before in human history, and the only sure projection is of continual growth and change. The English language looks set to become a world lingua franca, attendant with some concerns about linguistic imperialism.

The polarised positions of linguistic prescriptivists and descriptivists are perhaps resolvable through recognition of the paradox of stability and change, and greater attention to its implications. The writer's response to stability and change should be one of recognition and celebration. Celebration of stability and change is the curiosity to investigate the kinds of changes that occur over time and to enjoy the creativity and experimentation that can come from such investigation. Recognition of stability and change requires writers' and writing teachers' rigorous attention to language in use, not to unsubstantiated linguistic prescriptivism. Language change, and hence writing, is driven most of all by the need for efficient communication: for social interaction, for commerce, for creative expression. Avoiding ambiguity of meaning, which is anathema to efficiency of communication, requires the development of editorial skills that include the ability to be sensitive to both word-level and sentence-level nuance at the same time as attending to structure within an overall vision.

The continuing attention to writing guidance in the media, in books, and online is evidence of the interest and passion about language and writing that is another dimension of the human condition to communicate. Not only do humans have the instinctive need to communicate, but they have the unique capacity for metacognitive awareness of language that is the underpinning of all guidance about writing. The existence of writing guidance is built on the correct assumption that writing can be learned and taught. Understanding the conventions of writing, rather than prescriptive rules, is a vital area of knowledge required for writers. So it is disturbing that too much attention is given to old-fashioned views of language rather than to active promotion and engagement with evidence-informed understandings of language in the pursuit of better writing.

The most important thing that great writers' reflections on writing teach us is the paramount importance of vision, conception and, more simply, ideas for writing. The blank page is perhaps less intimidating if the ideas have been given sufficient time for incubation. For the most eminent writers, whose creativity stands the test of hundreds of years, immortality is a serious goal. For all writers, contemplation – and both conscious and subconscious speculation – is a vital precursor to writing, and a continuing part of the process of writing. Contemplation is increasingly challenged by the pace of modern life which requires writers to have the mental toughness and social ability to safeguard space and time. An overall vision or conception for writing is supported by the main threads, or lines of argument, that anchor writing and are a constant referent and sounding board in fiction, poetry and non-fiction writing.

It is universally agreed, from multiple perspectives, that reading is a vital key to writing. The ear of the writer is a part of *inhabiting* the world of the writer, as well as the more technical act to 'read like a writer'. Having an ear for writing, and reading like a writer, is an essential element of the work of competent and eminent writers alike. In relation to the attributes, knowledge and skills that writers most need, Maya Angelou was right when she added 'courage' to 'ears ears ears'. The ear of the writer is most of all developed through an insatiable curiosity about, and sensitivity to, the structures and language of different texts. The understanding of writing that follows from a writer's well developed ear is at all linguistic levels: forms of writing, topics, types of representation, structure, and use of words and sentences. Another essential benefit of such reading is in the identification of original ideas with value, warranted by in-depth attention to what has been written before. The type of writing to be read is not the issue as much as the act of reading and the thinking that accompanies it. The reading should be driven by the interests of the writer, and recommendations by others that the writer carefully weighs up. The types of texts read are ultimately reflected in the type of writing produced by the writer, something which sets up the tension between motivation for, and enjoyment of, certain types of texts versus the sense that other texts 'should' be read. Writers should follow their motivations for texts to read and engage with, whatever kinds of texts they may be.

The ear of the writer is also explained through the parallels between writing and music which are relevant to greater understanding of writing processes. In part this is because the origins of music are closely related to the origins of language, and they continue to occupy similar spaces. In particular, they both require composition of meaning through the articulation of their different building blocks. The sense of intonation, for music and for written language, particularly facilitates the editing of words and sentences until they reflect the authors' intended meanings. Rhythms, phrasing, and structures are key to writing and music. Sensitivity to rhythms in music and in words, and the phrasing of musical melodies and sentences are part of the writer's ear. As are the structures of written texts and music represented in main titles; chapters or movements; sub-headed sections or musical sections, such as the exposition, development and recapitulation of 'sonata form'. Melodies in music, which delineate musical structures, are like themes in writing – the powerful idea of the *leitmotif* for example. The chords and harmonies are the layers of textual meaning, for example, the multifaceted presence of the lake in relation to the characters' lives in Marylyn Robinson's book *Housekeeping*. And writers try and make sense of their craft and their art through musical metaphors. For example, the improvisational qualities that 'blowing like the tenor man' entails are a necessary disposition for writers. They capture the more ethereal aspects of creativity that continue to resist full neurological explanation.

The ear of the writer may be attuned through music. In music, there are composers and performers, and there are listeners. The listener who is not a musician may enjoy music for a variety of reasons, including background to other activities. But the trained musician will listen in a different way, typically with a different kind of intentness. Trained musicians will want to hear all elements, the base line, the harmonies, and the magic of the very quietest passages of music. They will be listening for the particular nature of the performance. If it is a piece they know well, then they will be comparing it with other performances that they have heard and/or performed in themselves. They will notice the notes that are slightly out of tune; they will notice the conductor taking an unusual tempo to the piece. The downside is that their ability to simply sit back and luxuriate in the emotional intensity of a brilliant performance, and to be transported, will be harder and harder to experience because the analytic musical mind will be at work. So although this capacity to listen is not without some negative consequences, its reward is the insights of craft and knowledge that it brings. Like the musician who learns to listen not just hear, the writer has to learn to read rather than just see.

The originality and value of creativity in writing will ultimately be determined by readers. For only a few writers, this creativity stands as a historic cultural landmark. But for all writers creativity is a part of writing. For very young children, it may be evident in the natural ways they express their thoughts in writing unencumbered by the conventions that they will necessarily have to learn, but that may also inhibit their creativity unless mediated by skilled teachers. Creativity can be present in all forms of writing, including fiction and non-fiction. The creativity of the mathematical proof or of the scientific advance is original and of value, but it is not created with the intent to create. Composition, in writing fiction and poetry, music, visual art, and dance, is not initially derived from a problem to solve, it is born from the need to be illusory in and of itself.

And creativity in any sphere does not happen without 'hard graft'. The almost universal condition of writers – sitting in their favoured writing place, starting the day early, seeking to write a set number of words in the allotted time – is striking. The afternoon switch to editing their writing, once the early drafting has taken place, but also attending to other forms of writing as part of communication within the writer's social world, is a practical reality but also time for more subconscious gestation of ideas and the solving of problems that emerge during the process of writing. The discomfort and discordance with a problem in the writing, perhaps the motivations of a character or the lack of focus in a line of argument, are an out-of-tune voice which needs to be listened to if the start of each day is to be as productive as possible.

Writing requires not just skills but also the development of knowledge. Knowledge informs the content of writing, whether non-fiction, fiction or poetry, but the writer's knowledge also needs to include knowledge about the craft of writing. The most relevant elements of the craft that call for attention are not straightforward to specify in advance because they differ from writer to writer. Knowledge about the craft for novice writers is guided by their teachers who, if they are good, differentiate their input in recognition of the knowledge required by individual students, hence the most appropriate knowledge is initially selected for novice writers. Expert writers also benefit from a range of teachers/advisors, but they are better able to independently select the knowledge required to improve their writing, by talking to other writers, and by reading a wide range of texts, including those about writing. Most professional writers 'teach' writing in some way or other. This teaching helps them write better because it requires the teacher to reflect on how writing works in order to help optimal learning. Tolstoy's story about his teaching writing, and his reflections on the process, was typical of the growth that all competent teachers experience. All writers can learn to write better by helping others to write, and by being receptive and reflective about writing feedback and guidance.

By looking in a multidisciplinary way, by looking at a range of writers and their reflections, and by focusing on the processes of writing as much as some of the products of writing, I have attempted to show in this book that there is a wealth of robust evidence that shows how writing works and hence how writing can be improved. Writing and its improvement are not only an area of interest to many people, they are also part of societal intent to improve literacy for young and older people alike. Teaching writing should be based on appreciation of the holistic nature of written language. *Undue* attention to the parts of writing, the letters, words, sentences and grammar, at the expense of the aims and structure of writing impedes writing development. One of the contributions that research on writing has made, particularly educational research, is a robust and clear view that holism is essential. For this reason, the repeated decisions by politicians worldwide to base language and literacy policies on 'back to basics', and old-fashioned grammar teaching based on their personal ideology rather than evidence, is unforgivable. And the lack of time for speculation, contemplation and incubation in formal education is one of the most troubling features of modern schooling.

The power of literacy is a global phenomenon. Governments around the world invest billions in their attempts to improve children's literacy, and hence life chances, but too often these initiatives are misguided. There is now sufficient robust research and theory to guide the promotion of practices and policies that would be more in tune with the needs of all learners. Too often, though, the learning and teaching of writing is dominated by what would have pleased Charles Dickens' famous character Gradgrind:

> Now, what I want is, Facts. Teach these boys and girls nothing but facts. Facts alone are wanted in life. Plant nothing else, and root out everything else.[5]

Dickens also reminds us what we must strive for, and the consequences of failing in the task:

> But, happy Sissy's happy children loving her; all children loving her; she, grown learned in childish lore; thinking no innocent and pretty fancy ever to be despised; trying hard to know her humbler fellow-creatures, and to beautify their lives of machinery and reality with those imaginative graces and delights, without which the heart of infancy will wither up, the sturdiest physical manhood will be morally stark death, and the plainest national prosperity figures can show, will be the Writing on the Wall.[6]

Written language can no longer be subsumed as a form of language of less academic interest than oral language. Writing is a dominant force in the world. Its instrumental power, for example in legal texts, is matched by its power to engage people through the artistic compositions of story and poetry and through its exponential rise in digital texts. The links with oral language are only part of the story of writing; much more pressing is further knowledge derived from understanding of the differences between writing and oral language.

Finally, this book raises the question about whether books about writing improve writing. Clearly, books can't literally teach people to write, as writing is a practical activity, an art, a craft and a set of skills and knowledge that can

[5] Dickens, *Hard Times*, 9. [6] Dickens, *Hard Times*, 287.

only be learned through reflective experience; this is one of the reasons why John Dewey's pragmatism is illuminative. But I am not as pessimistic as some who ask, 'If style guides are so good, then why is there a constant need for new ones?' One of the important things that an engagement with books and other sources about writing does is temporarily refocus the writer's mind towards the *ways* in which texts are constructed rather than on *what* is to be written. This is heightened metacognitive sensibility.

Whichever sources of guidance writers may choose, they need to be selective about the aspects they particularly attend to. Selection is based on a growing awareness of the writers' own strengths and weaknesses – a critically reflective stance. But, crucially, once particular pieces of guidance are absorbed, they need to be tested and reflected upon by forging them in writing. Writers are seeking the exact repertoire of knowledge that they need, which may not be needed by other writers. In effect, writers need to compile their own guide to writing that is uniquely related to their needs[7]. Theory is then fully realised in practice and, as a result, writing works.

[7] I'm grateful to my brother, and composer of music and text, Pascal Wyse for the idea of writers having their own personal guide to writing.

Bibliography

Alexander, R, ed. *Children, Their World, Their Education: Final Report and Recommendations of the Cambridge Primary Review.* London: Routledge, 2010.

Alvarez, A. *The Writer's Voice.* New York: W W Norton and Company Inc., 2005.

Amabile, T. 'Motivation and Creativity: Effects of Motivational Orientation on Creative Writers'. *Journal of Personality and Social Psychology* 48 (1985): 393–399.

Amabile, T. 'Social Psychology of Creativity: A Consensual Assessment Technique'. *Journal of Personality and Social Psychology* 43, no. 5 (1982): 997–1013.

Andrews, R. *A Prosody of Free Verse: Explorations in Rhythm.* London: Routledge, 2016.

Andrews R., C. Torgerson, S., Beverton T., Locke G., Low A., Robinson, and D. Zhu. 'The Effect of Grammar Teaching (Syntax) in English on 5 to 16 Year Olds' Accuracy and Quality in Written Composition'. In *Research Evidence in Education Library.* London: EPPI-Centre, Social Science Research Unit, Institute of Education, 2004.

Aristotle. *Poetics.* Translated by S. Butcher. Project Gutenberg, 2008, section XX.

Aubert, M., A. Brumm, M. Ramli, et al., 'Pleistocene Cave Art from Sulawesi, Indonesia'. *Nature* 514 (2014): 223–227.

Baines, J. *Visual and Written Culture in Ancient Egypt.* Oxford: Oxford University Press, 2007.

Banaji, S., and A. Burn. *The Rhetorics of Creativity: A Review of the Literature.* London: Arts Council England, 2006.

Barber, C. *The English Language: A Historical Introduction.* Cambridge: Cambridge University Press, 1993.

Barron, J. 'Completely without Dignity: An Interview with Karl Ove Knausgård'. *The Paris Review*, 2016.

Bashwiner, D., C. Wertz, R. Flores, and R. Jung. 'Musical Creativity "Revealed" in Brain Structure: Interplay between Motor, Default Mode, and Limbic Networks'. *Scientific Reports* 6, no. 20482 (2016): 1–8.

BBC Radio 4, *Codes That Changed the World: Fortran.* 6 April 2015.

BBC Radio 4. 'Meet the Vloggers'. *In Business*, 2015.

BBC Radio 4. 'Tales from the Stave', 2015.

Beal, J. 'Walker, John', Oxford Dictionary of National Biography. (accessed: 20 December 2016). Available at http://www.oxforddnb.com.libproxy.ucl.ac.uk/view/article/28499?docPos=8

Bell, J., and P. Magrs, eds. *The Creative Writing Coursebook.* London: Macmillan, 2001.

Biesta, G. *The Beautiful Risk of Education*. Boulder, CO: Paradigm Publishers, 2013.

Bissex, Glenda. *Gnys at Wrk: A Child Learns to Read and Write*. Cambridge: Harvard University Press, 1980.

Brande, D. *Becoming a Writer.* London: Papermac, 1983. 1934.

British Library. 'First Book Printed in English'. In *Learning English Timeline* (accessed: 28 November 2016). Available at http://www.bl.uk/learning/timeline/item126577.html

Bruner, J. *Child's Talk: Learning to Use Language.* Oxford: Oxford University Press, 1983.

Burchfield, R., ed. *The New Fowler's Modern English Usage*. Oxford: Oxford University Press, 1996.

Butterfield, J., ed. *Fowler's Dictionary of Modern English Usage (4th ed.)*. Oxford: Oxford University Press, 2015.

Castagnoli, L., and E. Di Lasco. 'Ancient Philosophy of Language'. In *The Routledge Companion to Philosophy of Language*. Edited by Gillian Russell and Delia Fara, 811–826. New York: Routledge, 2012.

Centre for Computing History. 'Commodore International Shows Its Commodore Pet 2001'. Available at http://www.computinghistory.org.uk/det/5947/Commodore-International-shows-its-Commodore-PET-2001/

Cerf, V., Y. Dalal, C. Sunshine, and Network Working Group. 'Specification of Internet Transmission Control Program December 1974 Version'. 1974. Available at http://www.rfc-base.org/txt/rfc-675.txt

Chomsky, N. *Syntactic Structures*. The Hague: Mouton & Co., 1957.

Clanchy, D. *From Memory to Written Record: England 1066–1307*. Chichester: Wiley-Blackwell, 2013.

Cooper, J. 'Quotations by Oscar Wilde in America'. In *Oscar Wilde in America*, 2016. Available at www.oscarwildeinamerica.org/quotations/took-out-a-comma.html.

Cosgrove, C. *An Ancient Christian Hymn with Musical Notation: Papyrus Oxyrhynchus 1786: Text and Commentary.* Tubingen, Germany: Mohr Siebeck, 2011.

Craft, A. *Creativity across the Primary Curriculum: Framing and Developing Practice*. London: RoutledgeFalmer, 2000.

Cropley, A. J. *Creativity in Education and Learning: A Guide for Teachers and Educators*. London: Kogan Page, 2001.

Crystal, D. *The Cambridge Encyclopedia of Language*. 3rd ed. Cambridge: Cambridge University Press, 2010.

Crystal, D. *Evolving English: One Language, Many Voices*. London: The British Library, 2010.

Crystal, D. *The Stories of English*. London: Penguin/Allen Lane, 2004.

Csikszentmihályi, M. 'The Domain of Creativity'. In *Theories of Creativity.* Edited by M. Runco and R. Albert, 190–214. London: Sage, 1990.

Cummins, J. 'Pedagogies for the Poor? Realigning Reading Instruction for Low-Income Students with Scientifically Based Reading Instruction'. *Educational Researcher* 36, no. 9 (2007): 564–572.

Daniels, P. 'Grammatology'. In *The Cambridge Handbook of Literacy.* Edited by D. Olson and N. Torrance, 25–46. Cambridge: Cambridge University Press, 2009.

Darnell, J., F. Dobbs-Allsopp, M. Lundberg, P. McCarter, B. Zuckerman, and C. Manassa. 'Two Early Alphabetic Inscriptions from the Wadi el-Ḥôl: New Evidence for the Origin of the Alphabet from the Western Desert of Egypt'. *The Annual of the American Schools of Oriental Research* 59(2005): 63–124.

Department for Business Innovation & Skills. 'The 2011 Skills for Life Survey: A Survey of Literacy, Numeracy and ICT Levels in England'. London: Department for Business Innovation & Skills, 2012.

Department for Education. 'The National Curriculum in England: Framework Document'. Department for Education. London: Department for Education, 2013.

Derrida, J. *Of Grammatology*. Translated by Gayatri Chakravorty Spivak. Baltimore: Johns Hopkins University Press, 1967.

Derry, J. 'Abstract Rationality in Education: From Vygotsky to Brandon'. *Studies in Philosophy of Education* 27 (2007): 49–62.

Dewey, J. 'Nature, Communication and Meaning: From Experience and Nature 1925'. In *The Essential Dewey: Volume 2 Ethics, Logic, Psychology*. Edited by L. Hickman and T. Alexander. Bloomington: Indiana University Press, 1998

Dickens, C. *Hard Times*. Introduction by Kate Flint. London: Penguin,1854/2003.

Edgehill, E. 'On Interpretation, by Aristotle'. The Internet Classics Archive, 2016. Retrieved from http://classics.mit.edu/index.html

Eggers, D. 'Dave Eggers' Wish: Once Upon a School'. TED, 2011. Available at https://www.ted.com/talks/dave_eggers_makes_his_ted_prize_wish_once_upon_a_school

Editors of the Paris Review. *The Paris Review Interviews*. Available at https://www.theparisreview.org

Eisen, C. 'Mozart'. In *Grove Music Online. Oxford Music Online.*: Oxford University Press., 2016.

Emerson, L. *Reading Writing Interfaces*. Minnesota: University of Minnesota Press, 2014.

Feldman, D. H., and A. Benjamin. 'Creativity and Education: An American Retrospective'. *Cambridge Journal of Education* 36, no. 3 (2006): 319–336.

Fowler, H. 'Plato, *Phaedrus*'. In *Perseus Digital Library*. Edited by G. Crane: Department of the Classics, Tufts University, 2016, 274.

Fowler, H. 'Plato, *Theaetetus*'. In *Perseus Digital Library*. Edited by G. Crane: Department of the Classics, Tufts University, 1985.

Freeman, H. 'Webchat: David Marsh Answers Your Questions about Grammar'. theguardian, 2013. Available at https://www.theguardian.com/books/booksblog/2013/oct/30/live-webchat-grammar-david-marsh

Freese, J. 'Aristotle, Rhetoric'. Rhetoric III, chapter 12, section 1. Edited by G. Crane: Perseus Digital Library, 2016.

Friedrich, M., and A. Friederici. 'Phonotactic Knowledge and Lexical-Semantic Processing in One-Year-Olds: Brain Responses to Words and Nonsense Words in Picture Contexts'. *Journal of Cognitive Neuroscience* 17, no. 11 (2005): 1785–1802.

Gazzard, A. *Now the Chips Are Down: The BBC Micro*. Platform Studies. Cambridge: MIT Press, 2016.

Geissmann, T. 'Gibbon songs and human music from an evolutionary perspective'. In *The Origins of Music*. Edited by N. L. Wallin, B. Merker, and S. Brown, 103–123. Cambridge: MIT Press, 2000.

Glennie, A. '"Don't Rely on Us for Good Grammar," Says the BBC: Broadcaster Is No Longer the Bastion of Correct English, Its "Style Chief" Admits'. MailOnline, 2014.

Available at http://www.dailymail.co.uk/news/article-2827798/Don-t-tune-good-grammar-says-BBC-Broadcaster-no-longer-bastion-correct-English-insider-admits.html

Goody, J. *The Interface between the Written and the Oral: Studies in Literacy, the Family, Culture and the State*. Cambridge: Cambridge University Press, 1987.

Goody, J., and I. Watt. 'The Consequences of Literacy'. *Comparative Studies in Society and History* 5, no. 3 (1963): 304–345.

Gourevitch, Philip, ed. *The Paris Review Interviews*. Vol. 1. Edinburgh: Canongate, 2007.

Gourevitch, Philip, ed. *The Paris Review Interviews* Vol. 2. Edinburgh: Canongate, 2007.

Gourevitch, Philip, ed. *The Paris Review Interviews*. Vol. 3. Edinburgh: Canongate, 2008.

Gourevitch, Philip, ed. *The Paris Review Interviews*. Vol. 4. Edinburgh: Canongate, 2009.

Government Office for Science. *Foresight Mental Capital and Wellbeing Project (2008): Final Project Report*. London: The Government Office for Science, 2008.

Graham, S., and, K. Harris. 'Evidence-Based Writing Practices: A Meta-Analysis of Existing Meta-Analyses'. In *Design Principles for Teaching Effective Writing*. Edited by R. Redondo and K. Harris, Leiden: The Netherlands (in-press).

Graves, D. H., *Writing: Teachers and Children at Work*. Portsmouth, NH: Heinemann Educational, 1983.

Grief, S., B. Meyer, and A. Burgess. *Effective Teaching and Learning: Writing*. London: Institute of Education, 2007.

Guardian and Observer Style Guide: C. Edited by D. Marsh and A. Hodsdon, 2016. Available at https://www.theguardian.com/guardian-observer-style-guide-c

Guilford, J. P. 'Creativity'. *American Psychologist* 5, no. 9 (September 1950): 444–454.

Halliday, M., and C. Matthiessen. *An Introduction to Functional Grammar*. 3rd ed. London: Arnold, 2004.

Harris, R. *The Origin of Writing*. London: Duckworth, 1986.

Hart-Davis, R., ed. *Selected Letters of Oscar Wilde*. Oxford: Oxford Paperbacks, 1979.

Havelock, E. *The Muse Learns to Write: Reflections on Orality and Literacy from Antiquity to the Present*. New Haven: Yale University Press, 1988.

Heinz, D. 'Ted Hughes, the Art of Poetry No. 71'. *The Paris Review*, no. 134 (1995): 1–25.

Hennessey, B. 'Intrinsic Motivation and Creativity in the Classroom: Have We Come Full Circle?'. In *Nurturing Creativity in the Classroom*. Edited by R. Beghetto and J. Kaufman, 342–365. Cambridge: Cambridge University Press, 2010.

Hermannsson, K. 'Economic Impact of Education: Evidence and Relevance'. In *The Sage Handbook of Curriculum, Pedagogy and Assessment*. Edited by D. Wyse, L Hayward and J Pandya, 873–893. London: SAGE, 2016.

Higgins, S, D. Kokotsaki, and R. Coe. *The Teaching and Learning Toolkit: Technical Appendices*. London: Education Endowment Foundation & The Sutton Trust, 2012.

Homer. *The Iliad*, edited by P Jones. London: Penguin Books, 2003.

Hughes, T. *Poetry in the Making: A Handbook for Writing and Teaching*. London: Faber and Faber, 1967.

Hughes, T. 'The Thought Fox'. *Ted Hughes New Selected Poems 1957–1994*. London: Faber and Faber, 1995.

James, K., J. Jao, and V. Berninger. 'The Development of Multileveled Writing Systems of the Brain'. In *Handbook of Writing Research*. Edited by C. MacArthur, S. Graham, & J. Fitzgerald, 116–130. New York: The Guilford Press, 2016.

Jewitt, C., and G. Kress. 'Multimodality, Literacy and School English'. In *The Routledge International Handbook of English, Language and Literacy Teaching*. Edited by D. Wyse, R. Andrews, and J. Hoffman, 342–353. London: Routledge, 2010.

Jones, R., and D. Wyse, eds. *Creativity in the Primary Curriculum*. London: Routledge, 2013.

Jung, R., M. Brittany, J. Carrasco, and R. Flores. 'The Structure of Creative Cognition in the Human Brain'. *Frontiers in Human Neuroscience* 7, no. 330 (2013): 1–13.

Kamler, B, and P. Thomson. *Helping Doctoral Students to Write: Pedagogies for Supervision*. London: Routledge, 2006.

Keefe, S. *Mozart's Requiem: Reception, Work, Completion*. Cambridge: Cambridge University Press, 2015.

Kellog, D., and A. Yasnitsky. 'The Differences between the Russian and English Texts of Tool and Symbol in Child Development. Supplementary and Analytic Materials'. *Dubna Psychological Journal* 4 (2011): 98–158.

Kerswill, P. 'Standard and Non-Standard English'. In *Language in the British Isles*. Edited by D. Britain, 34–52. Cambridge: Cambridge University Press, 2007.

King, S. *On Writing: A Memoir of a Craft*. London: Hodder and Stoughton, 2000.

Knausgård, K. *A Death in the Family*. London: Vintage, 2014.

Kress, G. 'Applied Linguistics and a Social Semiotic Account of Multimodality'. In *Theory in Applied Linguistics Research: Critical Approaches to Production, Performance and Participation*. Edited by T. Lillis, 49–71. Amsterdam: John Benjamins Publishing Company, 2015. Available at http://benjamins.com/#catalog/journals/aila.28.03kre/fulltext

Kress, G. *Learning to Write*. London: Routledge & Kegan Paul, 1982.

Kroon, D. 'Osi Reference Model (Open Systems Interconnection)'. ND. Available at http://searchnetworking.techtarget.com/definition/OSI

Kuhl, P. K. 'Early Language Acquisition: Cracking the Speech Code'. *Nature Reviews Neuroscience* 5, no. 11 (2004): 831–843.

Lifelong Kindergarten Group at the MIT Media Lab (Producer). About Scratch. (25 September 2017). Available at https://scratch.mit.edu/about/

Limb, C. J., and Braun, A. R. 'Neural Substrates of Spontaneous Musical Performance: An fMRI Study of Jazz Improvisation'. 2008. PloS ONE, 3 (2 e1679.). doi:10.1371/journal.pone.0001679.

Lowth, R. *A Short Introduction to English Grammar with Critical Notes. The Second Edition, Corrected*. London: A. Millar and R and J. Dodsley, 1794. 1762.

Mann, N. 'Thoughts of Chairman May'. BBC News, 2003.

Mann, T. *Doctor Faustus*. New York: Vintage, 1947.

Marx, K. *Capital: A Critique of Political Economy*. Translated by Samuel Moore and Edward Aveling. Moscow: USSR: Progress Publishers, 1887.

Mathiesen, T. *Appollo's Lyre: Greek Music and Music Theory in Antiquity and the Middle Ages*. Norman: University of Nebraska Press, 2015.

Mathiesen, T., D. Conomos, G. Leotsakos, S. Chianis, and R. Brandl. 'Greece'. In *Grove Music Online*: Oxford University Press, 2016.

McGilchrist, I. *The Master and His Emissary: The Divided Brain and the Making of the Western World*. New Haven: Yale University Press, 2009.

McLuhan, M. *The Gutenberg Galaxy: The Making of Typographic Man*. Toronto: University of Toronto Press, 1962.

Meek, M. *How Texts Teach What Readers Learn*. Stroud: Thimble Press, 1988.
Merriam Webster Incorporated. 'About Us'. 2016. Available at https://www.merriam-webster.com/about-us/faq
Michel, J.-B., Y. Shen, Aiden A., et al., 'Quantitative Analysis of Culture Using Millions of Digitized Books. *Science* 331, no. 6014 (2010): 176–182.
Miller, D., E. Costa, N. Haynes, et al. *How the World Changed Social Media*. London: UCL Press, 2016.
Milroy, J. 'The History of English'. In *Language in the British Isles*. Edited by D. Britain, 9–34. Cambridge: Cambridge University Press, 2007.
MIT Media Lab. 'About Scratch'. Available at http://scratch.mit.edu/about/ (Accessed: 25 September 2017)
MIT OpenCourseWare. 'A Brief History of the Internet'. 2012.
Montfort, N., P. Baudoin, J. Bell, et al. *10 PRINT CHR$(205.5+RND(1)); : GOTO 10*. Cambridge: The MIT Press, 2013.
Morley, I. 'A Multi-Disciplinary Approach to the Origins of Music: Perspectives from Anthropology, Archeology, Cognition and Behaviour'. *Journal of Anthropological Sciences* 92 (2014): 147–177.
Mulcaster, R. *The Educational Writings of Richard Mulcaster (1532–1611)*. Edited by James Oliphant. Glasgow: Glasgow University Press/James Maclehose and Sons, 1903.
Mulcaster, R. *Elementarie*. London: Thomas Vautroullier, 1582.
Nature. 'Internet Encyclopaedias Go Head to Head'. *Nature* 438, no. 15 (2005): 900–901.
Neuman, P. 'Mariner I – No Holds Barred'. In *The Risks Digest*, edited by Peter Neuman, 1989. Available at: http://catless.ncl.ac.uk/Risks/8.75.html#subj1.
Nicholson, R. S. 'Enhancing Creativity'. In *Handbook of Creativity*. Edited by R. J. Sternberg, 392–430. Cambridge: Cambridge University Press, 1999.
Office for National Statistics. 'UK Labour Market, February 2015'. Edited by Office for National Statistics. London: Office for National Statistics, 2015.
Olson, D. *The World on Paper: The Conceptual and Cognitive Implications of Writing and Reading*. Cambridge: Cambridge University Press, 1994.
Olson, D. *The Mind on Paper: Reading, Consciousness and Rationality*. Cambridge: Cambridge University Press, 2016.
Ong, W. *Orality and Literacy: The Technologizing of the Word*. London: Routledge, 1982.
O'Regan, J. 'English as a Lingua Franca: An Immanent Critique'. *Applied Linguistics* 35, no. 5 (2014): 533–552.
OED Online. Available at www.oed.com.
Oreskes, N., and E. Conway. *The Merchants of Doubt*. London: Bloomsbury, 2011.
Paris Review Interviews. Editors of the Paris Review. https://www.theparisreview.org
Parkinson, R. *The Rosetta Stone*. London: The British Museum Press, 2005.
Pinker, S. *The Language Instinct*. New York: Harper Collins, 1995.
Pinker, S. *The Sense of Style: The Thinking Person's Guide to Writing in the 21st Century*. London: Penguin Books, 2014.
Potter, M. Frege, Russell, and Wittgenstein. In *The Routledge Companion to Philosophy of Language*. Edited by G. Russell and D. Fara, 852–859. New York: Routledge, 2012.
Ramadhani, S. *Effect of tenure Regularization Program on Building Investment in Manzese ward in Dar es Salaam, Tanzania. (MSc)*, Enschede, Netherlands, 2007.
Ray, J. *The Rosetta Stone and the Rebirth of Ancient Egypt*. Cambridge MA: Harvard University Press, 2007.

Robinson, A. *The Story of Writing*. London: Thames and Hudson, 2007.

Robinson, M. 'Making an Impact: Authors, Articles, Almetrics'. In *British Educational Research Association Annual Conference*. Leeds. Taylor & Francis Group, 2016.

Rose, D. 'New Developments in Genre-Based Literacy Pedagogy'. In *Handbook of Writing Research*. 2nd ed. Edited by C. MacArthur, S. Graham and J. Fitzgerald. 227–243. New York: The Guilford Press, 2016.

Russell, B. *An Inquiry into Meaning and Truth: The William James Lectures for 1940 Delivered at Harvard University.* London: George Allen and Unwin Ltd, 1940.

Saussure, F. *Course in General Linguistics*. 1972. 1916.

Scanlon, S. Change Ringing Toolkit. 'Method Diagram Plain Bob Minor.' 2016. Available at: http://www.ringbell.co.uk/toolkit/index.htm

Schupman, E., and L. O'Flahavan. *Lone Dog's Winter Count: Keeping History Alive*. Washington, DC: National Museum of the American Indian, ND.

Seelye, J. 'Introduction'. In *The Adventures of Huckleberry Finn*. London: Penguin, 1985.

Shaffer, P. *Amadeus*. The Internet Movie Script Database, 2016.

Singh, Simon. *Fermat's Last Theorem*. London: 4th Estate, 1997.

Stein, M. 'Creativity and Culture' *Journal of Psychology* 36 (1953): 311–322.

The National Museum of Computing. 'First generation – WITCH & EDSAC' (accessed: 30 November 2016). Available at http://www.tnmoc.org/explore/large-systems

Thomas, F.-N., and M. Turner. *Clear and Simple as the Truth: Writing Classic Prose*. Princeton: Princeton University Press, 1994.

Thompson, D., D. Eggers, and C. Ware. '826 Valencia: Chris Ware's New Mural Tells the Story of the Human Race.' eye, Summer 2003. Available at http://www.eyemagazine.com/feature/article/826-valencia

Thomson, P. 'Writing About Research'. In *The Sage International Handbook of Educational Research*. Edited by D. Wyse, E. Smith, N. Selwyn and L. Suter, 957–973. London: Sage, in-press.

Truss, L. *Eats, Shoots & Leaves: The Zero Tolerance Approach to Punctuation*. London: Profile Books, 2003.

Tufte, E. R. *The Cognitive Style of Powerpoint*. Cheshire, CT: Graphics Press LLC, 2003.

Tusting, K., and D. Barton. 'Writing Disciplines: Producing Disciplinary Knowledge in the Context of Contemporary Higher Education'. *Ibérica* 32 (2016): 15–34.

Twain, M. *The Adventures of Huckleberry Finn*. London: Penguin, 1985. 1884

UNESCO Institute for Statistics. 'Literacy'. UNESCO, 2016. Available at http://data.uis.unesco.org/Index.aspx?queryid=166

United Nations. *The Millennium Development Goals Report 2014*. New York: United Nations, 2014.

United Republic of Tanzania Ministry of Education and Culture. *English Language Syllabus for Primary Schools*. Dar es Salaam: Tanzania Institute of Education, 2005.

University of Cambridge, 'Natural Sciences Tripos: Physics', 2016. Available at http://www.natsci.tripos.cam.ac.uk

University of Oxford. 'The First Part of the Elementarie Which Entreateth Chieflie of the Right Writing of Our English Tung'. In *University of Oxford Text Archive*: University of Oxford, 1582, section 1.1. Available at http://ota.ox.ac.uk/text/3176.html

Vernon, P. 'The Nature-Nurture Problem in Creativity'. In *Handbook of Creativity.* Edited by J. Glover, R. Ronning and C. Reynolds, 93–110. London: Plenum Press, 1989.

VidStatsX. 'One Hundred Most Subscribed People & Vlogs Channel Rankings List by Subscribers'. 2016. Available at https://vidstatsx.com/youtube-top-10-most-subscribed-channels

Vygotsky, L. 'Imagination and Creativity in Childhood'. [In Russian.] *Journal of Russian and East European Psychology* 42, no. 1 (2004): 7–97.

Vygotsky, L. *Mind in Society: The Development of Higher Psychological Processes*. Cambridge: Harvard University Press, 1978.

Vygotsky, L. *Thought and Language*. Translated by Alex Kozulin. London: MIT Press, 1986.

Vygotsky, L., and A. Luria. 'Tool and Symbol in Child Development'. In *The Vygotsky Reader*. Edited by R. Van der Veer & J. Valsiner, 99–175. Hoboken, NJ: Wiley, 1994.

Watkins, C. 'Observations on the "Nestor's Cup" Inscription'. *Harvard Studies in Classical Philology* 80 (1976): 25–40.

Wikipedia, 'World Wide Web'. Available at http://en.wikipedia.org/wiki/World_Wide_Web.

Wikipedia. 'List of Territorial Entities Where English Is an Official Language'. 2016. Available at https://en.wikipedia.org/wiki/List_of_territorial_entities_where_English_is_an_official_language

Wikipedia. 'Mariner 1'. Wikipedia, 2016. Available at https://en.wikipedia.org/wiki/Mariner_1

Wittgenstein, L. *Philosophische Untersuchungen. Philosophical Investigations*. Translated by G. Anscombe, P. Hacker and J. Schulte. Chichester: John Wiley & Sons, 2009. 1953.

Wittgenstein, L. *Tractatus Logico-Philosophicus*. Translated by C. Ogden. Project Gutenberg, 2010. 1921.

Worldometers. 'Current World Population'. Worldometers, 2016. Available at www.worldometers.info.

Wyse, D. *Creativity and the Curriculum: An Inaugural Professorial Lecture by Dominic Wyse*. London: IOE Press, 2014.

Wyse, D. 'Grammar. For Writing?: A Critical Review of Empirical Evidence'. *British Journal of Educational Studies*, 49, no. 4 (2001): 411–427.

Wyse, D. *How to Help Your Child Read and Write*. London: Pearson Education Limited, 2007.

Wyse, D. *Primary Writing*. Buckingham: Open University Press, 1998.

Wyse, D., and Cowan, K. *The Good Writing Guide for Education Students*. 4th ed. London: Sage, 2017.

Wyse, D., and U. Goswami. 'Synthetic Phonics and the Teaching of Reading'. *British Educational Research Journal* 34, no. 6 (2008): 691–710.

Wyse, D., and R. Jones. *Teaching English, Language and Literacy*. 4th ed. London: Routledge, forthcoming.

Wyse, D., N. Selwyn, E. Smith, and L. Suter, (Eds.) *The BERA/SAGE Handbook of Educational Research*. London: SAGE, 2017.

Wyse, D., and H. Torrance. 'The Development and Consequences of National Curriculum Assessment for Primary Education in England'. *Educational Research* 51, no. 2 (2009): 213–228.

Ziegler, J, and Usha Goswami. 'Reading Acquisition, Developmental Dyslexia and Skilled Reading across Languages: A Psycholinguistic Grain Size Theory'. *Psychological Bulletin* 131, no. 1 (2005): 3–29.

Index